Popularizing the Nation

POPULARIZING THE NATION
Audience, Representation, and the Production of Identity in Die Gartenlaube, *1853–1900*

KIRSTEN BELGUM

University of Nebraska Press

Lincoln and London

Library of Congress Cataloging-in-Publication Data
Belgum, Kirsten, 1959–
Popularizing the nation : audience, representation, and the
production of identity in Die Gartenlaube, 1853–1900 /
Kirsten Belgum.
p.   cm.—(Modern German culture and literature)
Includes bibliographical references and index.
ISBN 0-8032-1283-6 (cl.: alk. paper)
1. Die Gartenlaube.   2. Nationalism in the press—Germany—
History—19th century.   3. Group identity—Germany—History—19th
century.   4. Popular culture—Germany—History—19th century.
I. Neue Gartenlaube.   II. Title.   III. Series.
PN5220.G37B45   1998
053'.1—dc21   97-29654
CIP

Contents

Illustrations

Acknowledgments

This project changed shape repeatedly. The manuscript in its final form benefited from countless probing discussions with colleagues, helpful comments at conferences where I presented parts of it, and critical remarks of various reviewers. The discussion of national geography in chapter 2 was published as "A Nation for the Masses: Production of German Identity in the Late-Nineteenth-Century Popular Press," in *A User's Guide to German Cultural Studies*, ed. Scott Denham, Irene Kacandes, and Jonathan Petropoulos (Ann Arbor: U Michigan P, 1997). The material on national monuments in chapter 4 was published as "Displaying the Nation: A View of Nineteenth-Century Monuments through a Popular Magazine," in *Central European History* 26, no. 4 (1993): 457–74. Most of chapter 5 was published as "Domesticating the Reader: Women and *Die Gartenlaube*," in *Women in German Yearbook* 9, ed. Jeanette Clausen and Sara Friedrichsmeyer (Lincoln: U Nebraska P, 1993), 91–111.

This book could not have been completed without the collections of nineteenth-century German periodicals at several libraries: the Perry-Castañeda Library at the University of Texas at Austin, Memorial Library at the University of Wisconsin–Madison, and the Library of Congress. The University Research Institute at the University of Texas at Austin supported my work with two summer grants, and the German Academic Exchange Service enabled me to attend a summer seminar at Cornell University with Peter Hohendahl, who gave me the encouragement and inspiration I needed to undertake this project.

I thank my colleagues at the University of Texas and elsewhere who responded readily and with invaluable insight to various pieces of this work: Nina Berman, David Crew, Ann Cvetkovich, Michael Hanchard, Julia Hell, John Hoberman, Peter Jelavich, Irene Kacandes, Rudy Koshar, Anne Norton, Brent Peterson, Gretchen Ritter,

John Rodden, and Lynn Wilkinson. Thanks also to George Forell for Willard Lampe's collection of family magazines. I am indebted as always to many friends and teachers for their guidance and to my parents Kathie and David Belgum for their never-ending love and support.

This book is dedicated with gratitude to Forrest Novy, my partner in all things and my toughest reader, and to Morgan and Mariah, who repeatedly interrupted this project, but who sustain me.

INTRODUCTION: THE PRESS AND NATIONAL IDENTITY

In 1895 Germany's most popular magazine, *Die Gartenlaube*, boasted about its popularity by posing the rhetorical question "Who has never heard of the *Gartenlaube*?"[1] The magazine's claim to be a national household word was no exaggeration. From its very first issue in 1853, the *Gartenlaube* targeted the entire German *Volk* as its ideal readership.[2] In the next two decades it increased its circulation from a modest 6,000 to 385,000, thereby reaching a substantial portion of the German population. The decades of the magazine's growth, however, were also a period in which the exact dimensions of "the German people" were contested. The idea of publishing a magazine for "the people" and distributing it to a broad and dispersed national audience coincided in nineteenth-century Germany with the struggle for national unification and the eventual establishment of the German nation-state.

This book examines the intersection of the nation and the press in nineteenth-century Germany. It argues that the search for a national identity was inextricably linked to the early popular press. The identification of a reading audience as explicitly and inclusively national required an appeal to a mass readership; conversely, the concept of a mass audience was of major importance for the emerging consciousness of a German nation in the late nineteenth century. In the period when national identity in Germany most needed defining, the *Gartenlaube*, and other popular magazines, came forward to represent the nation to a mainstream readership. These serial publications were both a public repository of mythical memory of the nation and themselves a symbol of the modernity of the nation. By examining the representations of the nation and strategies of identity formation, this book studies the generation of mainstream national identity as an explicitly modern event. I propose that a detailed investigation of the sometimes contradictory images of the nation that stood side by side in these magazines can help us understand the problems and processes of constructing national identity.

Because it was far and away the most popular and successful periodical of its time in Germany, the *Gartenlaube* quickly established a trend for the press at large. By example it defined what it meant to be a mainstream periodical and provided a model that other magazines felt compelled to imitate. Even those magazines that wanted to distance themselves from its liberal politics, like the ten-year-younger *Daheim*, reacted to the *Gartenlaube* as a highly influential foil.[3] From its first appearance in 1853, the *Gartenlaube* characterized itself as a family magazine that strove to offer something to everyone. It provided a diverse, yet regular and predictable, fare of reading material for male and female, young and old. The lead piece in each issue was usually an installment of a serialized story or novel. The magazine regularly published poetry, short biographies of notable individuals, historical sketches, and essays about distant as well as familiar cultures and the arts. It featured a variety of topics that distinguished it from the cultural periodicals of its day, such as firsthand battle reportage from important wars and travel reports of life in foreign cities or the situation of German emigrants abroad. The *Gartenlaube* popularized scientific information with advice columns on human hygiene and essays on plant and animal life. It explained technological innovations and described modern industrial factories that might be of general interest. Although each issue ended with a brief section that contained announcements of newsworthy occurrences, the magazine did not focus on describing daily events as much as general contemporary concerns. Most of all, it always claimed to be above partisan politics.

The magazine presented this variety of material in an accessible and reliable format. The *Gartenlaube* was published in weekly issues averaging a modest sixteen pages that could be read easily in one week. Its language was straightforward and nontechnical. Readers rarely needed specialized prior knowledge in any field to understand the articles. In addition to general-interest texts, illustrations were central to its appeal as a family magazine. Like the magazine's prose, the images were immediately understandable, consisting of detailed woodcuts (later, lithographs and photos) of readily decipherable scenes. As the *Gartenlaube* became more successful and financially more secure, the number of illustrations in each issue gradually increased. Both the diversity of its offerings and its accessible format and tone contributed to the *Gartenlaube*'s popular appeal. The magazine's success in reaching a broad cross section of the German reading public lent credibility to the editor's claim that the *Gartenlaube* was an enlightener and entertainer of "the German people."

In the midst of this accessible variety, one theme, the German nation, emerged repeatedly in the pages of this nineteenth-century magazine and others like it. The *Gartenlaube* was by no means only interested in things German. It discussed other cultures and consistently published contributions on a variety of concerns that went beyond national interests. Many of its essays focused on concerns of modern life in general. Yet, discussions of German culture, German writers, German industry, German princes, and German landscapes played a dominant role. Numerous essays on national holidays, organizations, festivals, and military successes revealed the magazine's preoccupation with German identity. The *Gartenlaube* was, above all, a German family magazine, a magazine for the German *Volk*. That meant that its primary interest lay in appealing to all Germans, speaking for them and describing their lives, culture, surroundings, history, and future. Although the *Gartenlaube* and its editor-publisher were concerned with the nation, they were not advocates of a chauvinistic nationalism. At least in the first decades of its publication, jingoistic treatment of other nations was antithetical to the magazine's enlightened stance. Its liberal tradition meant that it favored German unification, but not necessarily a self-aggrandizing policy of Germany as a *Machtstaat*. The combination of the magazine's success and its dedication to providing the German populace with a sense of self makes the *Gartenlaube* a fascinating case for studying the problems and contradictions of generating a mainstream national identity.

The *Gartenlaube* is also an excellent source for such investigation because of its historical context; its founding and rise to prominence coincided with the important period in Germany's move to national unification. The magazine was started by a dedicated liberal, Ernst Keil, who had been a politically active publisher and proponent of a liberal conception of German unification prior to and during the German middle-class revolution of 1848. Keil launched the *Gartenlaube* in 1853 shortly after that failed revolution. In the following decade, he used it, in good liberal fashion, as a mouthpiece to profess his dedication to German unification. One example of this is that the magazine frequently celebrated liberal heroes from the first half of the century who had promoted unification. In the *Gartenlaube*'s second and third decades, it traced the progress toward political unity in the wars of 1864, 1866, and 1870 and reported on the national organizations that called for German unity outside state politics. A sign of its importance as a commentator on the creation of a German nation-state is the fact that it reached its greatest circulation in the first decade of the newly unified German Empire. The *Gartenlaube*'s definition of the nation and its formulation of what it meant to be German occurred against the background of momentous social change including industrialization, urbanization, and mass emigration. All of these concerns, as well as other economic issues, had a prominent place in its pages. In other words, the *Gartenlaube* constitutes an important historical document that not only ardently promoted the national idea, but also recorded the political events and social processes that accompanied Germany's unification.

The *Gartenlaube* documented this period from a clearly articulated political perspective. This is not to say that Ernst Keil's liberalism was the most important or always the most representative political position in Germany in the second half of the century.[4] Yet, an analysis of one magazine's shift in political values (as selective as they may have been) reveals much about the changes it had to make in order to continue to speak to and for a large segment of the nation. Ernst Keil had been sentenced to prison for his liberal ideas and publishing activity during the revolution of 1848. Undaunted, he carried many of his liberal convictions into the period of political reaction after 1848. His lasting goal was to educate his fellow Germans to active and responsible citizenship. He founded the *Gartenlaube* as an instrument of this liberal ideal, but in a repressive political climate of the early 1850s. His magazine thus marks the shift from the oppositional liberalism of the 1848 period to the national-liberal politics that would affirm Bismarck's policies in the 1860s. The *Gartenlaube* reveals the heritage of an older liberal conception of the nation while also showing how its own popularity had an effect on the presentation of the nation.

The *Gartenlaube* is also an ideal source for exploring the popular construction of national identity in general because of its attention to the family and to women readers. This magazine is an early document of the modern importance of "family" as a core concept of national identity. As only one of many periodical publications that called itself a family magazine, its appeal to the family as the heart of the German nation was representative of the century. The *Gartenlaube* explicitly addressed the entire German family in hopes of gaining a large audience and as part of its mission to educate as well as entertain the German people. This goal of national education, or "Volksbildung," determined both the tone and content of the *Gartenlaube* and similar publications: in later years the magazine included regular columns on household advice and puzzles for children. This definition of the nation in terms of the family also raises the issue of gender as it is tied to the nation. Even if the vitality or strength of a nation-state was defined in masculine terms, the truly popular national community, by definition, had to include women as members. Ernst Keil made a conscious effort to cultivate a female readership for his liberal magazine. In following the development of this magazine in the last half of the century, we can trace the changing significance of the family and women as participants in the German nation.

Finally, as a document that predates our twentieth-century immersion in the electronic media, the *Gartenlaube* can help us understand the early, intimate connection between modernity and the nation. By the late nineteenth century, the production and

consumption of magazines and newspapers were tied to technological innovations such as the telegraph, the high-speed rotary
printing press, and the railroad. As a source of information about
the latest technological advances, and being itself a product of recent innovations, the illustrated press was in an excellent position
to mediate between traditional and modern representations of the
nation. Because of its rapid and frequent publication, the press
was flexible in the images it presented. In the same weekly issue
it could retell mythical stories of national origins and argue for the
development of the newest defensive technology, all in the name
of the nation. An investigation of the *Gartenlaube*'s construction
and dissemination of national images (in pictures as well as essays)
reveals the tensions and ambiguities in early representations of the
modern nation. It also suggests that early forms of mass communication, as symbols of modernization themselves, were central to
the modern process of mediating national consciousness.

The *Gartenlaube* was born of a liberal goal of educating a national populace to autonomy and responsibility, a goal that still informs the self-image of the press today. This optimistic nineteenth-
century vision of the benefits of information for bourgeois society
had its roots in the Enlightenment. It grew out of a middle-class,
intellectual project of general education and informed public discussion of culture and politics that dates back to the eighteenth
century.[5] In addition to informing a general readership about a wide
variety of topics on a regular basis, most popular magazines openly
touted their own importance in educating the members of their
society. As it gained in popularity, the mass media became a highly
self-reflective industry that increasingly advertised its impact on the
formation and dissemination of ideas in the public sphere. Thus,
understanding the popular conception of the nation involves com-
prehending the popular press's presentation and representation not
only of the world, but also of the role the press played in the world.

THE PRESS AS A NATIONAL SPACE

At the center of this study lies the problem of German nation-
building that went beyond (and always goes beyond) political acts

of state power and authority.[6] Nationalism was a movement that involved not only the creation of a unified state and governmental structure, but also the mobilization of a national population. Various national organizations had been founded in Germany since the beginning of the nineteenth century. Ludwig Jahn's gymnastics society (first organized in 1811), the student fraternity movement (beginning in 1815), and an array of associated populist organizations and activities planted the seeds of German nationalism that sprouted and flourished in the years leading up to the revolution of 1848.[7] Organizations such as the singing and sharpshooting societies that blossomed in the decades before 1848 indicate the growing importance of the national idea in Germany. Yet, even these organizations did not grow beyond a few thousand members and consisted primarily of adult men. Beginning in the middle of the nineteenth century, the newly developed popular illustrated magazine and other widely distributed print texts played a seminal role in helping a broader German populace, of many generations and both sexes, imagine and continually re-imagine the nation.

My argument that the press was a crucial medium for imagining the nation is in part inspired by the work of Benedict Anderson.[8] His theory of "imagined communities" identifies print-capitalism as a key, although not sole, factor in the emergence of "a new form of imagined community, which in its basic morphology set the stage for the modern nation" (46). Anderson begins by noting that the spread of printing in the early modern period helped codify the vernacular languages.[9] At the same time, printing made it possible to reproduce texts in such quantities that they would conceivably be available throughout the entire region where a given vernacular was spoken. The development of print thus laid the groundwork for many geographically dispersed individuals to have contact with one another through common reading material. By participating in the same experience simultaneously, they could, without any direct, face-to-face contact, conceive of themselves as members of the same group. In other words, the medium of print helped establish the bond of a common language and the production of distributable texts that played a key role in the creation of modern Western nations. The centrality of print-capitalism to the notion of national identity means for Anderson that the concept of the nation is by definition modern.

Ernest Gellner proposes a similar argument about the modernity of the nation. Gellner considers cultural homogeneity a necessary precondition for the establishment of national consciousness.[10] He argues convincingly that a paradox of modern society is its simultaneous move toward specialization on one hand and standardization or nonspecialization on the other. Especially in the area of education, industrial society exhibits a great deal of uniformity: "The same kind of training or education is given to all or most children and adolescents up to an astonishingly late age. . . . The kind of specialization found in industrial society rests precisely on a common foundation of non-specialized and standardized training" (27).[11] Gellner argues that modern industrialized society appeals to egalitarian values such as universal literacy, standardized education, and broad access to forms of communication, not out of altruistic idealism or self-advertisement, but to sustain and reproduce itself. They are essential elements "in the effective working of a modern society" (29). Furthermore, national identity can only develop when the institutions that generate and perpetuate a homogeneous culture are in place.[12]

Although Gellner does not discuss the press in detail, he does include in his list of prerequisites for the sustained growth of modern society a "sustained, frequent and precise communication between strangers involving a sharing of explicit meaning, transmitted in a standard idiom and in writing when required" (34). One main vehicle of such communication and the creation of a homogeneous culture was, and still is, of course, the press. Specifically, the popular press of the nineteenth century was the first institution to move beyond a local readership to reach a national audience. The press was one of the few products that had regular contact with a geographically varied group of individuals. It was a simultaneous mediator, providing people who had no other connection with one another with the same information and images at the same time. In addition, the communication engendered by magazines, in contrast to books, was persistent and periodical. The same individuals and groups encountered such publications on a regular basis. Week after week, a growing audience shared access to common images and narratives of German history, world events, and modern life. Participation in this nationwide activity of reading the press made each reader a member of a new national community, a nation of readers.

The products of print-capitalism were modern in structural terms. The popular press of the nineteenth century epitomized and reinforced the modern aspects of immediacy (distribution on a regular basis) and simultaneity (universal access to the same material) that Anderson sees in even the earliest examples of industrial printing.[13] This periodicity not only established regular contact with a broad audience, it also allowed audience reaction to affect a given magazine's content and format. The popular reception of certain topics or authors in the press encouraged editors to modify the format and content of their product. The common practice of most nineteenth-century magazines of publishing readers' letters indicates the institutional concern within the press for reader involvement. The popular press of the nineteenth century thus became both a disseminator of national images and identities to a large national audience and a mechanism for that mass audience to participate in the process of constructing those images and identities.

This brings us to another important element of the press's modernism that Anderson and Gellner do not discuss. Beyond the structural concerns of distribution and broad access to a national population, a central aspect of the press's modernity was its location as a commodity within capitalist society. The commodity nature of the daily newspaper that Richard Terdiman has identified also applied to the weekly press: "Once it became clear that space in the newspaper could be *sold*, then *all* the space in the paper became potentially salable, potentially purchasable."[14] The limitations on affordable space in the pages of the illustrated magazine meant that all topics were in competition with one another for the attention of the growing mass readership. This has important ramifications for the present study, which is concerned with the construction of a national audience in the nineteenth century as well as with the representations of the nation it consumed. Even though the nation was a big winner in terms of the attention it received in the popular press, this competitive situation among topics meant that the nation also had to vie for its audience. The nation, like all other items that appeared in the press, was one commodity among others. Thus, the images of the nation published by the *Gartenlaube* must be understood in the context of the other interests the magazine represented.

MODERNIZATION AND THE NATION

Since the images of the nation that appeared in the popular press were subject to market pressures like all other goods, the press provides us with a useful tool for understanding what particular elements and aspects made the nation attractive to its contemporaries. To assess the symbolic value of the modern nation we need to ask not only how often the nation was presented as a focal point for reader identification but also how and in conjunction with what other images and ideals the nation appeared. This book considers the images of the nation and national identity presented by the *Gartenlaube* and also investigates the social, political, and aesthetic contexts that were important for the popular representation of the nation. With the advent of the press in the nineteenth century, the possibilities for representing the nation increased, but the structure of the press also frequently generated rather contradictory images. One complicated issue for the press was the relationship between the nation and history.

From its beginning, the *Gartenlaube* actively participated in the construction of a coherent and continuous national past. It selectively presented German history to generate a unified sense of the nation. Eric Hobsbawm has called this process of manufacturing a contemporary national identity from elements of the past the "invention of tradition." He suggests that the generation of a national historical myth is most likely to occur in a period of intense social change.[15] The modernization of nineteenth-century Germany that included industrialization, urbanization, migration, and eventually political unification (as well as division, if we consider the exclusion of Austrian Germans from the German Empire) made it a likely candidate for the "invention of tradition" when it came to the generation of a national identity. The *Gartenlaube* helped invent an unbroken national tradition by celebrating historical rulers, warriors, and cultural figures as well as contemporaries. It presented its readers with a long line of great German heroes such as Hermann the Cheruskan, Luther, and Friederich the Great. In doing so, it added to the ongoing process of constructing a myth of national origins and continuity.

This historical definition of the nation frequently stood in contrast to an explicitly modern presentation of Germany. As a modern phenomenon itself, the illustrated press was fascinated with topics of social, economic, and industrial modernization. Articles on technological and scientific innovation took up a significant amount of space in the *Gartenlaube*. Many of the magazine's essays and illustrations were devoted to explaining various aspects of modernization to a general audience. Essays about the growth of modern communication systems such as the telegraph constitute just one example of this interest. Invariably, the industrial growth of Germany and, especially after 1871, the German Empire's increasing international competitiveness were heralded as a sign of national strength. In other words, the magazine included numerous representations of the nation that stood in an uneasy alliance with an atavistic, historically rooted conception of the nation.

Such oppositions and the broad array of images of the German nation that appeared in the *Gartenlaube* should alert us to the fact that any construction of the nation is conflicted and contradictory. As the press developed into an increasingly dominant institution, it provided a powerful alternative to the official doctrine about the nation produced by the state or explicitly political agencies. This alternative was based on the generation of conscious and preconscious images of national belonging that preceded and followed the founding of a formal nation-state. Before the unification of the German Empire in 1871, the press was an important placeholder for a political definition of a nation that was awaiting fulfillment. After 1871 the press's vision of the nation often went beyond the accumulation of people into a unified citizenry, beyond the collation of geographical regions and governmental authority. After the founding of the German Empire, the popular press even continued to promote some images of the German nation that were not synonymous with the limits of Bismarck's newly established nation-state. The press reproduced constructions of national identity that spoke to more than a political sense of citizenship among its readers. It could appeal to a diversity of identities (based on region, gender, class, and religion), some of which were not recognized at the level of state authority. The press was thus an advocate of the German nation both in the absence of a unified state and sometimes in opposition to the state.

This flexibility of the press suggests that the study of nationalism and national identity must always consider identity in the context of other overlapping and at times conflicting interests. In the following chapters on the representation of German identity in the popular press, the nation will at times appear to be rooted in tradition, yet at other times epitomize modern society and its progress; at times be tied to public displays of social activity, but at other times be allied with the domestic sphere of middle-class women; at times go beyond all class differences, but at other moments spring forth from the very notion of bourgeois sociability. Rather than downplay or smooth out these disjunctures, this analysis of the press points to the necessity of difference and of including multiple identities in any successful popular construction of the nation. As paradoxical as they may seem, these varied, even contradictory, perspectives on the nation provide us with a more accurate sense of what the "nation" is, and how it operates in a historical moment, than would any list of typical national attributes.

READING SUBJECTS AND THE
STRATEGIES OF REPRESENTATION

The problem of identities brings us to the issue of the historical subject of national discussions and images. The contemporary readers of the *Gartenlaube* are long gone. References to their reactions to the magazine are rare at best. A thesis about the reception of this material might, drawing on reception theory in literary studies, posit an ideal or prototypical reader.[16] But the nineteenth-century popular press in general and the *Gartenlaube* in particular had a diverse readership, even more so than literature of that time. Because of the magazine's variety of material and, most important, because of its broad and varied audiences, it would be misleading to talk of a single *Gartenlaube* reader. Any conception of an ideal reader must take into account the range and identities of historical readers and also account for the possibility of numerous "ideal" readings.

Even though this book attempts to understand the parameters of national identity laid out by this popular periodical, it can only make approximations concerning the actual impact (if that indeed can ever be assessed about any historical factor) of the *Gartenlaube*'s images and essays. And yet, the popularity and success of this publication over many decades indicate that its images and essays struck a chord with a significant portion of the German population. More than any other contemporary example of the popular press, the *Gartenlaube* apparently found an attractive or intriguing tone for nineteenth-century, middle-class ears. The *Gartenlaube*'s regularity and consistency confronted each reader (or consumer) with the fact that he or she was doing what a large number of others were doing. The magazine encouraged an act of imagining that constituted the awareness of a common activity and thus a common identity.[17] Each image that was absorbed by this readership also emphasized commonalities among readers, describing the nation as a community of individuals with important similarities. In the case of the *Gartenlaube*, the nation can be redefined as an assembly of readers or reading subjects. If the periodical media offer the cultural historian one main indicator of popular tastes and interests, then the *Gartenlaube* is one of the best sources we have of nineteenth-century mainstream German identity.[18]

Several scholars have developed interpretive tools for considering the ideological components of identity. The most useful of these for this context interrogate the construction of identity by examining the prerequisite elements of political subjectivity. The activity of reading might be described by borrowing a phrase from Anne Norton's work on political identity; it is an "act of abstraction that enables individuals to recognize their common national identity," an act that, Norton claims, "establishes a collective capacity . . . for the process of differentiation and ordering characteristic of institutional rationalization."[19] As a literary scholar, Homi K. Bhabha pays particularly close attention to the processes of narration that constitute the identity of the subject.[20] In his own words, he has attempted to formulate "the complex strategies of cultural identification and discursive address that function in the name of 'the people' or 'the nation' and make them the immanent subjects and objects of a range of social and literary narratives" (292). Bhabha alerts us to the fact that the nation is not necessarily invoked in a uniform, unambiguous manner but rather remains ambivalently multiple and complex in its address to the reader (293–97). These concerns have informed the narrative focus of this project.[21]

In addition to considering the problem of representing the nation and national identity, this book also argues in favor of treating popular literature as an important textual source. In the last few decades many scholars have begun to take this material seriously as textual expressions that function according to the same principles as so-called high literature. The strategies of narrative perspective, identification, address, and focalization, to name some of the key concepts, are important tools for understanding the impact of the popular press on its readers.[22] The following chapters should demonstrate that detailed narrative analysis can be just as valid and useful for these works as it is for canonical literary texts. In this reconsideration of popular texts, the sociology of literature joins a critique of the canon.[23] Both are complemented by research in the field of publishing (*Publizistik*) which provides a rich resource on the demographics and the evolution of the periodical press, from the moral weeklies of the eighteenth century to the beginning of popular illustrated magazines and the family magazine of the nineteenth century.[24] This scholarship informs the following analysis of the production, distribution, and demographics of the nineteenth century's rapidly expanding periodical press.

Some scholars have suggested that cultural studies is concerned with the culture of the twentieth century.[25] This book is founded on the premise that popular reading material was an important element of literary and national culture of the nineteenth century. The analysis of the *Gartenlaube* presented here suggests that an examination of popular culture from earlier periods can yield important insights for the field of cultural studies.

The individual chapters of this book combine the broad issue of developing a mass readership with the operations of specific textual representations. The book is roughly chronological, from the beginning of the magazine's publication, through its most successful decades, to the end of the century as the *Gartenlaube* began to lose readers and could no longer claim to be Germany's most popular periodical. Each chapter deals with one or more themes that were of particular interest to the magazine in a specific decade. This thematic focus and organization is not meant to imply that those topics appeared only at that time or that there was no temporal overlap of various issues. Rather this selective thematic approach has been used to reveal patterns in a vast amount of material the magazine published over a fifty-year period. It shows how the magazine responded over time to the changing political configuration of Germany and the evolving issues of late-nineteenth-century modernization.

The first chapter outlines the backdrop for the *Gartenlaube*'s success in marketing its version of liberal politics and national cohesion in the second half of the nineteenth century. It discusses some of the magazine's historical precursors and the structural factors that allowed for the growth of reading and publishing. It pays particular attention to the *Gartenlaube*'s appeal to a middle-class, family audience that helped establish for the first time a nonpartisan and nonparticularistic social group, the mass audience, as the foundation for national identification. The success of the *Gartenlaube* was prototypical in developing both a personal and national reader appeal. This chapter sets the stage for the subsequent analysis of the magazine's thematic representations of the nation from the 1850s through the end of the century.

Chapter 2 examines the role of geography in defining the nation. The *Gartenlaube* and other family magazines borrowed a central preexisting discourse of national space in their representations of a continuous national identity. For instance, the popular series of essays on German landscapes and customs (including those of German emigrants) expanded the individual reader's knowledge of regional uniqueness at the same time it established a vocabulary of familiarity and unity. In focusing on a national geography from its very first issue, the magazine appealed to a traditional view of defining the nation even in the context of modern concerns. By looking at the *Gartenlaube*'s construction of a common geography in its first few decades, this chapter shows how the press, despite its modernity, initially relied on older, well-tested methods of constructing political identity.

By contrast, the next two chapters discuss definitions of the nation that can be considered a product of the modern era. They explore the magazine's rhetoric regarding technology and the impact of technological advances on political and social life. Chapter 3 identifies the fascination of this family magazine (beginning with its second decade of publication) with the role of technology in defending the nation, both in military conflicts and in the context of economic growth and industrial progress. The magazine's outspoken support in the 1860s of innovations such as coastal rescue devices and firefighting demonstrates how modern technology appeared at the center of a burgeoning discourse on public safety in the name of national stability.

Chapter 4 uncovers the magazine's later presentation of the nation as a mass spectacle. In the 1870s and 1880s, the German Empire celebrated its political power with the ambitious construction of national monuments. As the *Gartenlaube* reached the peak of its popularity, it distributed these images as symbols of unity, but it also interpreted them as signs of the nation's modernity and international competitiveness. The same interest motivated the magazine's presentation of national style and taste at world exhibitions. In such contexts, the nation itself became a commodity, a product being advertised at home and abroad to international audiences. This aspect of national identity was uniquely modern and inconceivable without the assistance of the mass media.

Chapter 5 analyzes the magazine's use of fictional narratives to consolidate the nation by speaking to a variety of constituencies. It considers in particular the way in which female readers were addressed by the *Gartenlaube*'s serialized stories and novels and shows how the tension between a traditional and a modern definition of the nation was tied on many levels to the problems of gender identity. The agents of Germany's historical change, the influential political and social members of the nation, were generally presumed to be men. However, as a family magazine, the *Gartenlaube* was highly conscious of the importance of its female readers. Women were explicitly addressed as part of the mass audience that constituted the national community. Yet, given the difference in gender identities in nineteenth-century society, the role of women in national concerns differed from that of men. Incorporating women into the definition of the nation meant combining national and domestic concerns. This chapter analyzes the early mass media's strategy of appealing to women readers as domestic participants in the national cause.

The final chapter examines the *Gartenlaube* at the end of the century. From 1885 to 1900 the magazine produced an ever-widening array of national images, from celebrations of Germany's new colonial empire to sentimental visions of rural German existence. These images point to an intersection of traditional and modern identities at the turn of the century. The increasing complexity and diversity of national representations in these years also coincided with a gradual decline in the magazine's popularity. This coincidence signaled a fundamental difficulty in uniting the disparate, contradictory interests that existed within Germany. It suggests that by the beginning of the twentieth century (at the latest) the modern nation had become too complex for the liberal goal of finding a unified representation that could speak to all Germans.

The decision to write a book on the construction of national identity raises several concerns for the author. First, it means tackling one of the most profound and powerful issues of contemporary society. The search for a national identity has been perhaps the most politically influential concern in the last two centuries. It has motivated the founding of states and political movements, and it has led to the destruction of societies and brutal persecution of minorities who have been excluded from the definition of the nation. Defining this phenomenon goes beyond the scope of any one volume. Most scholars agree that a conclusive definition for nationalism and national identity is elusive at best.[26] A comprehensive and satisfactory explanation for the appeal of nationalism seems even more remote.

Second, precisely because it has been such a powerful force in recent history, and perhaps also because it is so difficult to define, national identity has generated a vast library of scholarship. The first wave of research on nationalism was generally historical in its attempt to trace the path of the "nation" and "nationalism" as related concepts.[27] Much of the early work was an indirect response (in the 1920s) to the chauvinistic nationalism that led to World War I and then (in the 1930s and '40s) to the expansionist, racist nationalism of National Socialism.[28] Later work by sociologists tended to be more systematic, attempting to present a typology of national forms and movements.[29] In the last two decades alone, the nation and nationalism have inspired substantial historical and theoretical work by scholars in a variety of fields. This work has focused on such issues as the social development of national identity as a universally modern phenomenon (Gellner, Anderson, Hobsbawm), on the role of the state in the nation (Seton-Watson, Breuilly), or on the ethnic origins of nations and national identity (Smith).[30] These scholars have produced theoretical models and disciplinary perspectives that provide an at times overwhelming source of inspiration for the newcomer.

Finally, the study of national identity also raises personal concerns for the scholar. Regardless of the era or place under consideration, nationalism is relevant to all contemporary cultures. Because each of us is a member of a nation, we are all confronted with the problem of the nation when understanding our personal identity. Even those of us critical of nationalism as an activist movement are left in the awkward but unavoidable situation of defining ourselves against the backdrop of a national identity, one perhaps most frequently and vociferously put forward by those with whom we disagree. This mixture of public and private concerns makes the project of writing a book on national identity as stimulating as it is daunting.

The resurgence of national chauvinism and renewed notions of ethnic purity in Europe, and in Germany specifically, provide the ultimate backdrop for this project. The continued primacy and intransigence of national loyalties in political conflicts challenge us to understand at least a few aspects of this pervasive and often destructive social force. However, this book is not primarily about explaining the roots of chauvinism and racism as they entered national discourse in the late nineteenth century. Other scholars have contributed much to locating the origins of twentieth-century German nationalism by tracking the developments that preceded and led up to the events that have come to epitomize the use of brutality in the name of a nation: Nazi Germany and its culmination in expansionist warmongering and the Holocaust. Intellectual historians like George Mosse and Fritz Stern have looked at expressions of nationalism in nineteenth-century German intellectual work with this in mind.[31]

This book is also not about the construction of nationalist organizations in Germany at the end of the century. Historians such as Geoff Eley and Roger Chickering, to mention just two, have written articulately about the formation and success of nationalist organizations at the end of the century. They have pointed to the inflamed nationalist propaganda of patriotic societies that preceded and incited Germany's entry into the Great War.[32] To be sure, such organizations and ideologies were crucial to understanding the politics and, in particular, the foreign policy of Wilhelminian Germany. But despite their memberships in the millions by the early twentieth century, these groups did not represent the mainstream of German society.

What interests me, instead, is how and why, at a time of relative stability and normalcy, a large part of the German people imagined themselves as connected through the nation. This means trying to understand the mechanisms that already existed in the nineteenth century for constructing and disseminating images of national identity. This book offers a model for analyzing the relationship between the popular press and the development of political identity by examining the audience as a political subject and by showing how the search for a national identity in Germany was tied to the increased commercialization of cultural production. It also suggests that the nation, precisely because it is a constructed political identity based on a synthesis of many other identities, must be thought about in terms of the communication systems within society. The *Gartenlaube* serves here as material for such exploration. In its own time and place it was highly successful at constructing a sense of national identity that appealed to a broad readership. Its example might help us understand the processes and effectiveness of the mass media in our own time.

Popularizing the Nation

1

UNIFYING A NATION
OF READERS

In 1861 an article in *Die Gartenlaube* introduced its readers to the newest printing technology, the rotary printing press. The article's author expressed his admiration for the wonders of this new, steam-driven, Hoe "Ten-Cylinder-Type-Revolving-Machine" that enabled the *London Times* to distribute one hundred thousand copies of its paper "around the globe" each day. With detail typical of the *Gartenlaube*, the article described the size, speed, and specifications of this impressive innovation. Before doing that, however, the author lamented the comparatively dismal press situation in his homeland. "To my knowledge," he wrote, "no such wonder is in operation in Germany. Indeed, one could hardly make good use of it or feed it enough here. Police, taxes, and an old-fashioned, lazy manner of selling and reading newspapers, in other words, officials, the public, and newspaper entrepreneurs do everything in their power to ensure that no newspaper is published speedily, for a reasonable price, and in 100,000 copies." He proposed that such a modern printing press would only be possible in Germany "when the wings of our mental and material life are freed from the leaden weight of police fear and from our own clumsiness" (1861: 549).

Despite this gloomy picture of the nation's press landscape, the author went on to boast about the distribution success of the *Gartenlaube*. "Until now only one organ has made it to a circulation of over 100,000; it is not a newspaper, but rather the paper that the reader will not even have to look for if he reads the *Gartenlaube*" (1861: 549). The weekly magazine, which began publication in 1853 with printings of 5,000–6,000 copies, had grown in less than eight years to a circulation of 100,000.[1] In 1861 it was the largest periodical publication in all of Germany, but this was only the beginning of the *Gartenlaube*'s road to dominance in the German press marketplace. It was to remain the most popular magazine through the end of the century.[2]

Beyond serving as an advertisement for the magazine in which it was published, this essay from 1861 points to the main components of the nineteenth-century press as a modern institution. It identifies the creation of a mass readership as central to the success and vitality of the publishing industry; it mentions the new technology that would enable the press to produce circulations in the hundreds of thousands; and it cites the social and political factors, such as censorship and reader interest, involved in the growth of the mass press in any country. In Germany, as the essay correctly states, these factors first came together not with the daily newspaper but in support of a periodical genre that came to be known as the weekly illustrated family magazine.

The nineteenth-century popular family magazine generated the German press's first mass audience, and the *Gartenlaube* led the way.[3] By the 1860s, for the first time, this magazine had established a growing readership that spanned all of Germany. By definition, this early example of the mass media had implications for the nation. When the *Gartenlaube* spoke to the nation, it could be certain that a significant percentage of that "nation" was listening. Both in terms of the magazine's geographical reach and the variety of social classes and identities to which it appealed, the *Gartenlaube* had acquired a national audience. Before discussing representations of the German nation or German people that appeared in the *Gartenlaube* and similar publications, it is important to consider their potential impact. That impact was tied to the audience the *Gartenlaube* tapped so successfully, the readership that received and consumed the magazine's representations of the nation.

This chapter approaches the notion of the nineteenth-century magazine audience in three ways. It begins by tracing the history of the press and its readership in the early nineteenth century. The increase of reading behavior in the late eighteenth and early nineteenth centuries was a prerequisite for the development of the *Gartenlaube*'s national audience. Structural factors such as rising literacy levels, new print technology, and improved means of distributing the press made that mass audience possible. Second, the chapter describes the gradual emergence of the mass press in Germany. The inexpensive penny magazine, the illustrated weekly, and the family magazine all arose in the mid–nineteenth century. As founder and first editor of Germany's most popular magazine, Ernst Keil learned from each type of publication and devised an impressive recipe for success in the print press. Finally, the chapter closes with a definition of the national audience at the end of the century. From the beginning, the popularity of Keil's *Gartenlaube* was tied to the attention it paid to national concerns. But one magazine's representation of national identity does not fully explain the popularization of the idea of the nation. It is also important to understand that expansion of the press into a mass medium was an equally essential element in making the nation a truly popular concept. This chapter thus outlines the publishing context of the second half of the nineteenth century in order to provide the background for a subsequent discussion (in later chapters) of the *Gartenlaube*'s thematic construction of German identity.

ORIGINS OF THE MASS PRESS

Ideologically, the press was a child of the Enlightenment. Its distribution of general information and its call for critical reflection concerning social and political issues had their roots in the philosophical movement of the eighteenth century that proclaimed the intellectual emancipation of all individuals. The Enlightenment idea of a society of equal individuals emerged from a middle-class public sphere that developed in contrast to the nobility's traditional sphere of public representation.[4] This was a social space in which private individuals (generally members of the educated middle class) could convene to reflect on cultural, aesthetic, and moral concerns and express criticism.[5] One of the main institutions in which this critical discussion took place was the periodical press.[6]

3

It is not surprising then that the press grew along with the public sphere.

In Germany, an important vehicle for the public discussion of Enlightenment notions of morality and reason was the so-called *Moralische Wochenschriften*, or moral weeklies.[7] These periodicals began publication in the first third of the eighteenth century and flourished in Germany as they had in England and France.[8] They offered upper- and middle-class readers (both intellectuals as well as merchants and manufacturers) a forum for the exchange of ideas. They were intended to improve morals and facilitate a public discussion about aesthetic, intellectual, and occasionally even political matters of the day.[9] Authors of all persuasions discovered in this new medium a means for bringing their opinions and ideas to the public more quickly and easily than through books.[10] This early example of the periodical press constituted a regular and continuous form of communication that encouraged discussion and dialogue, often even soliciting responses or reader input (that it then supposedly published). As such, it had a dramatic impact on eighteenth-century society and thought.[11]

In addition to presenting new subject matter, the moral weeklies addressed a changing readership. For our case, the most significant shift was the often explicit acknowledgment of both men and women as readers. The first issue of Gottsched's *Der Biedermann* illustrates this.[12] This inclusion of women readers was a prerequisite for the eventual popularization of the illustrated magazine and the creation of a mass periodical press in the next century.[13] The circulation of the moral weeklies themselves remained nonetheless modest, rarely exceeding 400 copies.[14] Erudite references in these publications limited their potential reading audience.[15] Rolf Engelsing has also pointed out that the reading audience during the Enlightenment was well educated and relatively homogeneous; a significant differentiation of reader interests and characteristics did not take place until the nineteenth century.[16] In other words, these magazines constituted an early attempt at popular communication to a critically interactive audience. Their objective was education and the dissemination of information and they were often informal in tone and generalist in content. However, they were still far from

4

popular in terms of appealing to a wide audience. Their reception was restricted to a privileged segment of the population.

The development of the periodical press, from the eighteenth-century moral weeklies to the beginnings of a mass press in the nineteenth century, involved radical changes on several fronts. In terms of production, the early nineteenth century witnessed the advent of more efficient printing technology and distribution. These technological factors eventually combined to make the periodical press available to a broad audience. Alongside these structural changes were shifts in the political climate that also affected the development of a popular press. But availability and permissibility in themselves were still not enough for the development of a truly popular press. The new reading material also had to be appealing and accessible to a larger reading public. That presumed, first and foremost, a substantial increase in literacy, leisure, and reading interest in a large subset of the population.

These economic, technological, political, and social considerations were interrelated. It is difficult, if not impossible, to untangle their roles as factors of change from their roles as the result of other influences. But this distinction is not important to understanding their combined influence on the institution of the press. Throughout the late eighteenth and the nineteenth centuries, their cumulative effect was the emergence of the mass press. Without positing the priority of any one of these factors over the others, let us consider each in isolation in order better to understand its significance.

Literacy

The development of the modern press was ultimately all about creating an audience. Without the explosive expansion of the nineteenth-century reading audience there would have been no mass press. But what made this expansion possible? Certainly one necessary element for establishing a mass readership for the popular press was the ability of the national populace to read. The expansion in literacy from the eighteenth to the late nineteenth centuries in Germany was dramatic, although it is impossible to establish exact literacy rates with certainty.[17] Rudolf Schenda has estimated that the literacy rate in Germany in 1770 was approximately 15 percent. By contrast, one hundred years later the number of potential readers was about 75 percent, and by the end of the nineteenth century, closer to 90 percent of the population.[18] A similarly impressive growth in the number of children attending school and completing a minimum education also occurred in the nineteenth century, thanks to the introduction of mandatory schooling. In Prussia, for instance, the percentage of school-age children who attended elementary school increased from 60.6 percent in 1816 to 87.5 percent in 1864 and to 92.8 percent in 1900.[19] In addition to these increases in percentages, it must be considered that the population of Germany itself increased by 67 percent between 1816 and 1871.[20] These increases in literacy, basic education, and population do not of course mean that there was a parallel increase in the number of individuals who read on a regular basis. Yet most historians agree that of those individuals who could and did read, many more read the periodical press than books.[21]

Distribution

In addition to the growth of the population at large and the increase in literacy and education, the actual activity of reading depended on the availability of reading material. Given the difficulty of transportation in the early nineteenth century, where these potential readers lived mattered almost as much as their ability to read. The substantial shift of the rural population to the cities was itself a major force in expanding the actual reading population because city life meant greater access to new texts. The population in most cities increased by somewhere between six and ten times in the course of the nineteenth century, and that concentration of readers alone made delivery of periodical publications to a larger audience much easier.[22] For the still significant rural or small-town population, improvements in transportation helped increase readership. Expansion of roads and later railroads contributed to improved delivery of the periodical press on a regular basis.[23]

The greatest impediment to the distribution of the periodical press was government controls and regulations. Independent delivery systems of periodicals were not feasible until circulations increased substantially. Colportage, the house-to-house sale of subscriptions and delivery of magazines by traveling salesmen, was used but also expressly prohibited by law at various times in the nineteenth century. Postal systems, which were responsible for delivering most magazines, also established numerous regulations that limited circulation. By the late nineteenth century these restrictions were lifted somewhat and the fees for postal delivery of bulk periodicals decreased, in part due to the advances in transportation technology mentioned above. All of these factors played a major role in the rapid growth of periodical distribution by the final decades of the century.[24]

Censorship

As the *Gartenlaube* author quoted at the outset of this chapter was well aware, the political situation in Germany was also a central factor in the development of the mass press, not necessarily always in a supportive capacity, but certainly guiding and shaping its progress. Rudolf Schenda cites three main factors active in nineteenth-century censorship: church control, state laws, and moral watchdogs.[25]

For the press, state censorship was the most oppressive, since its goal of keeping citizens in a condition of political ignorance and subservience was at odds with the informational objectives of the press. The state made the periodical press, in particular, political newspapers, one of the main targets of its control. Any publication that led to political thinking or encouraged the organization of political groups was explicitly forbidden.[26] Although some smaller German states eased publishing restrictions after 1815, in Austria, Prussia, Saxony, and Baden strict censorship was maintained. In 1819 the repressive Carlsbad Decrees reacted to the growing national movement in Germany with increased severity. The result was that any publication of less than twenty sheets (320 pages) in length was subject to a thorough prepublishing review by the authorities. Only with the initially successful revolution in March 1848 were the restrictive press laws of 1819 lifted for a time.[27]

Nonetheless, even in times of extreme political repression, there was an active system for the public expression of opinion. Joachim Kirchner lists an impressive number and variety of magazines that began publication after 1815 (even under the constraints of the Carlsbad Decrees). Given the repressive state control of all aspects of the press, the diversity of these publications was considerable. In terms of distribution, however, these magazines remained limited. Most of them were regional publications that, because of their regional appeal, did not reach a national audience. And even in the area of "entertainment magazines," of which there were only a few, subscriptions rarely exceeded eight hundred. It was not until the 1850s, after the revolution of 1848, that the circulation of periodicals began to grow dramatically.[28]

Technology

While state censorship placed constraints on the content and thus the freedom of the press, it was in great part technological concerns that effected the development of a mass press in the early nineteenth century. The large-scale production of magazines and newspapers at a low cost was contingent upon an efficient and quick means of duplication. The most important inventions of the nineteenth century for the mass press were the cylinder printing press and the use of steam power in printing. In 1814 Friedrich König introduced his new cylindrical printing process that not only damaged less paper, but also drastically reduced printing time. With subsequent improvements in the printing press, within thirty years the number of impressions that could be made in one hour increased from four hundred to twelve hundred. By 1861 rotation presses, like the one described in the *Gartenlaube*, could produce between six thousand and eight thousand impressions in one hour.[29] The availability of quality paper in sufficient volume was another problem that was solved (at least partially) by the innovation of mechanized paper production over the course of the nineteenth century.[30] Still, because the machinery for mass production was so costly, consistent profits of a magazine had to precede and justify the economic investment that could make mass production possible. The result was a sort of vicious circle for the popular press: the size of a magazine's circulation in a sense determined its economic viability and thus its ability to enter the mass market. In sum, then, technological, political, demographic, and logistical changes in the second half of the nineteenth century all contributed to the growth of the print media into a mass phenomenon. The question that remains is which kinds of publications were in a position to profit most from this constellation of factors.

The Family Magazine

Two magazines for a general-interest audience benefited early on (in the 1830s and 1840s) from the structural changes described above. In the restrictive publishing environment prior to the German revolution of 1848, these periodicals experienced relatively little control from the censors, primarily due to their explicitly apolitical character. Both publications were precursors to the genre of the family magazine. The first magazine in Germany to reach a circulation in the tens of thousands was the *Pfennig-Magazin der Gesellschaft zur Verbreitung gemeinnütziger Kenntnisse (Penny Magazine of the Society for the Distribution of Commonly Useful Knowledge)*. This German publication, founded in 1833, was based on the English "Penny-Magazine."[31] As its title suggests, its price was low and its intention was to describe "the most important discoveries and inventions, unusual natural events, grand occurrences, interesting events, [and] the lives of famous men" (among other things) in an entertaining form. As an affordable, generalist periodical, it gained a circulation of 35,000 in its first year, and soon enjoyed a circulation of 100,000.[32] Joachim Kirchner suggests that the readership of this magazine included individuals from a variety of educational backgrounds, and that in this regard it was an important forerunner to the family magazine. Its essays in the areas of ethnology, religion, art history, and natural science suggest that its purpose was more to educate than to entertain.

Another magazine to gain a significant following was the *Illustrirte Zeitung (Illustrated Newspaper)*, founded in 1843. This magazine was not as affordable as the *Pfennig-Magazin* and thus had a more limited circulation. It reached a circulation of 8,500 by 1850. The reason for its high price was its inclusion of numerous finely reproduced illustrations in each issue, sixty-eight hundred of them in the first year alone. It was known for the excellent quality of these illustrations, but precisely because of the cost associated with them, the *Illustrirte Zeitung* never achieved the mass circulation of the *Pfennig-Magazin*. The appeal of illustrations in the *Illustrirte Zeitung* led the later family magazines to include illustrations on a regular basis in their weekly issues.[33]

By the middle of the nineteenth century, magazine production had adapted itself to the interests and expectations of an extended group of readers who for the most part had had little prior contact with publicist products.[34] As one German historian of the press summarized it, the *Pfennig-Magazin* was read by people who had earlier not even known what a journal was.[35] This trend of appealing to a broad audience expanded in the second half of the century with the advent of the family magazine; Kirschstein lists over 140 family magazines founded between 1850 and 1890. Thus, while the *Gartenlaube* was far and away the most successful, it was not the only family magazine.[36] In the 1880s several illustrated family and fashion magazines reached circulations thirty times that of publications with more demanding reading material.[37] Of all the new periodical genres of the nineteenth century, the family magazine had perhaps the most intimate connection to its readership.[38] These magazines carefully tailored their offerings and presentation to satisfy the presumed wishes and tastes of the broad middle classes who could afford them and had the education to read them. One contemporary summarized this process in the axiom: "The more subscribers a magazine has, the more certain it is that the taste of the subscribers will exert a substantial influence on its literary production."[39]

The content of the popular press as a whole distinguished it from other kinds of reading material that had (for centuries) reached a wide, geographically diverse audience. The Bible and song books, as well as almanacs, were the most widely read material of the eighteenth century, reaching readers from Bremen to Augsburg. But despite their presence within a national community, they devoted their attention to timeless rather than contemporary issues, appealing to eternal rather than temporal identities. The problem of national identity in nineteenth-century Germany was the stuff of the popular press and therefore new to the broad readership that had previously only had contact with what we might call "timeless" texts. Of course, the mass press did not immediately replace all other reading materials. The Bible and almanacs remained highly popular well into the nineteenth century. Rather than making such texts obsolete, the periodical press created and simultaneously satisfied a new desire for information about current events and developments, an interest in novelty that was to mark the modern age.

This distinction between timeless mass reading material and the popular press reveals a way in which Benedict Anderson's theory about the role of print-capitalism in the imagining of national community is framed too generally. Anderson's contention that novels of the early modern period could perhaps help create a mass national identity is valid, but he fails to note that the construction of an imagined national identity depends on a connection to contemporary life and on communication about contemporary life. Novels that dealt with contemporary relations, like the Filipino "Noli me tangere" cited by Anderson, may have lent themselves to a relevant imagining of national community.[40] Others, however, may not have. Just as the moral weeklies did not, in the first instance, construct a sense of national community because they did not reach a large enough audience, other popular texts that were of a timeless nature did not have an explicitly nationally cohesive effect on their readership because they were not concerned with contemporary social issues. The character of the mass press of the nineteenth century changed the role of texts in relationship to an audience. By directly addressing issues of national defense, viability, and industrial development as well as numerous social and cultural matters, and by constructing a coherent system of general public concerns, the popular family magazines of the late nineteenth century established a national discourse on identity.

GARTENLAUBE AS PROTOTYPICAL OF THE MASS PRESS

As we have noted, Ernst Keil's *Gartenlaube* was the most successful example of the nineteenth-century German family magazine. In many regards, Keil's magazine (like other family magazines) followed the pattern established by earlier serials in Germany. Like the *Illustrirte Zeitung* from Leipzig, it included texts from a variety of genres (fiction, travel writing, popular science), appealed to a wide range of reader interests, and incorporated quality illustrations into most of its articles. Like the *Pfennig-Magazin*, it was inexpensive, so as to encourage a large number of subscribers. And, finally, Keil envisioned the *Gartenlaube* as a magazine similar to Gutzkow's *Unterhaltungen am häuslichen Herd* (*Conversations around the Home Hearth*). It would be read in the family by young and old, male and female. But given these similarities, what explains the *Gartenlaube*'s astronomical success? Why did its circulation quickly grow from 5,000 in 1853 to 100,000 in just seven years, and to 385,000 by 1875?

In part, of course, the structural factors described above played a major role in the *Gartenlaube*'s numerical success. Without the greatly increased level of literacy that generated a large population of potential readers no magazine could have reached such a circulation. Without the new printing technology of the nineteenth century and the improved means of distribution, Keil could not have produced and distributed his magazine so inexpensively and quickly. In other words, Ernst Keil had the good fortune of founding his family magazine at a time when the press as a whole was expanding. In other countries as well, magazines were gaining similarly impressive circulations in the second half of the nineteenth century.[41] But these larger factors and the general growth of the periodical press do not explain why the *Gartenlaube*, in particular, enjoyed such great success. The family magazine was the most successful periodical genre of the period and the *Gartenlaube* the most successful of this genre. Why was its circulation after twenty years more than four times that of its closest competitor? How did it manage to keep its place as the most popular magazine in Germany for nearly half a century? We must look for the answer to these questions in the history and specific composition of the *Gartenlaube*.

A Liberal Magazine

From its beginning the *Gartenlaube* stood in the liberal tradition of the 1848 revolution. This political tradition was devoted to two causes: the guarantee of individual civil rights and freedoms and the unification of the German people.[42] Ernst Keil himself had an active publishing career in the years leading up to the revolution.[43] His first experience in journalism was as the editor (beginning in 1840) of *Unser Planet* (*Our Planet*), a magazine with contributors such as the notable liberal authors Robert Prutz and Louise Otto. Because of the threat of political repression, Keil changed this magazine's name in 1843 to *Der Wandelstern* (*The Planet*); at the same time he sharpened his progressive stance. In *Der Wandelstern* Keil called for improving social conditions for the masses and educating the German people as a nation, thus uniting the two ideals of liberalism: democracy and national patriotism.[44] Badgered again by censors and officials, Keil was forced to give up his editorship of the *Wandelstern* in 1845.[45] Undaunted by this political repression, in 1846 he founded *Der Leuchtturm* (*The Lighthouse*), a monthly magazine "for entertainment and instruction." Keil again experienced harsh censorship because of this magazine's liberal political position.[46]

The revolution in March 1848 changed the situation of the press in Germany. The initial successes of the revolution brought the end of censorship along with hopes for a united Germany. Keil's *Leuchtturm* celebrated this new era, but the revolution and freedom for the press were short-lived.[47] As the magazine's circulation grew past 4,000 in early 1849, it encountered renewed persecution. By 1850, Keil's magazine was forced to change its name and move from city to city in search of a tolerant haven for its outspoken views in favor of the republic, freedom of the press, and a united Germany. By 1851, it was finally closed down and Ernst Keil was arrested and sentenced to nine months in prison for breaking the reinstituted press laws of the postrevolutionary reaction.[48]

This prehistory to Keil's publication of the *Gartenlaube* is important for two reasons. First, Keil's earlier activities reveal the political commitment to liberalism that he never lost and that motivated the *Gartenlaube* from its beginning. Second, Keil's experience with the reaction after 1848 explains the changes he had to make to succeed in reaching an ever larger audience with his message of nationalism and liberalism.[49] Keil's idea for the *Gartenlaube* came while he was serving his prison sentence in 1852 for revolutionary publicist activity. With its initial publication in 1853, the *Gartenlaube* constituted a continuation of Keil's political struggle, but with different means.⁵⁰ His goal became to reach and enlighten the broadest possible segment of the German middle classes, because (as an early *Gartenlaube* article put it) freedom is only possible "in a relatively uniformly educated, uniformly virtuous society with the same interests" (1855: 424).⁵¹ Keil's publication objective of educating the German people to political maturity with the *Gartenlaube* was, from the start, dependent on reaching a large audience. Thus, both popularity and the generation of national identity were at the core of Keil's project.

The conservative post-1848 political climate in Germany severely limited the public form these liberal, democratic ideas could take.⁵² Keil's response to the censorship of the reactionary period was to cast his new magazine as neutral and apolitical. For this reason, the *Gartenlaube*'s self-introduction to its readers on the first page of the first issue was cautious and tentative: "Far from all political debates and disagreements in religious and other matters we want to introduce you to truly good stories about the history of the human heart and the world's peoples" (1853: 1). The professed harmless nature of the magazine's content was further tied to the ideal reading context of the middle-class family suggested in this same introduction: "When you sit in the circle of your loved ones on long winter evenings next to the cozy oven or with friends in the shady arbor in the springtime when the red-and-white blossoms fall from the apple tree—then read our publication" (1853: 1). Although the magazine was available in some public places such as lending libraries, it explicitly addressed itself to the family reading within the privacy of the domestic sphere, implying that its main targeted audience was the German family. The evocation of the peacefulness of an interior private space or of cultivated nature meant that the *Gartenlaube* could speak to the family within the security of the home, or what might be called the *"private Öffentlichkeit"* of mainstream German society.⁵³

The *Gartenlaube* was not alone in formulating this intimate response to the censorship of the post-1848 society. As noted earlier, one magazine that directly preceded Keil's and is considered to have been one of his models was Karl Gutzkow's family magazine, *Unterhaltungen am häuslichen Herd* (1852). The platform of this publication expressed the importance of the intimate familial space more explicitly: "There are times, when every conviction finds refuge in the family. . . . For us the domestic hearth is no thoughtless chatterbox . . . it is and remains for us the safe asylum of serious philosophy of life . . . a general union of humans as humans even when partisanship divides them."[54] Taken together, such statements, as well as the general popularity of the family magazine in the next few decades, suggest that the family was an important reserve in postrevolutionary German society.

This domestic agenda of the *Gartenlaube* was more than a preemptive measure against political censorship in a conservative era. The magazine's ability to define a national identity in late-nineteenth-century Germany was directly tied to its familial appeal. Put another way, the claim to represent the social attitudes of its audience rested upon the magazine's ability both to communicate its interest in the reader and to construct the broadest, most inclusive definition of that reader, whom (as we have seen from its introductory statement) it explicitly defined as anyone with family and friends. The idealized vision of the domestic family, emblazoned on the masthead of each weekly issue, changed only slightly over the decades. It depicted an extended family, in the circle of which a grandfather reads the magazine aloud to his children and grandchildren (see fig. 11).[55] According to the vision outlined in (or at least prescribed by) the magazine, the growing audience of the press was located in the intimacy and privacy of the domestic space. The *Gartenlaube* continued to identify the mass readership it gained during its first two decades as a nation living within the private space of home and family. Ironically then, the magazine's need to circumvent state control became part of Keil's recipe for success.

Building a Magazine Empire
In the most immediate sense, the success of the mass media in general, as well as any individual periodical publication, was directly tied to circulation—the number of subscribers that could be generated and maintained over a long period. Although the *Gartenlaube* was not the only family magazine of its era, its circulation far outdistanced its closest competitors.[56] According to available

circulation statistics, the *Gartenlaube* grew steadily throughout the first two decades of its publication.[57] In 1853 Keil's *Gartenlaube* began with a relatively modest printing of 5,000 copies, compared to the 15,000 and 50,000 of *Illustrirte Welt* (*Illustrated World*) and the *Illustrirtes Familien-Journal* (*Illustrated Family Journal*) in their second years, respectively.[58] Yet, within four years the *Gartenlaube*'s circulation had grown to 60,000, in seven years to over 100,000, and at the end of its tenth year had reached 180,000. Then in 1864, the publication of a story considered anti-Prussian by the censors caused the magazine to be banned in Prussia. This decreased its circulation by about 60,000, although that loss was quickly made up, and in 1867, when the Prussian ban was lifted, the *Gartenlaube*'s circulation rose dramatically to 230,000.[59] The increase in readership in these and subsequent years has often been attributed to the popularity of the magazine's new contributing fiction author, Eugenie Marlitt, whose works may have attracted female readers in particular.[60] Another source for this continuous and steady success, however, can be found in the magazine's dedication to the problem of defining Germany and German identity. In 1875, four years after the founding of the German Empire, the *Gartenlaube* reached its peak with a circulation of approximately 382,000.[61] This made the *Gartenlaube* the only periodical in nineteenth-century Germany to reach a circulation near 400,000, at a time when most daily newspapers did not print more than 4,000 copies.[62]

Not only was the *Gartenlaube*'s circulation unprecedented for Germany in the nineteenth century, its readership was considerably larger than the numbers of copies printed might indicate. The magazine's appearance in reading rooms, lending libraries, and cafes, as well as in the living rooms of many middle-class families, suggests that each copy was usually read by several people. Presuming at least five readers per copy, some historians of publishing have estimated a *Gartenlaube* readership in the millions. Given a total population of the German Empire in the mid-1870s of just over 40 million, the magazine certainly reached at least 5 percent of the total German population.[63] Even though this figure represents nowhere near a majority of the population, its significance was great. In addition to the fact that each issue was most likely read by several individuals, it has been argued that a cumulative reading practice increases the number of readers of a magazine in general.[64] In presuming that not always the same readers read each subsequent issue of a magazine, one can infer that a larger percentage of the national population read *Die Gartenlaube* than is represented by its circulation numbers, or even by a multiplication of the circulation by five.

The success of the *Gartenlaube* led to the founding of competitive magazines in the 1860s and later. The most notable example of this phenomenon was *Daheim* (*At Home*), which presented itself as a conservative alternative to the liberal magazine.[65] Another indication of the *Gartenlaube*'s popularity and name recognition was the founding of a magazine in Austria with the same title.[66] These publications followed a similar format and content week to week. As numerous as these imitators and competitors were, they never posed a serious threat to the predominance of Keil's magazine. It may be that its slight decline after Keil's death in 1878 was tied to a change in publishing policy that made distinctions between the *Gartenlaube* and other weeklies less substantial.

A National Community of Readers

In addition to winning an unprecedented readership, the *Gartenlaube* unified a community of readers that had not existed before in quite the same constellation. The significance of this new community can be understood in terms of geographical, regional, and class distribution. The development of this community stemmed from a popular or nonspecialized appeal that, ideally at least, transcended many social boundaries. The magazine's numerical success was more than anything a function of its decisive and explicit appeal to a readership that wanted to identify itself as German above all else, one that was interested in combining other social identities within the category of a common Germanness.

The *Gartenlaube*'s geographical distribution indicated that it acquired an audience that could be called national. The percentage of the national population the magazine reached was complemented by the geographical distribution of these readers. By the early 1860s, the magazine regularly reached audiences in all of the German lands. Although it was published in the southeastern city of Leipzig, the *Gartenlaube* was regularly subscribed to and read in distant parts of Germany.[67] Its reader letters from within Germany arrived from places as far apart as Königsberg, Freiburg, Kiel, and Munich. It reached large cities and small towns. The fact that the magazine could be found in all parts of Germany attests to its importance as a unifying disseminator of ideas and an index of transregional, that is, national interests. The nation of *Gartenlaube* readers extended beyond the bounds of what would eventually become the German Empire. The magazine reached German speakers in Austria, which, as we will see in the next chapter, was in keeping with its definition of Austrian Germans as part of the fatherland. The *Gartenlaube* even found its way beyond Europe to reach readers as far away as Siberia, Peru, and Australia. Collections from private subscribers abroad have landed in libraries in the United States and Brazil. The magazine itself boasted a distribution that included distant continents.[68]

The *Gartenlaube*'s variety of information made it attractive to many Germans. It generally did not reveal any particularistic preferences or loyalties. In rare instances, loyalty to its home of Leipzig in Saxony was noticeable in the narration of particular events, such as the German war of 1866, in which the southern German states were aligned with Austria against Prussia. However, as a rule, the *Gartenlaube* never limited itself to the events or issues of one region of Germany. It consistently presented concerns that were of interest to readers outside of Leipzig.[69] Daily newspapers and publications in the tradition of the penny magazine, by contrast, were much more closely tied to local concerns. An emphasis on local issues enabled the editorship of local or regional publications to establish a close connection to its readership.[70] However, with the advent of the *Gartenlaube*, the interests of the whole German *Volk* were regularly and successfully addressed by one publication. The *Gartenlaube* was the pinnacle of the *"Familienblatt"* ("family magazine") which integrated two previous kinds of publications: the nationally distributed magazines that were limited to a highly educated audience and the local magazines that appealed to the lower-middle classes.[71] Keil was able to maintain a personal, intimate tone with his readers. At the same time, the *Gartenlaube* became a model for subsequent family magazines in mixing a wide array of topics with a tone of reader familiarity.

The thematic content of the *Gartenlaube* that enabled it to move beyond a regional readership also appealed to a broad spectrum of reader interests in German society. Other serial publications had previously enjoyed a distribution to most German lands, but these had a much more limited readership. Scholarly or scientific journals that had subscribers in many parts of Germany rarely achieved a circulation beyond 1,000.[72] The same can be said for literary magazines that catered to a more highly educated audience and for this reason cannot be considered mass publications. Periodicals that examined political or economic concerns were published primarily for a professional audience and thus limited to an intellectual, professional subset of the national body. Only with the advent of the family magazine were many of these themes combined within one weekly publication and offered in a general and popularizing tone that was meant to incorporate as many readers of the nation as possible. Rather than addressing a specialist audience with a common foundation of expertise, the *Gartenlaube* fashioned itself as a popularizer of information. The initial outline Ernst Keil drafted for the magazine proposed that it "discuss the most important and relevant questions from nature in thoroughly popular letters."[73] Furthermore, Keil insisted that such contributions should be comprehensible to the most common artisan (*Handwerker*), but especially to women, and that in general it be "understandable to everyone."[74]

In addition to going beyond the limitations of regional audiences and specialized readerships, the *Gartenlaube* attempted to broaden its readership by transcending class differences.[75] As we have seen, Ernst Keil gave the magazine a pronounced liberal tendency from its inception, and that fact suggests that the magazine's readership was located solidly within the German middle classes. However, the *Gartenlaube* always attempted to address reader interests outside a narrow middle-class audience. One example of its intention of speaking to a lower-class audience is the series of essays intended explicitly for potential emigrants to the New World in the 1850s and 1860s, as we shall see in more detail in the next chapter. Another example is the fact that the magazine carried regular contributions by and about Hermann Schulze-Delitzsch, an advocate of working-class concerns and social reform.[76] The lower-middle-class or peasant members of the nation were always at least implicitly included in the *Gartenlaube*'s selection of material.

Like other family magazines, the *Gartenlaube* kept its subscription price moderate in the hopes of being accessible to a large audience.[77] Of course, even these prices were often beyond the financial means of working-class families, but lower-class readers nonetheless had some contact with the family magazine through lending libraries and reading rooms. Rolf Engelsing has documented that the *Gartenlaube* was a regular part of nineteenth-century lending library collections, where individuals who chose not to or could not subscribe could still read it. In some libraries it was the most highly represented magazine.[78] It was also generally available in common reading rooms (*Volksbüchereien*), even if it was not always the most frequently read publication there.[79] Some statements of contemporaries indicate that working-class people read the magazine as they happened to come across individual issues.[80]

IMPLICATIONS OF POPULARITY

The *Gartenlaube*'s popularity and unprecedented distribution throughout Germany was intimately tied to what the magazine became and how it saw itself. Its popularity was not just a marker of its ability to satisfy reader desires; it had an effect on the editor's estimation of the magazine and its import. Most notable is the right the magazine began to claim for itself by the 1860s to speak for the German nation. As we will see, from its very first issue the nation was a major focus of the individual contributions in the *Gartenlaube*. But only with the surge in its popularity did the magazine begin to present itself as a representative mouthpiece for the German *Volk*. The connection between the magazine's circulation and its ability to speak for the German nation was made clear at the beginning of 1861. In this ninth year of the *Gartenlaube*'s publication, its editor published a self-congratulatory note on the first page of the first issue, announcing that the magazine had surpassed a circulation of 100,000 copies before any other. This self-advertisement took an informal, personal tone, addressed "to our readers." But equally as important as this numerical success was the reason the editorship saw behind the magazine's popularity.

According to the logic of Keil's editorial commentary, readership expansion was indebted above all to the fact "that it [*Die Gartenlaube*] has the goal of being a German paper through and through" (1861: 1).[81] A thoroughly German magazine meant, according to Keil, that its contributions are German originals from German authors, that its illustrations come from German artists (not copies of French or English magazines), and that it discuss, above all, German life and aspirations. That such devotion to German culture was not merely part of a blind nationalism is evidenced by the prescription that all elements of the magazine should reveal a "love of the German fatherland . . . even in instances when one cannot speak highly of it." In other words, the "Germanness" of the magazine lay not in any loyalty to a state, but rather in a dedication to the German people that included self-criticism. This dedication was reinforced by assurances that future issues of the magazine would continue to be "thoroughly German" in the interest of continuing to satisfy its readership and in the hopes of increasing it. The contents of the volume from 1861, published after this notice, provide a good indication of what the *Gartenlaube* editorship believed constituted a "thoroughly German" paper in the second half of the nineteenth century. In the following summary of topics from the year 1861, we can get a clear idea of the national concerns the *Gartenlaube* generally raised.[82]

Every one of the *Gartenlaube*'s fifty-two issues in 1861 devoted some space to the problem or fate of the German nation.[83] Most prevalent, even in the absence of a current war, was the commemoration of martyrdom and military heroism in the name of the nation. The *Gartenlaube* attempted most frequently to rally its readers for the nation through tales of the foreign occupation of Germany by the French from 1806 through the Wars of Liberation in 1813.[84] In five articles labeled "From the Times of Great Trouble,"[85] the magazine repeatedly described the "iron suppression of the

German people by foreign despotism" (1861: 597). Its stated objective was to keep the memory of noble, patriotic deeds of heroic individuals alive in the minds of contemporary Germans so that the nation would be ready to defend itself again if necessary (1861: 630). These "simple, yet accurate sketches" of dedication to "the holy cause of the German people" (1861: 597) describe the lives of a bookseller, Palm, who was executed for his patriotic publications; of a nationalist newspaper publisher, Rudolph Zacharias Becker; and of a simple man named Born, who, although "just a shepherd," died by refusing to betray Germany even to save his own life (1861: 233–35). This last story ends with a clear message for contemporary readers: the defeat of Germans at Jena in 1806 pales in comparison with the determination and "beautiful" death of patriotic Germans such as this simple shepherd.[86]

The emotional appeal to a national identity is strong in such stories. Each of these three contributions is written in the emphatic, passionate style that also marked the magazine's serialized fiction. Although they are presented to the reader as historical accounts, they include information and perspectives that could not have been documented, such as the following psychological reconstruction of the shepherd Born's last moments: "Born was silent. Something seethed and welled-up in his breast. He could not become a traitor! . . . With bound hands he was led to the edge of the hill. In front of his eyes three soldiers loaded their rifles, he turned away. He was granted one half hour to come to his senses. Without a word, he sat down and fixed his gaze into the valley and on the distant mountain heights. His cheeks were pale. What emotions must he have felt!—a tear crept into his eye—he forced it back" (1861: 235).[87] The moral of all of these individual cases is that national pride and character rests not so much in outward success as in inner nobility and commitment.

These national themes appeared in a wide variety of genres in the magazine. Many essays about national military struggles, such as the Wars of Liberation or the hope of German nationalists to wrest Schleswig from Danish control, were published in the 1840s and 1850s in the form of reportage.[88] Other essays took the form of biographies and were listed as such in the volume's index. Poetry was also a common medium for praising national heroes, such as Theodor Körner (who was himself a national poet of the Wars of Liberation). Even the serialized fiction of 1861 paid tribute to solid German characteristics; for more than half of the year a novel by Otto Rupius, "Ein Deutscher" ("A German"), about a German emigrant to America described the title figure's responsibility, honesty, trustworthiness, and concern for others. At the end of the story, this commendable German hero (often referred to explicitly as "the German") is rewarded for these virtues with the hand of a lovely young heroine (1861: 548). Many of these texts were accompanied by illustrations. This breadth is significant to the extent that different reader groups may have been more attracted to one or another aspect of the magazine.[89] Thus, all groups of *Gartenlaube* readers would have been exposed to these images of national heroism and battle, even if they only read certain types of texts in the magazine.

The description of noble German spirit that pervades the fiction by Rupius, the biographies of national heroes, and reports of patriotic courage make up approximately one-sixth of the 1861 volume. But many other national concerns fill the other pages of this one year. The most striking aspect of the presentation of the nation in 1861, as in other years, is the diversity of national concerns. In this volume are included a poem calling for the end of German particularism (1861: 365–66), a poem and essay in support of building a German fleet (1861: 654–56, 696), the tale of a "German inventor" (1861: 648–51), reports about rescue stations on the German coast, (1861: 811–14), a reminiscence about Frederick the Great (1861: 375–77, 388–92), and a history of the Hohenzollern family (1861: 709–11) in which the interests of the dynasty are contrasted with the needs of the entire German population.

That year, the magazine also devoted particular attention to great figures in the history of German intellectual life such as Luther (1861: 485–87, 669–70), as well as to lesser-known honorables such as the "German Burgher's Daughter" from the sixteenth century (1861: 212–15). It mentioned contemporary figures of German culture such as the philosopher and theologian Schleiermacher (1861: 28–30, 39–40) who was characterized as "ready in word and deed to serve the fatherland," and the historian Dahlmann (1861: 164–67,

183–85), of whom it said: "From the misery and shame of the Bonaparte rule the young man developed a pious, loyal love of the fatherland" (165).⁹⁰ The "people's painter" Böttcher (1861: 645–46), the king of traveling, Karl Bädeker (1861: 52–55) ("a good man . . . a German patriot"), and the "German newspaper writer" A. Bernstein were also listed as notable Germans who had honored their people with great service. Individual articles often explicitly identified the reason for their publication as an obligation to the reading nation: "We have only fulfilled our duty when we introduce the readers of our paper to a man who can justly accept the thanks of the nation for his many years of unflinching and committed work in its service" (1861: 456).

Beyond the contributions of individuals, the national organizations that renewed national sentiment for many Germans caught the attention of the *Gartenlaube*. In this one year of 1861, the magazine featured three major national institutions: in reports it praised the gymnastics movement, singing clubs, and sharpshooting societies. In the first third of the year, the *Gartenlaube* published a speech by a Dr. Schreber from Leipzig about the necessity of gymnastic exercises for the defense of the state and fulfillment of the people's "cultural historical task." Schreber called for the creation of an extended system of education built on physical training that would both make the German people strong and unite them. This reform plan would give the German culture strength to defend itself against outside enemies (1861: 278–80).

Two other events in 1861 enabled the *Gartenlaube* to expound on its ideal of a united German state. The magazine reported on the "First German Sharpshooting Festival" in eight pages of text (two essays) accompanied by one single-page and one double-page illustration (1861: 524–28, 539–43). After reporting on the groups in attendance, the parades and festivities, and the shooting competition, the *Gartenlaube* summarized the political aspirations of this group and thereby brought its national message to a much larger audience. "It is indeed an important work, this Federation of German Sharpshooters; in peacetime with joyful festivities it will unite all the tribes of Germany and bind them together and immovably anchor the idea of national community in each one of them" (1861: 543). Again and again, the *Gartenlaube* emphasized the German diversity represented in all aspects of the sharpshooting festival, in those present, in those who donated prizes, in those to whom toasts were offered: Germans from north and south, east and west, from Tyrol and Schleswig-Holstein, Switzerland, and America.[91]

To the same extent, the magazine celebrated the success of the national singing festival in Nuremberg just two weeks later (1861: 571–74, 587–92). Again, the magazine included several illustrations. A double-page image of the singing clubs' procession against the backdrop of medieval Nuremberg depicts not only the excitement of the singing clubs, but also the enthusiasm of the mass of people in Nuremberg who have come out to greet the singers. The image further indicates the diversity of those present. According to the banners shown, they come from as far away as Kiel (in the northern Duchy of Holstein, which was still tied to the Kingdom of Denmark), about which the first essay remarked, "The good people from Kiel wanted to prove that they are Germans and feel German with body and soul" (572), and from Innsbruck in Austrian Tyrol. The festival is another occasion for the *Gartenlaube* to call for Germany unity. In almost every paragraph, the unity of diverse Germans is celebrated; the fact that the black-red-gold banner of German nationalists waved over the festival was heralded as a sign that all those gathered here distanced themselves from petty particularism (1861: 571). This report closes with the personal testimony of the author, who apparently was a participant: "And to you, you dear singing brothers down in the South, who have become dear friends of your northern colleagues through your solid, heartfelt being, to you I reach out once again in spirit the hand of brotherhood from my homeland. We have sung loyally with each other, and it created a glorious harmony as North and South united themselves so closely. Every song, however, that we sang together with you shall be a marker for us of German unity" (1861: 592). Subsequent volumes of the *Gartenlaube* continued this active interest in German gymnastics, singing, and sharpshooting societies.[92]

The extraordinary appeal of this magazine over its competitors has puzzled scholars of the press. Contemporaries and historians of the press have accounted for the *Gartenlaube*'s phenomenal success by insisting that Keil knew his audience and gave it what it wanted.[93] Others have suggested that the popularity of any family magazine lies in its intimate ties to its readership.[94] Statements by readers about their interest in the *Gartenlaube* and other nineteenth-century magazines are rare.[95] The source of an individual magazine's popularity must therefore be inferred. The intensity with which the German nation was celebrated and commemorated in this average year of 1861 strongly suggests that the *Gartenlaube* saw this discussion of the nation as the key to its increasing popularity.[96] Even if we trust the statements of the *Gartenlaube*'s editors, we must ask *why* this insistence on national identity attracted so many readers. Why was the concept of the German nation as presented by the *Gartenlaube* so appealing?

New interests and problems arose for most people in the late nineteenth century. Social changes such as urbanization, industrialization, and emigration altered family and social relations and meant that the elements of individual existence were no longer predictable, no longer simply rooted in traditions that could be learned from others. These changes were increasingly tied to political, economic, and technological events outside the purview of the individual. As common people felt the need to explore the elements outside their immediate surroundings in order to understand these changes, the periodical press was there to provide them with the information they sought. The turn of the middle classes away from a primary preoccupation with timeless texts to the purchase and reading of the temporally based press was a sign of general changing interests.[97] The press provided access to the changing contemporary world.

One product of this new era was increasing conflict among an individual's multiple identities. Many magazines responded to this by providing what was considered good, moral reading material for "the German people." For the *Gartenlaube*, identification with the nation was a way of transcending conflicting and competing identities. The magazine's initial greeting to this national audience was printed on the first page of its first issue in 1853. Before summarizing the proposed contents of this new publication, the editor began: "Greetings to you, dear people, in the German land!" (1853: 1). This greeting, written in the second-person plural, informal "you," was friendly and informal. It immediately included all readers in "the German land," using the singular form of land, rather than the numerous German lands, to denote a nation united in spirit, if not yet in political terms. The focus on the nation for the liberal publicist Ernst Keil was an ideological program, but it also was the right concept at the right moment for integrating multiple identities and helping readers comprehend their changing social situation. One could argue that popularity was awarded the magazine that best helped its readers understand their place in the modern century. The point of identification was the nation, and liberals like Ernst Keil entered the second half of the century with a repertoire of representations of the nation.

With this national agenda, the *Gartenlaube* made the claim to speak for as well as about the nation. It repeatedly identified itself as a mouthpiece for the nation. The *Gartenlaube*'s explicit appeal to the entire nation as its audience enabled it to approach the status of a mass publication. Given this fact, it is important to understand what image of the nation appeared in this new medium. What did this intimate involvement of the periodical press with its readers and their desires mean for the image of the nation that emerged in the most accessible and widespread public forum in the late nineteenth century? The relationship between the mass media and its mass of readers, and the relevance of this new relationship for the construction of national identity, is what we will explore in the following chapters. These chapters outline the ingredients of the *Gartenlaube*'s successful national recipe.

2

PLOTTING A NATIONAL GEOGRAPHY

T he primary community of the popular illustrated magazine
was the middle-class family. This social group had the education, literacy levels, and leisure time to enjoy a weekly
publication. It could also afford individual subscriptions. Yet, even
if the family was the main subscriber and the primary target audience of the *Gartenlaube* and similar magazines, it was only one of
the readerships to which the magazine appealed. The genius of the
Gartenlaube and the key to its success was its ability to integrate
multiple social and cultural identities within its texts and images.
Our main concern here is the way in which the *Gartenlaube* formed
a national sense of self in the period of its greatest popularity. How
did it speak to an aggregation of Germans from a wide range of
geographical areas and thus with different local and regional loyalties? One way it did this was by citing geography as the basis for a
national community. It introduced the German nation as a community in space and provided an implicit map of the national space for
its readers. In the *Gartenlaube*, geography became a reliable means
of identifying and defining the nation.

"HEIMATH!": CREATING A FAMILIAR TERRAIN

The very first issue of the *Gartenlaube* reveals both the geographical
definition of the nation and the narrative construction of Germany
as a common homeland, or *Heimat* (arch. *Heimath*). In its slight
(eight-page) first number, the magazine greeted its readers with the
story of a German in America. This contribution appeared in the

form of a letter written by an emigrant to his brother in Germany.[1] The narrator begins by characterizing the place he had left behind in idealized terms. The first paragraph of this supposedly authentic, personal text is worth quoting in greater detail.

> It was a beautiful Sunday morning, as I took my leave from you and our homeland [*Heimath*]. On the fields lay the warm spring sunshine, and the birds sang their hymns to the heavens and from the towers of our small hometown the bells rang and called the pious to church. We stood on the mountain and looked down into the local [*heimathliche*] valley to which my most beautiful and lovely memories are tied. I will never forget that moment. You had thrown your arm around my neck, we did not speak, we only looked into each other's eyes and pressed our hands together and thought about the past. Yes, home, lovely home! [*Ja, die Heimath, die liebe Heimath!*] (1853: 5)

The image here is of a universalized homeland. The requisite elements of this description—Sunday morning, warm springtime sunshine, singing birds, towers and church bells, mountains, and a familiar valley—describe many German small towns. This passage is devoid of any specific regional markers such as names, invoking instead a generic geography. Its characterization of *Heimat* depicts an original and unchanging image of the German landscape.[2] Thus, while this first contribution is ostensibly about one particular German and his experiences abroad, its effect is to present a generally recognizable image of Germany for a variety of readers. Geography functions as a sign of similarity and familiar coherence. *Heimat* becomes a term that signifies Germany as a whole as well as a local or regional homeland. It helps establish a geographical commonality that can represent a unified and coherent image of national space.

The *Gartenlaube* presented German geography, as it did most of its subjects, in easily understandable images and language. In keeping with the magazine's appeal to a broad readership, its descriptions were not only readily accessible to regionally diverse audiences, they also appeared in a form that made the various regions, despite their differences, somehow familiar to all readers.

[handwritten margin note: generalizations]

The *Gartenlaube* was constantly confronted with a twofold task when introducing its readers to new landscapes. It had to emphasize the novel, unfamiliar aspects of those regions that made them worth describing, yet, at the same time, it needed to ensure that those places were recognizable as parts of a single larger, cohesive national space. Familiarity depended on narrative and visual presentation. The result was a textual process of generalization that discussed the specificity of a regional identity in order to emphasize its broader German relevance. The popular magazine, as a mediator of information and images, created a spatial vocabulary of the nation on several levels. The *Gartenlaube* could both familiarize its readers with geographical terrains and shape these places according to its own interests. More than that, it generated a national space in the minds of its readers that was not limited by political boundaries. The *Gartenlaube* helped establish a definition of the German nation as a community in space that both preceded the nation-state and stood in an uneasy alliance with it after 1871. In the process, the magazine itself became an important space for national imagining.

A geographical approach to defining the nation had a long tradition in Germany. For centuries, Germany lacked the unified political state authority of France and England. It had no metropolis like Paris or London that defined a central national culture. For the early nationalists of the nineteenth century, focusing on a German geography was one way of insisting on the unification of a regionally fragmented nation. Thus, the idiom connecting geographical regions was available to the *Gartenlaube* and other popular magazines in their attempt to define the nation. These publications thus often relied on this traditional representation of the German nation. This chapter begins with a brief overview of discourses on the nation as a community in space that predated the rise of the popular press.

GEOGRAPHY: TRADITIONAL DISCOURSE ON NATIONAL IDENTITY

The preoccupation with the geographical extent of the nation was in part a result of the fragmented political landscape of the Holy

Roman Empire of the German Nation. This amorphous political empire had lacked cohesion since the sixteenth century. Its political power and authority had been continually contested by particularistic regional rulers and shaken by the religious split of the Reformation.[3] At the end of the eighteenth century, its military and economic effectiveness lagged behind that of England and France.[4] Political disunity caused many thinkers to look to issues outside of political power to define the German nation.[5] Intellectuals of the German Enlightenment such as Friedrich Karl Moser and Gotthold Ephraim Lessing found the essence of the German nation in its culture, in the *Kulturnation*.[6]

Culture was also central to the nation in the work of Johann Gottfried Herder, who is often considered the father of German nationalism. Herder contended that language and culture were the constitutive elements of a people's or nation's identity.[7] In his major work, *Ideen zur Philosophie der Geschichte der Menschheit* (*Reflections on the Philosophy of the History of Mankind*) (1782–84), Herder emphasized the importance of geography for a people's cultural tradition and sense of self.[8] Although Herder also placed great emphasis on the role of education and contact with other cultures, geographical location was central to his notion of cultural formation: "Some sensitive people feel so intimately close to their native country, are so much attached to its soil, that they can scarcely live if separated from it. The constitution of their body, their way of life, the nature of work and play to which they have been accustomed from their infancy, indeed their whole mentality, are climatic. Deprive them of their country, and you deprive them of everything."[9] For Herder, geography and regional climate combined to shape a people's culture[10]; every nation and every people acquired a personality from these forces.[11]

This connection between culture and geography was taken up by Johann Gottlieb Fichte, who adopted Herder's contention that a national language is the most significant and precious offspring of a people's character.[12] Although Fichte shared a founding role with Herder in contributing to a cultural rather than an overtly political form of nationalist thought, he departed from Herder's universal acceptance of all cultures as equally legitimate. The notion of German superiority entered Fichte's work after the defeat of the German armies by Napoleon in 1806. He outlined his nationalism in the 1807 *Reden an die deutsche Nation* (*Addresses to the German Nation*), a series of public lectures that were meant to inculcate a "true and all-powerful love of fatherland" in his compatriots in the face of the "degradation of our whole nation" by a foreign power.[13] In these addresses, Fichte became an advocate for an aggressive political nationalism by insisting on a hierarchy of cultures (45–50). He contended that the superiority of the German language was founded on the fact that Germans had "remained in the original dwelling places of the ancestral stock" and thus "retained and developed the original language of the ancestral stock" (47). For Fichte, this continuity of place and language implied a greater development of the German language's philosophical richness. As an unmixed, unpolluted language, German enabled its speakers to think more clearly and profoundly than did neighboring languages, which were based on linguistic borrowing. Fichte's notion of Germans as an "eternal people" was tied to a spatial conception of the nation and to the idea of geographical continuity.

The use of geographical ties was one of the consistent refrains of many nineteenth-century German nationalists who followed Herder and Fichte. In response to what the publicist and bookseller Johann Philipp Palm called Germany's "deepest humiliation," a phrase for which he was executed by French occupation forces, numerous German intellectuals organized to inspire in their defeated people a sense of defiance and the beginning of a national movement.[14] Notable documents of this national sentiment came from activists like Friedrich Ludwig Jahn, the father of the German gymnastics movement, and the professor and poet Ernst Moritz Arndt. Jahn cofounded the German Federation in 1810 and organized youths in gymnastics associations with the goals of national education and self-defense. In the same year, he published his treatise *Das deutsche Volkstum*, which proposed a recipe for the nation's resurrection.[15] Elements Jahn considered central to the self-assertion of a viable new German nation included a dedication to national education, support of the Protestant church, and the liberal ideal of a popular constitution. But it also included physical activities such as wandering by foot through the fatherland, which involved both training the body and exploring the German countryside. For Jahn, familiarity with German geography was central to defining and defending the nation.

Ernst Moritz Arndt's influential poem, "Was ist des Deutschen Vaterland?" ("What Is the German's Fatherland?") (1813) epitomized the main concern of many German nationalists. Arndt wrote his famous lines shortly before the expulsion of Napoleon from Germany, at a time when Germany still lacked political unity. The song's response to its repeated question, "What is the German's Fatherland?" was a listing of geographical regions and a constant insistence that none of the regions alone (Swabia, Prussia, the Rhineland, etc.) could satisfy the call for a German homeland.[16] In Arndt's poem, Germany included but superseded all of these specified areas. This long, rather repetitive poem became an early hallmark of the national movement in Germany and had a tremendous appeal precisely because it listed so many of these German lands (Bavaria, Styria, the Marser, the Mark, Westphalia, Pomerania, the coast, the Danube, Tyrol, Switzerland, Austria, etc.). Arndt concluded this list of places ("Where'er resounds the German tongue, Where'er its hymns to God are sung") with the demand that "All Germany shall be the land!"

For the next six decades, the image of Germany as a diverse yet spiritually united geographical space was populist in tone. The dream of a unified Germany was particularly prevalent in liberal writings that hoped to conjoin national unity with political and economic freedom. Perhaps the most famous and enduring example was Heinrich Hofmann von Fallersleben's "Deutschlandlied" ("Germany Song") from 1841. The twentieth-century context of this song was frequently chauvinistic; the refrain "Deutschland, Deutschland über alles!" took on ominous overtones when sung by German soldiers in World War I and as an official anthem of the National Socialist state. However, in the context of the nineteenth-century national movement, this refrain initially meant to say that a unified Germany was more important than any of its individual parts. The poem's first and most famous stanza used Arndt's strategy (although in abbreviated form) to identify Germany by its geographical regions, as a place bounded by rivers on the west, east, and south, and by coastline on the north ("from the Maas to the Memel, from the Etsch to the Belt").[17]

Giving the disparate German lands political coherence, as Arndt and Hofmann von Fallersleben did in their poems, was a major political issue for the entire century. It is not surprising that a liberal magazine like the *Gartenlaube* appealed to the same tradition of defining the German nation in geographical terms. From its beginning in the mid-1850s the *Gartenlaube* repeatedly provided a geographical outline of the nation as part of its call for national unity. The magazine's interest in geography as the foundation for the nation is an example of how the mass press borrowed from and participated in the political and intellectual trends of its day.

THE NATION AS A COMMUNITY IN SPACE

From its first issue, the *Gartenlaube*'s use of geography to describe the German nation took two main forms: one concerning the German lands and one involving German individuals abroad. The first characterized a national territory through careful discussion of the various German regions. The *Gartenlaube* systematically unified the nation by appealing to the commonalities and interrelationships among these various locales. Its insistent portrayal of an internal German geography began quite early. In its third year of publication the magazine launched a series entitled "Land und Leute" ("Land and People"). Initially, these essays took an ethnographic approach to describing regional landscapes, dress, and customs. Although this practice was perhaps most common in the 1850s and 1860s, it was not limited to the period before the founding of the Bismarckian nation-state. Even after 1871 the magazine continued to present the nation in terms of a sum of lands, a collection of "fatherlands."[18] The nation that the *Gartenlaube* posited through geography as a constant or eternal phenomenon was not necessarily synonymous with the geographical terrain of the German Empire. This indicates that the *Gartenlaube* was interested in defining a national identity that went beyond the political unification of Germany and beyond the limited notion of citizenship in a state.

In the second regard, descriptions of Germans in other geographical settings helped define membership in the German nation. Germans abroad were celebrated as important representatives of the nation. Their inclusion in the national community was based on a concept of nation, or *Volk*, that was older and by implication more permanent than the modern nation-state. Some of the early articles were intended, among other things, to educate a populace considering emigration about the dangers and pitfalls, the scams and hazards that awaited the unwary emigrant. By the 1880s the emphasis of these essays on Germans throughout the world had shifted to a proud presentation of German achievements in other nations. The most extreme example of this, as we shall see in chapter 6, was the depiction of German colonial exploits in the non-Western world. Calling emigrants "German" suggested continuity of the German nation not only over time, but also beyond the arbitrary limitations of state borders. The foreign landscape, vegetation, and climate these emigrants confronted abroad became a foil against which the practices and cultures of the German nation could be described and praised. In this geographical presentation of German identity, the entire world was a potential stage for the nation.

HOLDING THE CENTER: A GEOGRAPHY OF GERMANY

From its beginning the *Gartenlaube* was dedicated to representing the diversity of regional characteristics as part of a German national whole. It depicted a national geography in visual images and textual information. Several aspects of this presentation of a German geography are of particular interest. In the first place, the selection of regional spaces presented not only a diverse cross section of the national landscape, but more particularly an outline of the nation, a perimeter or periphery that might be seen as protecting and circumscribing a stable center. Secondly, the choice of places portrayed was dependent (even if tangentially) on the explicit political conflicts that affected the nation's geography. Thus, the border regions that were contested in one way or another were particularly important at specific moments (Schleswig and Holstein in 1863 and 1864, Tyrol in and after 1866, Alsace after 1870). Finally, as descriptions of a national terrain, these images privileged rural scenes and spaces over the urban life of the city. Cities were included, but not as frequently as the countryside. The predominance of rural spaces suggests that they were most easily tied to the continuity or constancy of a national identity. The magazine summarized the purpose of these introductions to regional cultures as explicitly national: "It is a satisfying task to offer them to the German people as newly won treasures, since we can never become acquainted with enough lovely and good things about our fatherland, in order to always hold it in greater and holier esteem" (1864: 502).

In its first three decades, the *Gartenlaube* presented a steady offering of geographical images of the nation. The "Land und Leute" series itself (which began in 1855) lasted for almost three decades, culminating with the fifty-second contribution under that same heading in 1882. These essays reported on geographical regions and their inhabitants from throughout the German-speaking area of Europe. Thus, "Land" meant Germany and "Leute" implied ethnic Germans, or occasionally minorities, living within German regions. The dual principle of inclusiveness and diversity motivated the selection of these articles.

Each sketch of local culture varied in emphasis, yet all adhered to a standard style and content. The fourteenth essay in the "Land und Leute" series illustrates this format. In presenting the region of Betzingen near Tübingen, it begins by noting the beauty of a Sunday morning in late May. It then describes the approach to the village including the geological formations, their larger context (this range is "the last terrace step before the Swiss Alps"), and the names and spatial orientation of landmarks ("on the farthest left side in the east . . . the Hohenstaufen, . . . on the farthest right side in the west the Hohenzollern") (1864: 438). The essay describes the people of this area, first from their external appearance: the characterization of traditional peasant dress fills six long paragraphs, itemizing such details as the variety of colors, fabrics, patterns used, describing the dimensions of the women's bodices and accompanying accessories, and introducing the reader to the regional names for various articles. A discussion of the social significance of traditional clothes, that is, that nonvirgins may not wear the white apron, is followed by a lengthy description of important customs and celebrations: for marriage, baptism, funerals, Christmas, "egg hunting," cock dancing, and the "*Karz*," a winter courting ritual. The essay also discusses the history of the region, praising the local population's resistance to the French in 1796, tracing costumes back to medieval times and the residents themselves back to the last great migration of peoples before the Middle Ages.

Like other essays in the series, this one combined two strategies for presenting a local culture to the *Gartenlaube* readers as part of the German nation. On the one hand, the presentation speaks the language of scientific objectivity. It categorizes this space and orients the reader with typologies (of geographical formations) and names (of mountains and articles of clothing). The accompanying illustration of young women and men in the village allows the reader to verify the descriptive detail with a visual presentation. The essay affirms its authority to report by noting which things were witnessed directly ("we were able to convince ourselves with our own eyes") and which were based on local testimony ("about that we gathered no information") or historical documents ("a charter of Emperor Maximilian I from Worms from September 17, 1495") (440). Even when the author lists customs (such as the winter courting tradition) that would not have been visible in late May, the time both of the supposed visit to Betzingen and of the narration, he insists on comprehensive description.

On the other hand, the description contains numerous points for reader identification. It begins with positive associations ("What a wonderful feeling") and repeatedly affirms the pleasing character of the place: mountains with forests and rocks lie "in the richest glow"; villages "glisten and sparkle under the beautiful spring sky" (438–39). It employs similes and metaphors from common experience (a mountain "that spreads out its lowest layers like a petticoat") to make this landscape and its culture recognizable. Finally, even in its difference, this region is made familiar. The relationships between the sexes, the problems of morality are said to be "just like in the city." This presentation does not look down on rural life in Betzingen, but rather, through contrast and comparison, argues that it is just as "complicated" as urban existence. Specific events (like the occupation of the French) tie the history of this region to national history. Both are characterized as an unbroken chain of tradition. In other words, while describing its uniqueness and particulars, the *Gartenlaube* uses a variety of strategies to draw a connection between this place and the national whole.

In their accumulation, these lessons in German geography generated a common national identity by familiarizing readers from various German lands with diverse German regions. Essays featured areas from the far north, islands in the North and Baltic Seas such as Sylt and Amrum (1856: 180) and Rügen (1889: 120–21, 392–93); central regions such as Upper Franconia (1858: 260) and Thuringia (1856: 117), and southern places such as the Black Forest (1868: 148, 356, 874) and Tyrol in Austria (1868: 228). Occasionally, several articles in one year would focus on a particular region, but usually the presentations continually changed focus within this broadly circumscribed national space. Essays on regions from the north would alternate with those about southern, eastern, western, or central areas. Reports were generally evenly distributed among the various corners of German-speaking Europe, thus suggesting that all regions should be included in the space of the nation.

Despite this emphasis on inclusiveness and diversity, not all regions were given the same amount of coverage in the *Gartenlaube*. The selection of places that were depicted in illustrations and described in adjoining essays followed a consistent pattern of outlining the boundaries of the ideal nation. In 1855, for instance, the year the series "Land und Leute" began, three "German" regions were depicted in visual images. These were Helgoland (1855: 374–75), Canton Zurich (1855: 435–38), and the harbor of Königsberg (1855: 572–74, 587–90).[19] This attention to areas in the farthest northwestern, southern, and northeastern reaches of German-speaking Europe presented an outline of the nation in the vein of Hofmann von Fallersleben's "Germany Song." Here, as in earlier depictions of the nation, the extent of a cultural nation was described in ideal terms by its farthest geographical outposts.

In this instance, of course, the Helgoland island is in English possession and the Canton of Zurich is part of Switzerland, but in each case the significance of these regions for German identity and history is made clear. In the case of the Swiss canton, one author writes: "On this ground we encounter many a memory, many a historical kernel which we have seen develop grandly far away. It was no small piece of German history that had its seemingly small beginnings here" (1855: 437). From the outset, the geographical focus outlined a German cultural and linguistic nation, not a political one. In the ensuing decades, the Alps of Switzerland or Tyrol, although they lay outside the German Empire, played as important a role as those of Bavaria.

Even when the presence of non-Germans in these border regions is mentioned, the contributions of Germans help the magazine posit a national characterization. The description of Königsberg focuses on the cosmopolitan atmosphere in this harbor city. It presents the foreign sailors and merchants who migrate through the city as interestingly exotic. Germans, by contrast (listed as Königsberger, Stettiner, Memler, Hamburger), are the stable, familiar citizens who provide the backdrop for a colorful interchange of foreign languages and national characteristics. The strangeness of the Slavic customs and languages described in the essay affirms the familiarity or commonality of various Germans one would encounter in this city. Even the cultural judgment of the Germans is presumed to be uniform and constant. The example characterizing the Dutch predilection for burping shows this clearly: "They behave publicly in opposition to what we understand by respectability and decency, with the tone of belching that one commonly calls burping" (1855: 572). The "we" of the text reveals a first-person plural narrative voice, but also expresses a German narrative position. This "we" stands for the German residents of Königsberg, the narrating subject, and the *Gartenlaube*'s reading audience. It implies agreement among all three groups on social matters; it posits a national unity of opinion for Germans, the potential and ideal audience of the essay.[20]

Besides positing a contrast between German cultural standards and those of other peoples, the essays on border regions were important for outlining the national space in terms of its frontiers. In his seminal work on the history of the United States, the historian Frederick Jackson Turner argued that the frontier was as important to the concept of American national identity as the older, uncontested space of the Atlantic Coast—and perhaps more important. Turner wrote in 1893, "The true point of view in the history of this nation is not the Atlantic coast, it is the Great West."[21] Although the development of the United States in the nineteenth century differed in many respects from that of Germany, both shared one significant feature—unfinished nation-building. Germany's unification in 1871 might be compared to the closing of the American frontier. Each respectively established the confines or limits of each nation in space. The portrayal of national space in the pages of the *Gartenlaube* seems to bear out the relevance of Turner's notion of "frontier" for Germany in the second half of the nineteenth century. The outer reaches of German territory received more attention than other parts of the nation. The following discussion is concerned with this symbolic value rather than individual descriptions of frontier regions.[22]

Frontier regions that were politically contested seemed to be especially significant; they appeared with disproportionately high frequency in *Gartenlaube* essays. Generally, regions that had a substantial ethnic German population, but were under the political jurisdiction of a neighboring state, were the object of more frequent reports in the family magazine. These areas were of particular interest for a geographical circumscription of firm and stable national boundaries. This relevance was directly tied to historical or political conflicts of the nation in the nineteenth century. The provinces of Schleswig and Holstein in the north, for example, had served as a focal point for advocates of German unification and national strength since the 1840s.[23] Their control by the Danish crown was contested by German nationalists in those provinces, and their call for independence was picked up by nationalists throughout Germany. In the Frankfurt Parliament of 1848, the liberation of Schleswig and Holstein from Danish control was a powerful rallying cry for liberals and conservative nationalists alike. Interest in this cause resurfaced in the 1850s but was not resolved in Germany's favor. In 1863 the issue of the provinces' unity and independence from Denmark became a major cause within the German national movement. Bismarck, as prime minister of Prussia, recognized the usefulness of the provinces as a key to national mobilization under Prussian leadership. In the spring of 1864, along with Austria, the Prussian military wrested this territory from the Danes in a matter of weeks.[24]

In 1864 the *Gartenlaube* published, not surprisingly, at least fourteen essays dealing with Schleswig-Holstein and the "Schleswig-Holstein War." But even in the years leading up to this war, it included essays on the culture and landscape of this region as a way of integrating it into the German nation and establishing it as a fixed element of the national frontier. The *Gartenlaube*, for example, featured these provinces and their German residents in a series of six essays called "Aus den Landen des verlassenen Bruderstammes" ("From the Lands of the Deserted Brother Tribe") in the first part of 1864, before the outbreak of the war, as well as during the war.[25] Before that, ten contributions, poems as well as essays, concerning this region appeared in the years 1860–63,[26] and an additional six essays under the series heading "Vom verlassenen Bruderstamm" ("Of the Deserted Brother Tribe"), in the years 1861–62, indicate the overrepresentation of this frontier region in the outline of the nation.[27] By contrast, only a total of fourteen essays appeared between 1853 and 1871 (almost a twenty-year period) dealing with the areas of Hessia, the Electorate of Hessia, Saxony, Brunswick, Württemberg, and Hanover combined.

These essays portrayed the Germans of Schleswig and Holstein as easy points for national identification; they profiled a common matron who loyally and fearlessly showed her dedication to the German national cause in 1860 by intrepidly providing German troops with butter (1863: 62–64) and a simple apothecary who unjustly lost his business because of the Danes, yet remained "a brave fighter among the Germans in Schleswig" (1861: 712–14). In addition, there were numerous essays describing the linguistic persecution of Germans in schools and churches (1861: 664–66; 1862: 825–28; 1863: 809–13). In all of these instances, the specific dialect, the food, and the festivals of the Germans in this region are described as a way of introducing these members of the nation, yet making them familiar: "All around the city lives a decidedly upright and competent peasantry that distinguishes itself by an alert, healthy understanding, by a rare intelligence, by a forceful industrial spirit, by charitable convictions, and by a truly German sensibility" (1864: 75).

Another example of the magazine's insistence on a secure—and securely German—frontier was the case of Alsace. This province along the Rhine that for centuries had French-speaking as well as German-speaking residents, and had alternated between French and German rule, was taken by Bismarck as part of the Germans' victory over the French in 1871. In 1872, under the heading "Vom wiedergewonnenen Bruderstamm" ("Of the Regained Brother Tribe"), two essays appeared concerning Alsace and Lorraine.[28] Beginning in 1874, the *Gartenlaube* mounted what could be described as a narrative campaign to outline the importance and Germanness of the Alsace for its readers. Three essays (part of the "Land und Leute" series) appeared in the year 1874 alone, and several others about such topics as the Cathedral in Strasbourg or farmers of the region appeared in the next two years.[29]

In discussing the traditional cultures of the region, including games, dances, and a typical wedding ceremony, these essays from 1874 present Alsace as a region with values and roots similar to those of *Gartenlaube* readers. As with all the other "Land und Leute" essays, these are a mixture of ethnographic description of dances, traditional dress, and food. It is interesting to note that just three years after the incorporation of Alsace into the German Empire these essays make no mention of the Franco-German war. Although the war had certainly been a major topic in the magazine for over a year, it is noticeably absent in the cultural depiction of this region.[30] Rather, the detailed descriptions of traditions and customs are repeatedly tied to the narrator's euphoria about "the lovely homeland (*Heimath*)!" As in the *Gartenlaube*'s very first texts from 1853, here, too, the appellation of "*Heimath*" implies a cultural commonality within the nation.

An examination of the first essay in this series about the Alsace region shows how such an introduction to regional culture in the *Gartenlaube* contributed to establishing the boundaries of the nation. The author describes his hometown in Alsace (which remains unnamed), devoting particular attention to the games and dances of the young people. This selection of cultural events (like those in the other essays) enables the magazine to present Alsace in terms of traditions that have endured. The region is thus characterized by the things that have remained constant there, not by novelties or social change. These items are brought to life in detailed descriptions (of the shape and color of buttons on youths' vests or the specific cut of girls' shoes) that complement the illustration and emphasize the traditional character of this place. These constants are brought together with a broader German past when the narrator compares these costumes to those in neighboring German areas. To remind the reader of the German (and not French) quality of these costumes, the narrator informs his reader that this is a version of the Allemanic costume that can be found in parts of Swabia, the Black Forest, and the Hanau region of Baden. The women and girls wear skirts similar to those found in Bern Oberland, an ethnically German part of Switzerland (1874: 376). In other words, these traditions are made familiar by being described in a language that emphasizes their nonexotic, nonforeign, easily understandable character.

Above all, however, the element of this essay that shapes Alsace into an important part of Germany is the position and attitude of the narrator. In many *Gartenlaube* texts, the narrator provides readers with an accessible point of identification. In this case, the first-person singular narrator opens the essay with an extended comment that includes himself: "'Hurray! Soon I will again be in the beautiful homeland, so rich in glorious pastures, vineyards, woods, and meadows. Soon I will move again among this comfortable people that, under the veneer of the modern age, has not lost its original freshness in customs, traditions, and dress'" (1874: 373). The narrator praises both the landscape and the people for having maintained their original character. Once again, "*Heimath*" becomes a generalized, broadly applicable name for the national homeland.

Indeed, what the narrator first sees in his town reminds him of his own childhood there. Scenes, such as a group of young boys waiting for girls to call them for a game in which each girl gives her beau a bouquet she has picked, stir his memories of an earlier era

(1874: 373). This unchanging, idealized vision of regional and national identity resurfaces in the final paragraph of the essay: "What a beautiful, harmless time of youth, when all coarser impulses are silent! It is the time of purest love. The children love as their parents did; they take each other's hand through the open hedge of the neighbor's yard" (1874: 376). By describing this region as the embodiment of his own experience of Alsatian life, the narrator creates a universal landscape of cultural memory for his readers.[31]

In this description, there is no discussion of anything French in conjunction with the Alsace region. France (from whence this narrator had come before returning to his homeland) is simply marked as "the foreign land." The recent war between France and the united German states under Prussian leadership has no place in this characterization of Alsace as German. Political border disputes become irrelevant as a timeless culture is presented as the true, authentic bearer of this region's identity. The politics of the present are erased from the landscapes as they appear in these geographical and ethnographic sketches. With a rhetoric of continuity— "The memory from the time of youth awakens!" (1874: 373)—the frontiers of the German nation were secured in cultural terms that preceded (and by implication could outlast) the contemporary German nation-state.

A final example of the *Gartenlaube*'s preoccupation with a frontier region shows that the popular press was not only interested in those territories that were part of the existing German nation-state after 1871. Indeed, the notion of an ethnically based nation required that the magazine go beyond the political boundaries of the state to insist on the larger category of a cultural and linguistic nation. One of the main questions involving Germany's size in the nineteenth century concerned Austria. In the first half of the century, calls for a united German nation-state drew responses that were split between the so-called "greater German solution," according to which all German-speaking lands would be included, and the "smaller German solution," which excluded Austria.[32] The inclusion of Austria was initially advocated by many 1848 liberal nationalists, some of whom hoped to avoid an imbalance of Prussian power within Germany. Eventually, however, the National Assembly of

1848 voted in favor of a smaller German solution, in part due to the counterrevolutionary position of Austrian elites.[33] In 1866 Prussia won a quick and decisive war against Austria and her southern German allies that gave military support to the smaller German solution. Bismarck's war against France in 1870 resulted in the unification of Germany without Austria.[34]

The boundaries of the German Empire were not the only measure of nationhood in the years that followed, however. The exclusion from the nation-state of a large German-speaking region did not mean that Austrian Germans were no longer part of the German nation in the minds of many. The *Gartenlaube* and its editors, for example, devoted considerable attention to the Germans of Austria. Between 1871 and 1873 (the first two years of the German Empire), the *Gartenlaube* published eight essays on Tyrol; from 1881 to 1901 it published a total of thirty-seven. The essays on Tyrol that appeared in 1872 are revealing in their narrative tension. The three contributions focus on experiences of being in the mountains as a German tourist, such as a visitor's interaction with a guide or another local resident, and surviving a near-fatal accident. These essays on tourism emphasize the affinities between Germans and Tyroleans and insist on a bond in life and death (1872: 61; 1872: 505; 1872: 534).

Even as late as 1884, an essay about the Krain region close to the Adriatic was entitled "Verlorenes deutsches Land" ("Lost German Land"). This essay began: "Where have the times gone when German speech, German song, and German tales resounded deep into Istria and to Friaul! Where—it will soon be asked—have the times gone, when as in the days of the blessed Federation we dreamed that one day the tricolor of a united Germany would wave from the towers and Schloßberg roofs of Laibach, from the walls of Gradista, from the palaces of Triest, that was always our German port on the shimmering Adriatic!" (1884: 460). The area of Siebenbürgen also surfaced in the *Gartenlaube* in the 1880s as a German region that must be maintained as an island of German culture to offer a defense against Slavic "unculture."[35] Frequently referring to German parts of Austria as the lost, betrayed, and deserted "brother tribe," the magazine implicitly adhered to an ethnic definition of the nation that transcended territorial disputes or political boundaries. This attention to German regions outside the German Empire implied a cultural, ethnic community and presumed that the nation was an archaic, eternal entity.[36] In this respect, the *Gartenlaube* became a compensatory visual space for the ideal nation that existed in the imagination and beyond political realities.

BEYOND BORDERS: EMIGRANTS AND EXPLORERS

Although the *Gartenlaube* welcomed the founding of a political state to encompass and represent the nation, it generated conceptions of national identity that could be considered alternatives to mere citizenship in that nation-state. The examples, cited above, of including members of other German-speaking regions in Europe as brother tribes of the nation was one instance of this. Another instance was the common bond established among *Gartenlaube* readers. The editors were proud to advertise the magazine's worldwide distribution and implicitly tied this global readership to a German nation: "The *Gartenlaube* is read in all corners of the discovered world, in America, Africa, Australia, even in inner Asia and in northern Siberia, just as far as the German tongue resounds."[37] This reference to the dream of Ernst Moritz von Arndt, "as far as the German tongue resounds," repeated the idea of a grand German fatherland that is oblivious to political borders and includes all regions where German is spoken.

Another prominent example of this continued dream of a greater fatherland was the magazine's discussion of German emigration. The essays of the *Gartenlaube* that focused on emigration and settlement colonization clearly reveal that, when necessary, national identity could be transported to new places in the world. In the age of emigration and European imperialism, the flexibility of a spatial nation was an innovative, but not surprising, addition to the traditional notion of a national homeland.[38] The second half of this chapter focuses on the magazine's discussion of individual German emigration (mostly to the Americas or Australia) and its implications for national belonging. The effect of commercial colonization in Africa and Asia will be discussed in chapter 6 as a different phenomenon, since it included the issue of German political, economic, and military control over other regions.

During the first decades of the magazine's existence, Germany experienced two great waves of emigration.[39] In the first few years of its existence, the *Gartenlaube* ran eight essays on the lot and fate of German emigrants in their travels or as newcomers to another country. This publication paralleled the first wave of emigration that lasted from 1846 to 1857. Another thirteen essays and notices appeared between 1863 and 1874, roughly coinciding with what has been called the second wave of nineteenth-century German emigration.[40]

Before the founding of the German Empire, the *Gartenlaube* functioned as a mouthpiece for emigrant concerns and as advisor to the nation. It repeatedly published essays that warned its German readers about the pitfalls and possible hazards of emigration. Essays advised potential emigrants not to sign contracts that were vague or did not guarantee them complete passage to their foreign destination, and not to believe the oral promises made by dubious agents in harbor towns. Other notices warned the uninformed German about false promises made by the Peruvian government (1867: 815–16) and pointed out that some colonies supported by the Chilean government were in areas that were still contested by indigenous peoples (1868: 496). Another essay identified problems with the mining district in Venezuela (1869: 690). In general, emigrants were seen as a national group that needed to be protected from the dishonesty of others and their own ignorance and gullibility. At least until the political unification of the German Empire, the *Gartenlaube* saw the task of informing and thus protecting the unwary German about the dangers of emigration as the responsibility of the press.[41]

All of these essays treated potential and established emigrants as members of the German national community. According to the *Gartenlaube*'s writers, emigrants carried their nationality with them into the new country and might keep it forever. Even much later generations, those born in the new country, were often identified as "our compatriots" (1885: 531) Although numerous contributors wrote about the situation of German immigrants in various places, such as the United States, Brazil, and Australia, the uniformity with which they argued for certain issues indicates a concern on the part of the magazine as a whole that Germans who leave their homeland not lose their identity. This included their language and culture, but first and foremost it included their nationality and understanding of themselves as Germans.

Thus we find a *Gartenlaube* author in 1864 critiquing a book about emigration to Brazil, in part, because it takes the side of the Brazilian government in wanting Germans there to adopt Brazilian citizenship, which the author contends is at odds with a "German-patriotic" stance (1864: 351). This contributor instead argues for maintaining German identity in the new country by teaching German language and customs (1864: 351). Another essay from the same year about a group emigrating to the United States praises the emigrants as they proudly assert: "And rest assured that we will remain, in our house and hearts, upstanding Germans. . . . The black-red-gold banner will also grace our roof abroad" (1864: 87). In an essay from the 1880s about German emigration to Australia, E. Jung bemoans the fact that Germans are threatened with losing their "nationality" by being submerged into the general English population (1885: 532). With these contributions, the *Gartenlaube* supported the maintenance of German identity abroad. The magazine's authors repeatedly argued that the nation could and should be exported to places outside the borders of even a unified German nation-state.

Despite the liberal tendency of the magazine, it was not immune to racial typologizing. In an essay about Brazilian emigration, one author suggested that since a state already existed in Brazil, German immigrants there, no matter what their number, would lose their identity in the mixing of races: they would serve as "fertilizer for a mixed race, which will never manage to play a significant role in the great drama of peoples" (1864: 350).[42] Such a characterization implies a theory of racial dilution and the inferiority of a people who compromise their racial identity. Given this notion of national purity, it is not surprising to find that Germans in the *Gartenlaube* were acclaimed as the best newcomers to other countries. Essay after essay suggested that the work ethic and skill of the Germans made them the most desired by all governments:[43] "Again we have proof that foreign nations always look for Germans whenever they want someone to fill a position of responsibility" (1863: 304). But even more notable than the comparison of Germans with other (European) immigrants in these new countries is the way in which Germans were discussed in the context of their new country and culture. In most situations, the *Gartenlaube* presents the rest of the world through German eyes. Other cultures thus remain the novelty, even when it comes to a discussion of the newcomers, that is, Germans, in that "new" context.[44]

In order to understand the role that the *Gartenlaube* set for itself in defining a national space, let us consider the example of German emigration to one country. Brazil was one of the distant places to which popular magazines devoted considerable attention. Although actual German emigration to Brazil paled in comparison with that to the United States, it was nonetheless the second most popular destination for German emigrants.[45] This fact, combined with the more exotic character of Brazilian geography, climate, and culture made it an ideal place for the magazine's implicit exploration of German identity abroad. Two essays, in particular, demonstrate how the presentation of Germans abroad (be they emigrants or scientific explorers) established a positive cultural identity for the nation.

In *Gartenlaube* essays about Brazil, Germans confront obstacles such as jungles, raging rivers, and mosquitoes. In all of these discussions, nature is presented as strange and perplexing. It is not surprising that the drastically different terrain, flora, and fauna of South America should be depicted as fascinatingly exotic for the nineteenth-century German reader. Yet, the extensive narration of encounters with this aspect of Brazil is not as revealing as what is missing from the characterization of the travelers' and emigrants' experience there. The essays rarely include encounters with other humans who might confront the German narrator, and thus the German reader, with their own difference. The reader gains the odd impression that these Germans are the main residents of this new place. There are scattered references to an unspecified landlord or to unnamed slaves, characters who for lack of detailed description remain disembodied and narratively insignificant. But, for the most part, non-German inhabitants, be they native Indians or descendants of earlier immigrants, are absent or at best serve as decorative backdrop. In other words, this foreign place becomes an enchanting terrain upon which the German can define himself.

One example is an article written by a German who spent fourteen years in Brazil. The characterization of German life in Alfred Waeldler's ("Christmas Memories from Brazil") is a "faint reflection" of the celebrations that occur in Germany.[46] The assertion of Brazilian inadequacy compared to German traditions is maintained throughout the essay.[47] It begins with the description of the problems of creating a Christmas tree in the absence of pine or fir trees. An innovative carpenter begins with a coat rack that then must be transformed with bushels of green leafy vines. Despite this small victory over the lack of appropriate foliage, the author laments that Brazilian weather makes for an extremely hot Christmas evening. The narrator then recounts adventures resulting from local conflict (but only among German colonists). These are followed by the author's reminiscences of the Christmas traditions of his childhood in Germany. Waeldler includes a poem he had written years earlier in which he imagined his distant relatives in Germany celebrating Christmas. His poem (written in Northern German dialect) summarizes in melancholy stanzas the typical activities of his parental home during this holiday and contrasts them with his own loneliness.[48] At the end of his set of stories, the author is euphoric at finally spending Christmas back in his "*Heimath*," a thrill that reminds him of his childhood and of the wonders of the German celebration. He notes how this festival will also please his little daughter with a lit tree that is much more beautiful than all the lightning bugs in the Brazilian rain forest. In sum, this contribution to the *Gartenlaube* strikes a somber note about being divorced from the homeland. It informs German readers that Germans in Brazil maintain this holiday as best they can, but that the terrain of Germany, especially its snow and *Tannenbaum*, are the essence of Christmas. In their hearts, these German colonists remain German and maintain their original heritage.

German exploration plays a similar role in the *Gartenlaube* to that of emigration. Articles glorified the work of German specialists in charting new territory around the globe. The title of an essay from 1875 indicates the German perspective that dominates articles in the *Gartenlaube* about the exploration of foreign lands. "Die weißen Flecken unserer Landkarten" ("The White Spots on our Maps") describes Brazil as a place deserving the interest and attention of researchers, a place in need of present-day exploration. Although a list of previous explorers is included, Brazilians themselves are absent from the essay. The only "locals" who appear are native Indians (*Ureinwohner*) who are mentioned as ideal objects of study for German ethnographers. Brazil is cited as a source not only of valuable raw materials for industry, but also of material for modern scientific investigation; its forests yield treasures of glorious woods, textile fibers, and oils for German factories, products for German medicine, and new species for the natural sciences.[49] As in the essays about German emigration to Brazil, this distant land becomes a space to be occupied and explored by German experts, a resource to be harvested for German profit.

In the illustration accompanying one essay, the *Gartenlaube* reader sees three individuals measuring and charting an otherwise open wilderness. The most pronounced of these figures is the author (and illustrator) himself, Keller-Leuzinger (1875: 477). This illustration receives the following elucidation: "The researcher cannot find a more beautiful or pleasant setting, as our illustration shows him, with the sextant or rather the reflection-circle in his hand and ready to measure the height of the sun. Underneath the massive branches of a Uauassú palm (Attalea) a lightweight table is set up which holds the carefully tended chronometer. The gaze is cast afar from the high shore across the wide river and its islands crowned with palms" (1875: 479). Via description and illustration the *Gartenlaube* reader is included in the action of the researcher ("the gaze is cast afar"). The implication of these two views is that Brazil is a geographical space lacking scientific analysis and categorized knowledge. As Mary Louise Pratt has demonstrated in her work on eighteenth- and nineteenth-century travel writing, this position concerning the "rest of the world" was standard for most

Western descriptions.[50] Pratt argues that since the Enlightenment, European travel writing often saw its *raison d'être* in categorizing and organizing knowledge about "unknown" places.[51] In our context of German national identity, this kind of reportage reaffirmed the magazine readers' confidence in the German *Volk* and discouraged any questioning of German culture and traditions as they came in contact with those of other peoples and places.[52]

A later essay by the same author on the construction of a road in an inland area of Brazil also emphasizes the knowledge and technical skill of German experts who are key to completing the project.[53] Again, this essay praises the capabilities of the German engineers and erases the local individuals and their competencies and skills. There is no mention of the residents of this area or the usefulness of the road, not even of the local crews who no doubt made its completion possible. The work, frustrations, even the existence of non-Germans are made invisible for the *Gartenlaube* reader. Instead, we hear of the determination with which the Germans struggled against foreign elements and succeeded.[54] In descriptions of Germans encountering a new place, the tenacity and strength of the German people took center stage. The characterization of Germans abroad enabled the *Gartenlaube* to affirm a catalogue of national virtues that included technical skill, industriousness, and tenacity.

In the second half of the nineteenth century, the German nation could not be understood without the context of other parts of the world. The reality of mass emigration and the eventual issue of colonialism near the end of the century (as we shall see in chapter 6) challenged the traditional definition of the nation. In the popular press, this was expressed by the incorporation of distant lands into a broad national imagination. The *Gartenlaube* saw itself as defender, supporter, and advocate of the *Volk* at home and abroad. To be sure, the geography of German-speaking Europe was the main interest in this liberal magazine's attempt to define the nation as a cohesive entity, but in "the rest of the world" as well, Germanness was to be defended and preserved. National identity, based as it was on a sense of ancient and lasting ethnic identity, could extend well beyond the nation's political borders. In this geographical and thus traditional view of the nation, other parts of the world were also useful as a setting for characterizing German identity.[55]

The geographical information the magazine offered its readers was central to its larger purpose to educate as well as entertain its readership. The *Gartenlaube* provided a summary of the various traditions, costumes, and landscapes of diverse parts of what needed to be understood and envisioned as Germany. The nation was geographically centered in the media even before it acquired the centralized power of the nation-state. Essays on the culture and landscapes of Germany in the *Gartenlaube* constituted a significant part of the nation-building that preceded the founding of the German Empire in 1871. But even after 1871, the German nation continued to be imagined in the *Gartenlaube* as something larger than the specific state boundaries of the *Kaiserreich*; the landscape of the nation potentially included all regions of the world where Germans lived and worked.

In fact, the German nation was identified as existing wherever and as far as the pages of the *Gartenlaube* reached. This inclusive definition had a dual implication for the press. It enabled the magazine to address all of its readers, that is, potentially any German speaker anywhere in the world, as part of the German nation it was in the process of describing. The project of narrating and imagining the nation incorporated these readers into a potential national audience. At the same time, the popular family magazine could define itself as a national publication precisely because it addressed (and reached) an unprecedentedly large audience. It became a national, people's publication by attending to the dimensions of the nation. Ethnic Germans throughout the world figured both in its readership and in its geographical characterization of the nation, even after the constitution of a political "Germany" in 1871.

This larger conception of the nation does not mean the *Gartenlaube* was challenging the existence and legitimacy of the German Empire. Viewing the national space as larger and more complex than the boundaries of the Empire was not a consciously oppositional act. It was rather a logical outgrowth of the press's own role as an important and highly visible national space. With a readership that gradually grew to mass dimensions, the press became an influential mouthpiece of national imagining. The *Gartenlaube* presented identities not just as reflections of life or as concrete, realistic alternatives to lived reality, but always also as a space of textual and visual compensation.

3

IN DEFENSE OF THE NATION

This is how it stands at present with this German invention. . . . Should it really first fall into foreign hands of another country, in order to return to Germany as, for instance, something English and therefore something good? Is it necessary to remind our fellow countrymen of König and Bauer and the fate of the rapid press, in order to inspire them to act more justly toward German inventors?–Gartenlaube *1862: 59*

The modern mass media was flexible and highly adaptable in its presentation of the nation for a mass audience. As we have seen in the preceding chapter, it absorbed a stock of national images that existed prior to and independent of the popular press. But it was also open to new influences. As a modern innovation itself, it was by definition the logical site for modern representations of the nation. The popular press reported on inventions of the rapidly developing industrial world. The *Gartenlaube*'s interest in presenting the latest technological developments to its readers was part of its liberal goal of educating the population at large to political maturity. Such maturity depended on information about the functioning and rapid changes of the industrial age. However, these innovations were also the emblem of progress that was at the center of a liberal goal of strengthening and unifying the German nation.

The attention the *Gartenlaube* devoted to technological advances was closely tied to its construction of the nation. Establishing a connection between the German nation and modern inventions implied two things: that the German nation was internationally competitive in the present and, as a corollary, that the nation had a future as well as a past. The emphasis on a national future, on the nation's participation in processes of modernization, did not make the exploration and appropriation of the past obsolete. On the contrary, the "invention of tradition" became an important backdrop to the concrete inventions of the future.[1] The viable nation had to be situated firmly between an identifiable and laudable past and an understandable, powerful vision of the future.

From the first year of its publication, the *Gartenlaube* regularly included articles on recent technological innovations. These articles introduced the reader to practical products such as the gas oven (1853: 339) and the sewing machine (1853: 478), as well as new materials such as an industrial resin called gutta percha (1853: 351; 1854: 126). In most cases, a picture of these innovations accompanied a wealth of details concerning the devices' composition, functioning, and applications. These presentations were anything but dispassionate; they exuded enthusiasm and excitement that were also expected of the reader. Authors praised the increased productivity these devices allowed; they saw in them the unprecedented solution of problems, and they often discussed future applications. But beyond being touted as specifically useful, these inventions were explicitly tied to the well-being and general productivity of the nation. An article on a steam-powered digging machine, for example, credited this innovation with having helped German peasants, who until recently had clung to older methods, catch up with those in other countries.[2] The *Gartenlaube* presented these innovations not only as advances made by technological research, but also as events of national significance.

The patriotic stakes were raised considerably in the 1860s when discussions of technology in the *Gartenlaube* took on the tone of national fervor. This was partly tied to the changing political climate within the German states. Bismarck's war against Denmark in 1864, and then his quick and decisive victory over Austria in 1866, united many liberals behind him. The National Liberal party increasingly supported his politics in the Prussian parliament and the parliament of the North German Confederation. As a member of this party, *Gartenlaube* publisher and editor Ernst Keil seemed to find favor with the successful Prussian foreign policy. Prussia's primacy on the battlefield provided the popular press with unambiguous images of strength and unity for the entire nation. The affirmation of technological progress and innovation entered discussions of the nation's military prowess. The press celebrated industrial and technological inventions as sites of cooperation that could unite all Germans in a common effort.

This chapter focuses on three features of this link between industrialization and the unification of the German nation that appeared repeatedly in the *Gartenlaube* and other family magazines in the 1860s and early 1870s. The first feature that consistently incorporated the discussion of technological innovation into the construction of the nation was a persistent discourse on public safety and security. This interest in public safety ranged from the improvement of local firefighting services to the creation of coastal rescue devices and stations.

A second interest was the promotion of German inventors and their inventions as national property. Several magazines celebrated German inventors as modern crusaders in the national cause. The *Gartenlaube* launched an aggressive campaign to rally national support for the underwater devices of Wilhelm Bauer. Like the coastal rescue stations, many of Bauer's creations were also intended to save lives and goods, but some also had more explicitly national applications as weapons in time of war. Bauer was just one example of the individual designer who became a point of identification and was supported in the name of national unity and cooperation.

A third topic that tied technological progress to the fate of the nation was military conflict. The three so-called wars of unification, 1864 by Austria and Prussia against Denmark, 1866 between Austria and Prussia, and 1870 by the united German states against France, were centrally important to a definition of Germany. Although there were significant delays in the weekly illustrated magazines' reporting on these wars and individual battles, these conflicts held the attention of the press for a long time.[3] The press discussed the technology of warfare as a means of affirming the modernized nation.[4]

SAFETY AT SEA AS A NATIONAL CONCERN

Compared to the other major nations of Europe, Germany had relatively little coastal area per square mile of country. This fact was highly significant in Germany's process of nation-building. In Britain and France, to name only the two most prominent and powerful western European states, the myth of the coast was an important element of national lore. Fishing culture as well as seafaring trade had a long, powerful tradition in each country. In Germany, by contrast, the profession of seaman was part of a limited regional identity. It helped characterize the specific quality of lower Germany, the salty image of the Lower Saxons and Frisians. Historically, the coast was of regional rather than national import. In the nineteenth century, the seacoast entered the regional literary works of North German authors like Theodor Storm and Fritz Reuter, who soon became known as national writers.

As we have seen in the previous chapter, one important national task of the popular family magazines of the second half of the century was to introduce all German readers to the geographical and regional variety of the "fatherland." The international reputation and history of the Hanseatic League gave port cities like Hamburg, Lubeck, and Königsberg a transnational element. The specificity and local color of these areas were presented as part of German heritage and brotherhood without obliterating their difference. This was done, I have suggested, to inculcate a traditional national link among the diverse German readership in order to demonstrate a historical bond within Germany.

To be effective for a modern reading audience, however, this bond could not remain antiquated. It needed a contemporary relevance to make it a viable part of modern German society. One approach of the press was to launch participatory appeals for an all-German identification with the North of Germany. This appeal focused on the German coasts, in particular, on the threats to ships, their passengers and goods from storms and the rocky shoals that were a common fixture of the coastline. Several coastal rescue organizations (*Rettungsvereine*) had been founded by the 1850s in a few regions and cities, and in 1854 some of these were united into a central organization (*Centralverein*).⁵ In the wake of a terrible storm that struck the small Bremen harbor town of Vegesack in 1860, there were some attempts to create a truly national organization, but no such overarching organization materialized. There remained only the local associations, such as those for the mouth of the Elbe or in Bremen.⁶

The press adopted this regional issue and helped bring it to national attention. Beginning in the early 1860s, magazines like the *Gartenlaube*, the *Illustrirte Zeitung*, and *Daheim* (after its founding in 1864) spoke out in support of a *national* rescue organization for the German coast. The *Gartenlaube* first presented the construction of sea rescue devices and organizations to its audience as an urgent national mission in 1861. In a four-page article entitled "Rettungsstationen an deutschen Küsten: Eine Mahnung an die deutsche Nation" ("Rescue Stations on the German Coasts: An Admonition to the German Nation"), the magazine introduced the main categories that would continue to dominate the popular press's discussion of this concern with national safety (1861: 811–14). These categories included (1) a comparison of Germany with other countries that had already founded such united efforts (Britain, France, the Netherlands, and "even" Denmark), and (2) a discussion of the magnitude of the threat, which was underscored by statistics about the number of ships sunk, the number of lives lost, and the value in goods destroyed in shipwrecks that were never recovered. Furthermore, each article appealed directly to a national audience to unite against what it described in the most urgent terms as a national threat. In this process, the distinctions between the coast and the interior, north and south, big city and small town were put aside. The cooperation of all was demanded and regional divisions were challenged by appeals to the inherent unity of the German people.

For most of the 1860s the *Gartenlaube* included annual articles on this issue; substantial articles appeared in 1861, 1862, 1865, 1866, 1867, and 1868. Each essay outlined the attempts to found national organizations for "rescue operations at sea" and mentioned the equipment that had been developed (such as rescue boats and lines that could be sent to a stranded ship by rocket). Often, these articles were complemented and magnified by other contributions printed in close proximity on storms at sea, the heroic deeds of a Dutch rescuer, or numerous other innovations for sea use.[7] In each case, the issue of dangers at sea and attempts to provide security for people and goods were consistently framed as national concerns.

In order to demonstrate the general interest in the popular press for this topic, we turn here to one of the *Gartenlaube*'s competitors in the 1860s.[8] For the family magazine, *Daheim*, this interest in safety at the coast amounted to a veritable campaign in its first year of publication. In this year alone the magazine published twelve separate articles and notices about rescue boats (lifeboats) or rescue organizations.[9] For half of the year, it made public at the end of every other issue the list of financial contributors to the cause.[10] No doubt this campaign presumed some knowledge already made available by the series of articles that appeared in the *Gartenlaube*, but the intensity with which *Daheim* hoped to shape its audience's views became clear in its initial onslaught of essays.[11]

Despite their criticisms of other publications, the editors of *Daheim* were no doubt interested in copying the influence of other magazines. *Daheim* discussed the notion of the press's influence explicitly in its first year. In its third issue of 1864, it featured a notice about the success of the daily London paper, the *Times*. It agreed with a "famous French publicist" that a newspaper should have no opinion of its own, that it would last longer if it submitted to public opinion (1864: 40).[12] Yet, the next issue of *Daheim* challenged this view by pointing out the substantial influence among the English population of the newspaper. Noting how the *Times* had energetically argued against railway speculation in 1846, even though that sector brought the newspaper up to £500 a day in advertising income, *Daheim* insisted that the paper exerted pressure on public opinion as much as it registered it.[13] According to this German weekly magazine, the protests of the *Times* were also central to ensuring the English army was adequately outfitted during the Crimean War. The details of this story are not as important as the clear interest on the part of *Daheim* in the social function and power of the press. With this background, it seems that *Daheim*'s campaign for the German *Rettungswesen* beginning in issue number

18 and escalating in number 22 was launched with the confidence of being able to effect change.

As in the *Gartenlaube*, the appeal in *Daheim* identified the construction of rescue stations with boats and rocket-launched rescue lines as a national mission. The first story that appeared, "Das Rettungsboot" ("The Rescue-Boat"), narrated the dramatic rescue of twelve seamen from their stranded ship off the Frisian island Langerooge. This essay established the tenor of the magazine's subsequent contributions in praising the bravery, strength, and dedication of coastal residents. It closed with a plea for financial support for the proposed equipment, so that many more success stories could be told in the future. The magazine repeatedly emphasized that this problem "is a matter of the people."[14]

At the same time, *Daheim* held England up as the model for such endeavors: in 1864 it noted that the English people had donated 140,000 Thaler in the previous year for such projects and had helped save 470 lives. The author of one article posed the rhetorical question: "Should Germany, should Prussia not measure up to England, should our fatherland, that considers itself the cradle of civilization, stand accused that it does not deserve this title?" A few weeks later another contribution on this topic announced that England's "royal-life-boat institution" had saved a total of 13,568 lives in a period of forty years since its inception in 1824.[15] These comparisons were used to insist that Germany needed to coordinate its splintered attempts into a national effort to save the victims of coastal disasters. After contrasting the situation in Germany with that in England in issue 20, the magazine directly asked its readers for financial donations to this national cause. It devoted the first page of issue 22 to an appeal to its readers: "No, we are convinced that it is not a lack of good will that closed the heart and hands of the German people to such noble purposes. We know that only its unfamiliarity with maritime relations is responsible for this."[16] The *Gartenlaube* pursued the same strategy as *Daheim*. It challenged its readers to continue their national service: "The endless calls for help, which our newspapers bring, wherever fires or floods take place anywhere in the German fatherland or also elsewhere, prove through their success in an always uplifting manner the charitable sensibility of our nation" (1861: 811). In other words, each magazine (both *Gartenlaube* and *Daheim*) saw its task as educating the populace through its articles and then engaging this newly informed public in support of a national undertaking.

Such appeals were central to involving the readership of a popular periodical in the construction of the nation. They constituted advertisements for the national cause, in this case, securing the national coast. But because the magazines were serial publications, their repeated treatment of any topic could become effectively self-referential. In the process of repeating articles and announcements about the rescue stations and lifeboats, *Daheim* could also remind readers, and frequently did so, about its own role in making the public more aware and better citizens.[17] Its initial call for financial contributions in issue number 22 of the year 1865 was repeated in issue 24, which also included a list of donations. Another list of donors and their contributions appeared at the end of issue 26. Issue 29 included an essay that added urgency to the topic of rescuing seamen and their passengers. This essay was written by a Captain Werner, the head of a corvette ship, the same individual who had written numerous articles for the *Gartenlaube* in previous years. Werner's essay prepared the reader for the contribution campaign that opened the following issue (issue 30). This piece, entitled "Die nächsten Ziele des Rettungswerkes zur See" ("The Next Goals of the Rescue Work at Sea"), was a direct call to readers for financial support and again was written by Werner.[18]

In this appeal, Werner not only repeated much of the information that had already been mentioned, he also expressly praised the efforts of *Daheim* and of the *Daheim* readers who had contributed to the cause. After announcing that with the sum already collected (820 Thaler) the work on the rescue project could begin, he proceeded to tell the readers what this would involve, thus including them in its ideas and development. From the perspective of an expert (Werner's expert status had been established in his personal account of seafaring in the previous issue), this author reminded his readers that although some devices were already in service, the ultimate success of such a project would depend on the implementation of new technology (lifeboats and rescue-line launchers).[19] In this essay, readers were told about the improvements that had been made with their contributions, as well as about future plans for the project. They became knowledgeable participants in this national event, informed of the details and the development of the endeavor as a whole. The voice of the expert, both praising and appealing to the readers as active members of the nation, resurfaced at the end of this essay: "Already I give my sincerest thanks in the name of my colleagues to all noble donors, who participated in this enterprise and contributed to the creation of the first rescue station amidst the people on our Baltic coast."[20]

Daheim explicitly took credit for the support its readers had given the project: the station that was constructed with these donations would be named "Daheim" and the first boat to be launched from it also carried the magazine's name.[21] Its test run was described in a detailed announcement that celebrated its use of the newest techniques, including a self-emptying valve.[22] Aspects of such construction were spelled out in even more detail in articles in the *Gartenlaube* and the *Illustrirte Zeitung*.[23] Not only was *Daheim* the supporter of this technology in name and deed, but it consistently reminded its readers that innovations put in the service of national safety were proving themselves worthy, and thus capable of convincing initial skeptics.

Given the exhaustive investment of time and space in this project and the unending interest of the popular magazines in allying themselves with such a cause, we need to ask what motivated this investment. Why should the coastal region of Germany have played such a strong role in the presentation of and argument for national cooperation? The first thing that comes to mind is the German struggle with Denmark over the provinces of Schleswig and Holstein. These northern coastal provinces had to be defined in the process of this struggle as seminally German. This conflict lent itself to a publicist preoccupation with the north as the focus of German solidarity. While troops from several German states fought on the battlefield for the Germanness of Schleswig and Holstein (in the 1850s and then, successfully, in 1864), the popular print media launched and pursued a press campaign for defending the German coast against natural threat. Two years later, the victory of Prussia over its inner-German competitor Austria also set the sights of the German nation as a whole on the north, on the strong military state of Prussia, whose ships would have to defend the nation against foreign aggression from the north.

This notion of direct national defense is supported by the fact that the magazines interspersed these essays and announcements about coastal rescue devices with essays on the construction and growth of the Prussian navy.[24] This attention to military use and control of the seas also grew over the years. Although the danger of shipwreck and the deeds of the German organization were discussed in later years in *Daheim*, as they were in the *Gartenlaube*,[25] the importance of the Prussian and eventually the Imperial German fleet took precedence.[26]

But there seems to have been more at stake in the press's preoccupation with the dangers on the coast than the defense against a foreign enemy. Indeed, the enemy in all of these articles is the sea itself, nature in the form of natural storms. Why should these national magazines that were published for the most part in the major publishing center of Leipzig far away from the sea be obsessed with the northern coast? The problem at issue here is both borders and security. For a nation in the struggle of defining itself, the security of its borders is crucial. National borderlands can be liminal spaces which help stabilize a national center. The coast and the sea to the north of Germany, although not part of the territory of most German states nonetheless constituted a clearly defined edge of the ideal, unified German state. They were at the same time an unpredictable, wild frontier that posed a constant challenge to the success or strength of the nation. The discourse on lifesaving boats and rescue stations for the shipwrecked can be seen as a response to this threat. These stations functioned as a means of uniting the nation in common activity, but they were also a symbol that gave coherence to the idea of the nation.

The seamen in these stories of danger acquired a role similar to that of the frontiersmen of the American West. In their activity, grit, determination, and bravery they became agents of national salvation and unification.[27] By encouraging the rest of the nation to come to their aid with this system of coastal rescue devices and organizations, the press allowed the entire nation to center itself by participating in this German frontier experience. Thus, the prodding of these articles (in *Daheim*, the *Gartenlaube*, and the *Illustrirte Zeitung*) that insisted on the German ability to match the work done by the English, the Dutch, and the Danes was not a matter of international one-upsmanship. It was rather a matter of achieving what these peoples seemed to be able to achieve along their coasts: the unification of the nation along its border, the stabilization and assertion of national identity where it counted the most, on the frontier. The magazines insisted that this cooperative national effort would help overcome the divisions between city and countryside, interior and coastal regions, north and south. National cooperation was, to be sure, an important part of imagining the nation, but for a nation that was desperately seeking to eliminate many intranational divisions, it was also important to conceptualize a final border, to fix a clear and indisputable boundary for the entire nation at once. For this purpose the northern coast proved to be a powerful metaphor. Another metaphor was that of the inventor as national hero.

TECHNOLOGICAL PROGRESS: WILHELM BAUER

One German invention dominated the *Gartenlaube* in the decade of the 1860s more than any other single subject. The story and creations of the inventor Wilhelm Bauer appeared in twenty-six articles, illustrations, and announcements in the years 1861–1864 alone. The focus of these discussions was the underwater devices that Bauer had invented for various purposes: salvaging sunken vessels, pursuing maritime research, and conducting warfare. Bauer was credited with creating a man-powered submarine during a conflict with Denmark in 1849. A few years later he developed an apparatus capable of carrying men 100 feet below the water's surface, and a system for raising vessels off the seafloor by attaching empty balloons to their hulls, then inflating these via long air hoses (pumped from a ship on the surface).

The *Gartenlaube*'s veritable crusade in support of Bauer and his underwater inventions outdid its interest in any other technology or single topic, except perhaps each of the national wars. Most of the essays in this press campaign were written by Friedrich Hofmann, a friend of Bauer's, who provided impassioned descriptions of Bauer's achievements and his unfortunate neglect at the hands of the German states. Hofmann's detailed articles and the pleas for financial donations regularly printed by the *Gartenlaube* at the end of each weekly issue argued for national recognition and support of Bauer's work. As in the case of the coastal rescue stations of the same period, one might ask, what was this work and why did a magazine like the *Gartenlaube* take it up so actively?

There are several answers to this question. In the first place, Bauer's devices and technology lent themselves to the *Gartenlaube*'s objective of informing its readership about the changing world. The descriptions of Bauer's inventions included a broad range of information about basic principles of physics (water pressure, etc.), mechanical apparatuses (air pumps), and new materials (rubber diving suits, etc.). These articles were part of the larger project of educating the German populace. But beyond the simple novelty of these devices, the attention devoted to Bauer was tied to the national importance of modernization. Not only was technological innovation repeatedly claimed as a German achievement, but article after article insisted on the active participation of the nation in the support and encouragement of technology and inventors. The inventor became a resource of the nation and the success or failure of the nation was tied to its participation in the modernization process.

Finally, this series of articles (like those in *Daheim* that campaigned for support of the coastal rescue stations, and which were probably inspired by the example of the *Gartenlaube*) established a bond to the readership through its activist quality. The magazine repeatedly contrasted the nation to the various German governments that had failed to notice what was in their best interest. According to the rhetoric of these essays, the nation was something different from these governmental groups, something larger and above them. The nation consisted of the people, and hope for the nation lay only in their activity. The magazine used the case of Bauer the inventor to bring its readers to the aid of the nation. As a rallying point for national action, the magazine took responsibility for raising national consciousness by providing information and appealing to its readers for involvement. Along with the modernization of the nation came the press's strategy of nationalizing the masses, creating a nation of readers who were responsible agents of the idealized national body.

Germany in the 1850s and 1860s lacked a nation-state that could speak in the name of all Germans. Before Bismarck's successful wars of unification (and the growing support throughout Germany for Prussia), the path German unification might eventually take was unclear. This lack of a coherent political trajectory was particularly distressing to those interested in national unification. In various *Gartenlaube* articles, this disunity, the political patchwork character of Germany, was seen as detrimental to all Germans. Friedrich Gerstäcker, a popular author who traveled throughout the world, reported that the security of individual Germans' rights abroad was severely restricted because of this. Gerstäcker pointed out that in foreign countries where Germans were beginning to be active, for example, in many parts of South America, the existing system of consuls from the various German states was ineffectual in guaranteeing German citizens their political and economic rights. In terms of trade as well, he suggested that ships sailing under one German flag would be treated with more respect and understanding than the scattered and confusing presentation of multiple state insignias. For Gerstäcker, the problem lay not only in the lack of a German nation-state, but also in the petty politics conducted by most German governments (1862: 590–91).

The same accusation arose in the context of technological modernization. The author of numerous articles about Wilhelm Bauer insisted again and again that the reason for the lack of support for Bauer lay in the regional fragmentation of Germany. Just as Gerstäcker called for the use of a common German representative (emissary) and a common flag abroad, Friedrich Hofmann pleaded for a common patent system so that young German inventors would not have to find the time, energy, and money to apply for a patent in each German state (1862: 566). The failure of the *Bundestag* and the German governments to agree to a common patent regulation, he insisted, had forced young inventors of little means to leave Germany and seek patents elsewhere (1862: 566). Hofmann argued that the mental property of the German nation, its ideas and creations, were being lost to other countries. In other words, the German political structure was doing the nation and its technology a disservice.

The root of the German problem, however, was identified as more than this lack of organization and internal cooperation. The devotion of Friedrich Hofmann and the *Gartenlaube* to the cause of Wilhelm Bauer and his innovations was consistently presented as the direct result of the explicit unwillingness of German states to support the man and his machines. Hofmann's essays repeatedly raised the question: in the absence of the state, who else can come to the aid of such national works? As an implicit answer and evidence of its own willingness to take on the national responsibility, the *Gartenlaube* launched a press campaign for Wilhelm Bauer and his inventions.

The *Gartenlaube*'s strategy for creating a national dialogue on the issue of modernization began with the trusted and familiar biographical approach to a new topic; the individual inventor was characterized as the son of the nation. Yet, beyond that, he was also acclaimed as an unsung hero who then could be rescued from oblivion by the press. By characterizing the inventor as a neglected son of the people, the press (in this instance, the *Gartenlaube*, although other magazines participated in this approach as well) could define its own task as singing a hero's praises. In this manner, the press became a self-appointed national institution. This role was part of the press's self-definition as mediator and informer of the people. To understand this process, let us take a brief look at the number and kinds of essays the *Gartenlaube* published on Wilhelm Bauer from 1861 to 1865.

Hofmann initiated the long series of articles on Bauer in late 1861 with a three-page essay entitled "Ein deutscher Erfinder" ("A German Inventor") (1861: 648–51). From the essay's title alone, the supposed national import of Bauer and his work was clear; he was above all else defined as German, a German inventor. Hofmann's article asserted that Bauer's unfortunate fate, of not finding support for his work, was sadly also quite German. The remedy for this situation was an appeal to the nation. The essay closed with the exclamation: "It is the duty of the nation to call the German inventor into its service, it is its duty to announce not that this man can, but rather that this man must be helped!" (1861: 651). This outcry concluded the story of Bauer's success and determination, but also his abandonment and neglect at the hands of various (German and non-German) governments. This essay about Bauer's heroism born of national devotion began with Bauer's personal history.

Bauer's story fit in well with the issue of national cooperation in the name of German defense and public safety since he was a Bavarian who fought in 1849 in northern Germany against the Danish troops. As a cannoneer and born in a landlocked part of Germany, he had a national, creative inspiration that outdid the northern German seamen on their own terrain. According to this story, as Danish ships bombarded German soldiers on a Baltic beach, Bauer watched a seal leap through the waves. He developed the idea of a man-powered vessel that would be as maneuverable as a seal and could dive beneath the waves and attach mines to Danish ships (1861: 648). Such inspiration was described in this article as the product of national dedication: "The love for his comrades in arms, the honor of the fatherland, the hatred of the enemy were the spurs to his invention, its first and only purpose could be nothing other than the decimation of the enemy fleet" (1861: 648). As if to confirm the populist national quality of Bauer's inspiration, Hofmann noted that the construction of Bauer's prototype was supported not by princes, but by Bauer's fellow soldiers.

National combat provided the initial context for the story of Bauer's invention, but in the logic of Hofmann's narrative, this war was soon replaced by the struggle of the individual innovator against the skepticism of the age and the absence of financial and state support. Bauer became the lonely captain of his vessel, who attempted a trial run to a depth of 100 feet in the company of two sailors. As the submarine ran aground and lost its pumps, all three men were faced with death and the sailors became despondent, one threatening Bauer's life: "What emotions, what thoughts must have torn the heart and head of this good, well-behaved, always so loyal, courageous and serving sailor, that with a crazed look he pulled out his knife and, confronting the master, called to his friend: 'Witt, I won't die alone! The one who brought us here must fall, too!'" (1861: 650). The subsequent tale of their escape from a watery grave was the result of Bauer's clever scientific mind overcoming the sailors' lack of understanding. This heroic story had all the elements of an entertaining tale: drama, violence, suspense, pathos-filled dialogue, narrative climax, even the revelation of the hero's name only at the end of the tale. In case some *Gartenlaube* readers missed this initial story, they were repeatedly referred to it in later articles on Bauer and his innovations. The details themselves were also repeated, and his further fate (as a patriot forced to wander through other countries in search of support for his dreams) was subsequently outlined in detail (1862: 621–23; 1863: 555).

As a national hero, Bauer joined the ranks of other innovators to whom the *Gartenlaube* paid homage. Technological innovations in general became a favorite concern of the magazine. Bauer's underwater inventions were repeatedly described in their usefulness, not only for military purposes, but also for peacetime applications, such as research on underwater plants and animals, uses in the pearl industry, and in conjunction with other technologies that, as we have seen, also captured the imagination of the press: the telegraph and the lifeboat (1865: 667–70). The idea of a floating underwater telegraph cable was again presented as the creative idea of a German who had unfortunately found too little national support, so that now it was being advertised by other countries as their invention (1865: 478–79).

Bauer was repeatedly characterized as typical of the breed known as the "patriotic inventor." His fate was presented as parallel to that of Joseph Ressel, who, the *Gartenlaube* claimed, was the true inventor of the ship propeller, but who had also suffered the injustice of not receiving support and encouragement from his native country (Germany). Likewise, for the *Gartenlaube*, the first inventor of the telegraph, or at least of the principle idea behind such transmission of information, a physician from Mainz named Soemmerling (1865: 318–20), was yet another example of how Germans were not credited for their inventiveness, not sufficiently honored for their modernizing influence. The repeated references to Bauer's story in the context of articles about other German innovators and inventions enabled the *Gartenlaube* to impress upon its readers the significance of Bauer's undertakings.

The *Gartenlaube*'s repetition of the individual stories surrounding Bauer's activity, as well as the recitation of various facts, was also extensive.[28] For instance, the story of Bauer's attempts to lift the steamer Ludwig from the bottom of Lake Constance was documented in detail in several articles: this began with five full-length essays in 1862 in issues 4, 21, 36, 39, and 48. These were followed by updates in issues 27, 29, and 32 of the year 1863. What should we make of this obsession with one man and his innovations? The magazine introduced an article in 1865 with the almost apologetic appeal for its readers' forbearance: "We ask all readers of the *Gartenlaube* not to pass over the following article because they fear they will find something purely technical or already repeatedly discussed, rather, if they have a patriotic heart, to let the fate of a German man and a German cause of honor beat next to their heart, so that it can warm to sympathy and action for both" (1865: 478). In this concluding article, the lone innovator was seen not only to evoke the honor of the nation, but also to depend on the appeals and support of the press itself.

At the center of all the space devoted to Wilhelm Bauer stood the German nation. At stake in each article was not only Bauer's work and fate, but also his service to the nation and the apparent unwillingness of the nation to recognize it as such. For the *Gartenlaube*, the inventor embodied the modernization upon which the viability of contemporary Germany depended. If the nation saw that the protection of its coasts or the development of a new German navy fleet were important to its survival, then the work of a Wilhelm Bauer would also have to be defended and supported as part of the national cause (1861: 651). The magazine's devotion to Bauer's work was based on the conviction that modernization and technological innovation had to become national priorities. But it was also based on the premise that the nation was inherently a modern phenomenon.

THE PRESS AS MODERN UNIFIER OF THE NATION

The intensity with which the magazine championed Wilhelm Bauer in the public domain reveals the key strategy of the popular press in constructing the nation. The *Gartenlaube* used its existence as a mass medium to rally its audience behind causes it defined as national. Again and again the magazine positioned itself as a mouthpiece of the nation in the absence of a unified nation-state. In the case of Bauer, the capabilities and importance of new technology were identified in the *Gartenlaube* as goods of the nation that could either be neglected and thus squandered (given up to other nations who wisely put them to use) or treasured, tended, and employed to return profits for the good of the nation many times over. The same might be said of the popular press's discourse on public safety or, as we shall see, on war.

But how were the inventions promoted by the *Gartenlaube* nationalized? What made them more than instances of modernization in a general, transnational sense? One means of giving these innovations a national context and quality was the issue of the inventor's nationality. We have seen how the individual fate of Bauer (and Soemmerling and Ressel like him) took on attributes of the lonely hero fighting for his nation even in the face of disappointment and rejection. Certainly this often repeated narrative of national devotion and perseverance was part of the national mystique of modernization. Perseverance became by extension a quality of modernization that the nation could not afford to reject.

On a more practical level, however, the *Gartenlaube* appealed to its audience to turn the information of such articles into national activism. This took the form of the organization of committees to collect funds that would directly support individuals, groups, or in the case of Bauer, research and development. Like the magazine *Daheim* in its support of rescue stations on the coast, the *Gartenlaube* took up such collections for victims of fires and floods, for the German poet-in-exile Freiligrath, for the war injured and the widows and orphans of soldiers (after the war of 1866, especially). As we shall see in the next chapter, after unification it encouraged its readers to help finance the project of finishing the national monument of Hermann in the Teutoburg forest. With these pleas to its audience for monetary support of national causes, the magazine directly involved itself in the overt construction and reconstruction of the nation. In these contexts, the magazine was pursuing its liberal agenda, but it was also setting the course for a definition of the nation and national concerns.

At the end of its eleventh issue in 1862, the *Gartenlaube* published a direct appeal entitled "Ein Wort für Wilhelm Bauer: um Unterstützung seines 'deutschen Taucherwerkes' zum Heben und Bergen untergegangener Schiffe und Güter" ("A Word for Wilhelm Bauer, in Support of his 'German Diving Work' for Raising and Securing Sunken Ships and Goods") (1862: 176). In this prototypical appeal, the magazine claimed a right and an obligation to speak in the name of the nation. Its strategy was simple: it first recalled its own role (through publication of two articles) in relating Bauer's arduous climb from a lowly position. It then informed its readers of financial donations that had already reached *Gartenlaube* in support of Bauer's projects and encouraged further support with reference to endorsements by notable institutions and authorities. The appeal also suggested a unified strength of the press by calling for other magazines and newspapers to print similar calls for support.

This particular appeal closed in the same way appeals for many other causes in the *Gartenlaube* did. It reminded its readers that the *Gartenlaube* not only was taking up a national cause, but was also, as a nationally distributed publication, in a position to bring its message to diverse members of the nation: "With this we send our greeting in all directions into the dear fatherland" (1862: 176). Again, it is important to recall that the magazine's primary objective was not to generate a German nation-state. But as its popularity grew, the popular press was *de facto* communicating on a national scale that could be claimed by few other organizations and by no single German state.

After this call for donations, the magazine could reinforce its legitimacy in speaking for the nation (just as a state would need to) by pointing to the response from its readers. Each weekly issue listed their contributions to this cause, including the person's or group's name and city and the amount donated. It began to include them in its growing list of national participants, as national heroes on a modest scale. With each list it announced to its readers that this same readership or audience constituted the contributors to the nation. The assurance that more names would appear in the next issue served both as reward for the readers who contributed and as confirmation of the *Gartenlaube*'s power to speak to a wide range of members of the national community. By giving its readers credit for their participation, the magazine asserted its authority to recognize their contributions.

As the sum of these contributions to the cause gradually increased, the magazine continued its celebration of Bauer's work in extensive and repeated appeals for support endorsed by experts. This activism on the part of the *Gartenlaube* took on grand proportions in the magazine's presentation of itself. By repeatedly listing itself as participant and coordinator of this collection drive, for instance, the magazine could raise its own stature since it consistently recognized its own work in supporting this cause. Thus, it could portray its effort as a national activity. The mass media became the much needed mediator and intermediary in national causes in the face of the political fragmentation and particularism of German state institutions. In keeping this issue in the purview of its audience, which was then equated with "the German people," the *Gartenlaube* advertised the national role of the press: "Our determined efforts to disseminate knowledge and to realize it [must] appear as justified to everyone" (1862: 331). The press adopted for itself the voice of the absent state authority in defining the needs of the nation and organizing the means to meet these needs.

Inevitably the press began to compete with the state as unifier of the people. The magazine repeatedly affirmed its role in mediating for the nation at the same time it incessantly noted the refusal of German governments to support Bauer's work in its experimental stage. Years after launching its initial campaign in support of Bauer, it portrayed its dedication to this cause as unflinching: "[We never] let ourselves waver for a moment in our conviction about the fundamental correctness of the clever experiments of this man of the people, rather we supported them energetically because we held this to be our national duty." The *Gartenlaube* cited the danger of losing Bauer's work to other nations and argued that it stood alone at the head of a movement to rescue this national treasure. With this activism, the press shifted its role from informer and enlightener of the people to national servant and political unifier in a disunited political climate.[29]

WARFARE AND PROGRESS

In addition to usurping the role of the state in its discourse on national unification and cohesion, the *Gartenlaube* also minimized the state's significance. Even in the case of the wars of the 1860s, which eventually contributed to the political unification of Germany, the states played a relatively minor part in the narrative the popular magazines presented. Instead, the soldiers, their struggle, and weapons were in the forefront of the magazines' tales of national battle. Warfare has always lent itself well to rallying unity and, in the case of Germany, it is commonly agreed that Bismarck's unification from above was primarily the result of his aggressive foreign policy, his genius about when and why and how far to fight a war. It is not surprising, then, that popular magazines of the 1860s directed a great deal of their attention to the progress and outcome of the Prussian (or German) wars that gradually helped define the German nation in political terms. What must concern us here, however, is the way war was portrayed as part of the national cause in the nineteenth-century press.

Of course, the public conception of the progress of war in the nineteenth century differed substantially from the technological horror of war that became the legacy of World War I. In the nineteenth century, the civilizing mission of the Western world relied on industrial production and the wonders of modern technology to demonstrate its superiority over those parts of the world it intended to conquer and dominate. The Great War that savagely turned such inventions on Europeans threw the civilizing potential of such innovations into question. In this conflict, technology combined with nationalist hysteria led to mass death in the trenches and massacres that would forever change the world's conception of military conflict. As Michael Adas has argued, the mechanized slaughter of

World War I severely undermined the European fascination with its technological progress.[30]

Perhaps because the national wars of the nineteenth century did not produce carnage and devastation to the same extent, they were also not the object of harsh critique in the public realm. Indeed, in the nineteenth century, technologies of military power and control, such as the needle-gun and the steam-powered battleship were rather the objects of pride and fascination. As such, they provided an ideal focus for a discourse on national strength. These specific developments, which received detailed attention from the popular press, were paralleled by new kinds of reporting on events of war that became available in the late nineteenth century because of the increased speed with which information could be transmitted and events presented to a mass audience.

Bismarck's strategic wars of unification held the attention of the populace; they were the subject of extensive documentation and commentary in daily newspapers and in the popular weekly press. This attention continued for several years after the conflicts themselves ceased. It is interesting that these events did not necessarily enter the pages of more exclusively cultural periodicals. The monthly magazine *Westermanns Monatshefte* (also *Zu Hause* and *Illustrirte Welt*), for instance, made no reference to the Prussian–Austrian War in the year 1866. Such publications were less interested in day-to-day political events than in presenting culture and discussing general social values. For the weekly magazines, however, contemporary events, especially those that had an immediate impact on the definition of the national self, played a central role. Events of war often occupied up to two-thirds of the space in a weekly issue of publications like the *Gartenlaube*, *Daheim*, and the *Illustrirte Zeitung*.[31]

The representation of the war of 1866 in these periodicals had two functions with regard to national identity. In the first instance, war figured as a sign of national activity; battles were events that involved almost all Germans and directly affected the future stability and shape of German politics. Because readers of popular magazines hailed from all German regions and states, the reports on war had to avoid loyalty or preference for one side in favor of a language of commonality or neutrality that would not offend. In the second instance, the war offered readers a set of events in which the latest innovations, such as railroad transportation, telegraph communication, and modern armaments could be discussed at length. Technology even became a useful way to explain and accept the defeat of the southern German states and the victory of the Prussians. In this direct way, the outcome of war came to mean the progress of the nation in technological terms.

The presentation of the 1866 war, while following the events in a loose chronology, was less about a precise reconstruction of individual battles than about a presentation of the conflict as a "*Bruderkrieg*," or a war between brothers. The magazines, whether they tended to sympathize with Prussia or with the Austrians and its allied *Bundesarmee*, used the opportunity of this major German event to talk about the fate of the German nation and the ultimate goal of national unity. This concern with the nation led to a pattern of representation that can be summarized as follows. First, there was an interested description of the modern character of this war. Then, as the war progressed, articles included an increasing number of gruesome characterizations of the suffering caused by war: injury, pain, and death. Finally, in the reporting that appeared quite a while after the war had been over (with the normal delay of several weeks for the publication of articles) the magazines again turned to the riveting subject of war technology.

Articles that introduced the mass readership to the events of this intra-German war often mentioned the technological innovations that made their wartime debuts. In most of the articles in *Daheim* and the *Gartenlaube*, for instance, there was at least one reference to the new breech-loading needle-gun of the Prussians, or to the use of the telegraph for communication in the field and the railway for war transportation. Although the railway had already existed in Germany for thirty years, there were still regular articles celebrating its expansion (in 1866 the *Illustrirte Zeitung* carried several articles on new routes in Russia), or on developments such as a movable bridge to allow for riverboat traffic where railway bridges were needed. The usefulness of the railway in a German war constituted a noteworthy innovation in the eyes of the press.

The *Gartenlaube* and the *Illustrirte Zeitung* carried articles that pointed explicitly to the railway as a sign of the modernization of warfare. In its second article about the mobilization for the war, the *Gartenlaube* described the use of the "steam steed" ("*Dampfroß*"), to transport soldiers and the traditional steed of war, the horse, to the front. The picture that accompanied this essay showed cheerful, excited soldiers loading their horses onto a train to prepare for their departure.[32] An early article in the *Illustrirte Zeitung* pointed out the irony of this modernization more explicitly: the picture it offered its readers of horses in a transport wagon was meant to depict "the difference in means of assistance between modern and earlier forms of warfare . . . the former mediator of rapid movement, the horse, is taken onto the back of the stronger 'steam steed.' "[33] Both essays described the modernization of war as an interesting and entertaining novelty. The slaughter of battle had not yet entered the pages of the magazines; it took weeks for reports and especially illustrations from the front to be published and distributed. The press focused on the applications of new technology to war as its readers waited for descriptions of the fighting at key battles like Langensalza, Gitschin, and Königgrätz to appear.

The next and longest phase of reporting on the various battles between the Prussian and the Austrian and Saxon forces, by contrast, highlighted the destructive effect of modern technology in war. In reports that tended to favor the Prussian side, there was occasionally an enthusiastic commentary on the speed and efficient reloading of the new Prussian guns, the so-called breech-loading needle-guns. One *Gartenlaube* reporter in the field exclaimed: "Now come here, loyal needle-gun, give our comrades time and air!" (1866: 470). Yet, such euphoria about Prussian superiority in technological matters was dampened by sobering reports on the casualties of war, the wounded, the suffering, the deaths. Essays focused on the victims of battle languishing in field hospitals and on the horrible details of their maiming and primitive amputations.[34] Indeed, images of war losses and devastation dominated the reports from the field. Several articles pointed out that the tragedy of a war of brother against brother meant that every death was a loss for Germany.[35]

Despite these negative details, however, there was an overt attempt by the press to compensate for the destructive and divisive nature of this war by insisting on a national commonality through it all. Throughout the reporting, the existence and health of the nation was depicted as dependent on these losses. A *Gartenlaube* essay from mid-July put this ideology of sacrifice for the nation in the mouth of a young Saxon woman who was anxious about her brother in the field: "He expressed repeatedly and—I am convinced—with complete candor, that he would gladly give his life as a sacrifice if in that way a service could be paid to the fatherland of Saxony and the greater, grand, beautiful Germany. He was however, always in a struggle with himself concerning which side was in the right, Prussia or Austria. He loves our beautiful Saxony with his whole heart, but above all else he values the freedom and unity of Germany" (1866: 473). Because of the inner-German nature of this war, magazine reports praised the heroic efforts of Saxons, Austrians, and Prussians alike. All were characterized as valiant in their struggle for their respective German fatherlands, as the young woman said of Saxony. All were identified as heroes, as skilled and devoted warriors.

The magazines' interest in supporting the national idea occasionally inspired depictions of these battles as brotherly meetings rather than as a war of brother against brother. Essays emphasized that these diverse German soldiers (whether Austrian, Saxon, or Prussian) got along well in the field hospitals: "Many of the soldiers from all three armies, Prussians, Austrians, and Saxons, who are heading for recovery walk and sit here . . . they stand and sit among each other with no animosity" (*Gartenlaube* 1866: 462). The war had united them in a common experience: "The Prussians shared their bread with the captured and wounded enemy; the hard lot had brought them all close together and one could observe groups that were as endearing as they were interesting" (*Daheim* 1866: 645). Essays reported that the soldiers were nursed back to health (if possible) without discrimination, and if they died, "they will be buried with military honors, whether friend or foe" (*Gartenlaube* 1866: 457).

This common link between the various German soldiers was highlighted by a linguistic-ethnic sense of Germanness. *Daheim* repeatedly revealed a xenophobia that characterized non-Germans as somehow inferior to Germans. The soldiers who spoke differently, who had an ethnic distinction, such as Croats or Czechs in the Austrian forces, were called misguidedly superstitious (*Daheim* 1866: 696). This judgment was not made of their German Austrian colleagues. Likewise, the Bohemian peasants who were witnesses to the war were described in pejorative terms as speaking a "horrendous gibberish" (*Daheim* 1866: 682) and were mocked for their fear of the Prussian troops. Their impoverished homes were ridiculed and found wanting in comparison to those of German peasants, a generalization that may or may not have had a foundation in reality: "O you sad bohemian home—how different is your aspect from our peaceful, often so friendly peasant cottages!" (*Daheim* 1866: 681).

Finally, in the last phase of reports on this war of brother against brother, the subject of technology returned. Along with later reports that drifted in from the front, eventually labeled "reminiscences from the battle," the magazines again devoted most of their space to issues of normalcy, the concerns of daily life, essays on hunting, historical figures, and natural science (a volcano or mountain range). With the war at a safe temporal distance and the destruction over, these magazines returned to the topic of war technology. Articles surfaced in all three magazines on the needlegun, the Krupp cannon, and other examples of munitions fabrication. *Daheim* was the first publication to present what seems to be a direct interview with Nikolaus von Dreyse, the locksmith who spent decades of his career developing the new quick-loading gun and marketing it to the Prussian military.

In its lead essay, *Daheim* presented Dreyse as "a genuine burgher," a modest man who takes little of the credit for this invention and insists that it still needs much improvement. In *Daheim*'s depiction, Dreyse is typically German, a man whose modesty is symbolized by the phrase "Pray and work" carved above his front door (1866: 658), and who struggled like a hero to push his new technology through against heavy opposition within the military community. Despite the "victory" of his quick-loading needle-gun, this humble man saw each military victory and his current fame as only part of a larger, longer process. For him, the salvation of the German nation lay in keeping one step ahead of the other nations that would likely adopt this new system (1866: 660).

The *Gartenlaube* also published an essay on Dreyse that was longer than *Daheim*'s and written on the basis of interviews with those who knew him. It followed the same personalized yet hero-izing story. According to the *Gartenlaube* version, Dreyse began working on the improvement of the rifle when he stumbled upon a battlefield after the Battle of Jena that epitomized Germany's defeat at the hands of Napoleon's army in 1806. Although the details of the gun's design and its production were central to this essay, they did not provide its narrative power. The *Gartenlaube*'s story of this invention was a tale of revenge, of innovative energy applied for a national cause. Prussia needed a better weapon and Dreyse spent his career making it (1866: 628–31, 640–43). From the title alone, the point of this story is clear; "Preußens militärischer Luther" ("Prussia's Military Luther") was a rebel, a man who stuck to his opinion even in the face of serious opposition, but who, in the end, would change the course of German history. This gun had political implications for the nation. In Dreyse's own words: "The North German Federation will also be the Needle-gun Federation" (1866: 642). For the press, modern technology was not only central to winning national battles, but also to giving the nation a definition and sense of unity.[36]

The same national implications applied to the press's discussions of Alfred Krupp's arms manufacture.[37] The titles given to Krupp by the popular press suggested an imperial power: "Der Kano-nenkönig" ("The Cannon King") (*Gartenlaube* 1866: 819), "Fürst Kanonendonner" ("Prince Cannon Thunder") (*Daheim* 1867: 312). Grandiosity notwithstanding, in these essays, Krupp joined the list of German inventors who struggled and suffered for their nation. Despite his obvious willingness to sell his weapons to any power in Europe, the press made Krupp into a national hero like Wilhelm Bauer. He emerged from these stories as a man who wanted to use his inventions to support his homeland, but was sometimes overlooked, and who had to look elsewhere for clients. The press's search for unifying national heroes led it to characterize Krupp, who was in truth an aggressive industrialist who cared little for national boundaries, as a devoted son of his nation.

To be sure, in the extensive reporting in the weekly popular press on the war between Prussia and Austria, technology did not completely replace the traditional war narrative of soldierly valor and bravery or the notion of loyalty to a ruler. But the press exhibited its fascination with the innovations in war technology as a special and excitingly new aspect of popularizing the national battle. Technology, even in the context of a war that was acknowledged as brutal and destructive, could be a rallying place for the nation. Ultimately, the popular magazines portrayed it as a neutral terrain on which to recoup the embattled, embittered nation. The inventions could be characterized as specifically and simply German, taking their national identity from their inventors. They became, quite literally, a means for inventing the nation in modern garb. In other words, the representation of national security in time of war, as well as public safety, went hand in hand with a new discourse on the importance of industrial progress and innovation for the nation.

These stories attest to the power and skill of the popular press in introducing technology as a key to political unity. Periodical mass publications were fascinated with technology in most forms. In part, this revealed the modernity of the press itself. Innovation provided the backdrop for the press's own extensive growth around the middle of the nineteenth century. The numerous articles on telegraph and printing technology, as well as railway transportation and postal communication, suggest the press's dedication to promoting the basis of its own production and dissemination. Improvements in speed and quality of these sectors meant that the press could look forward to even greater expansion and influence.[38] But the presentation of new developments in these magazines was more a reflection of the press's agenda than a representative cross section of technological advance.

The magazines' interest in innovations devoted to public safety, such as firefighting and rescue ships, was part of this larger fascination. The selfless, humanitarian quality of such projects also highlighted the progressive aspects of inventions. The property and numbers of lives saved from destruction became part of a heroic presentation of technology. Critiques of the effects of modernization explicit in the work of authors like Wilhelm Raabe were not part of the press's presentation of Germany's industrializing society. Nor were the social disruptions that went hand in hand with industrialization the focus of the periodical press. The erosion of craft and skilled labor trades that the author Max Kretzer thematized in his novels was elided in the pages of these magazines. Technological innovation was presented instead as a vigorous and singularly useful ingredient of contemporary life and work.

This one-sided praise of modern technology suggests that the image of the nation had to be competitive in the most modern terms. The nation was not only a traditional phenomenon, as the essays and images of national geography had suggested. For the popular press, the people's support of coastal rescue stations and the historic work for the nation of Wilhelm Bauer and Wilhelm Dreyse epitomized this modernity and competitiveness. They were direct responses to specific threats, either natural disasters or the danger to national borders posed by military foes. In each case, the illustrated magazines celebrated technological advances as the source for national survival and vitality. They presented a forward-looking picture of the nation that stood in stark contrast to its other strategy of "inventing tradition." This material suggests that the explicitly modern mass media had to incorporate the aspect of modernization into its affirmation of the nation. The depiction of the nation in industrialized, technological terms did not conflict with an "invention" of the nation that recycled the past. By the 1860s both were essential components of a successful, marketable nineteenth-century image of the nation.

4

SPECTACLE FOR THE MASSES

Her small finger can just be grasped by two adult hands, her thumbnail is nine centimeters wide and eleven centimeters long . . . and ten couples can dance in the interior of her torso. [Description of the Germania monument on the Niederwald]–Gartenlaube *1883: 553*

T he mass press exhibited a deep fascination with the products of industrial society. As we have seen in the preceding chapter, the fabulous speed and performance of these technological wonders were recited like a litany. Elements of modern production took on a life of their own within the popular press. In the 1860s these impressive images of a modernized nation were most frequently tied to some clear application of national defense or civil security. By the 1870s, however, they also served to concretize national cohesion when put in the service of representation per se. Just as machine power, efficiency, and technological innovation were emblems of national health, the immense dimensions of modern products depicted in the popular press added a sense of spectacle to the representation of the nation.

Two kinds of image were central to the *Gartenlaube*'s spectacularization of the German nation. The first was directly related to the public celebration of the nation: the national monument. Numerous structures erected in the late nineteenth century represented the strength of the nation and the glory of its military and political successes. While isolated projects were launched in Germany in the first half of the century, the construction of monuments became a national obsession with the founding of the German Empire in

1871. These massive monuments paid tribute to the political power of the newly established empire as highly "visible" examples of national production. In the first decades of the empire, the popular press followed the use of modern technology in these structures as a barometer of national health and vitality.

A second image that repeatedly filled the pages of the popular press was the spectacle of modern industry. Magazines consistently glorified the productive power of modern industry and new sites of manufacturing in Germany. These detailed accounts of industrial production from various regions were meant to attest to the stability of a national economy. Interest in the newest products of the era inspired a fascination with the international exhibition. These fairs were attended by thousands of visitors who wanted to see the remarkable creations of the industrial age: the largest block of forged steel, the newest telegraph technology, or luxurious tropical gardens in the midst of northern Europe. Despite their "international" character and name, however, these exhibitions were forums for national self-presentation. Reports that appeared in the popular German press emphasized that these wonders of technology were a measure of national strength and competitiveness in a modern world. The spectacle of viewing and the pleasure of reading about the latest trends and designs were part of a specifically national discourse of emergent modernity. Other problems of industrial modernization, such as the economic crisis of the 1870s, paled in comparison to the *Gartenlaube*'s fascination with the spectacle of the modernized nation.

Monument construction and industrial production enjoyed substantial coverage in the popular illustrated magazines from the late 1860s to the 1880s. For the millions of readers who could not attend the industrial and trade exhibitions or witness the unveiling of new national monuments (or even visit them later), the popular press was a means of encouraging and enabling national participation. In the first decades of the German Empire, the considerable space these popular magazines devoted to depicting organized spectacles increased. In general terms, information about new developments in technology was part of the people's education (*Volksbildung*) that the press sought to give its readers. Detailed articles that discussed the functioning of steamships or the composition and installation of the Atlantic telegraph cable were like essays that introduced readers to elements of their own physiology or the basics of botanical development. This information about the modern world was intended to make readers informed citizens, but it often entered the service of the national cause. In discussions of industry and technology, education to civic responsibility and informedness coincided with a patriotic support of the nation. The mass press presented modern innovations in the context of national strength and as part of a discourse on the nation as spectacle.

My use of the term "spectacle" has been inspired by the work of Guy Debord but departs somewhat from his usage. Debord, in analyzing late-twentieth-century French society, understood that the commodity as it surfaced in consumer exchange, and especially in advertising, functioned as more than a simple item for sale. In interpreting the power and pervasiveness of the commodity in modern society, he argued that the spectacle it generated was "the existing order's uninterrupted discourse about itself, its laudatory monologue."[1] Debord tied the spectacularization of twentieth-century society to the transmissions of the electronic media in particular.[2] But already in the nineteenth century, the rapidly emerging mass press experimented with representations in which the national spectacle could become an item of consumer desire. These spectacles of the nation in the nineteenth-century popular press operated to distract their spectators from issues that confounded the stability of the nation, such as economic crises or internal political conflict. At the same time, of course, they helped represent the national idea. In bringing these images to a national audience, the press constructed a spectacle of state power as a force that was rooted in the populace at large, in the rapidly emerging mass readership.

NATIONAL MONUMENTS

The earliest image of the spectacularized nation in the *Gartenlaube* was the national monument. The magazine's essays about these colossal structures enabled the representation of the nation within a single image. Historically, nation-states have erected monuments to embody their power and legitimacy clearly. Yet, despite their apparent physical stability, the meaning of such massive structures has always been subject to alteration and reinterpretation. They provide an intriguing place to explore ambiguities that emerge when a complex social phenomenon, like the nation, is given a unified representation.

In the nineteenth century, German production of monuments was particularly pronounced. Especially after the founding of the *Kaiserreich* in 1871, Germans witnessed the proliferation of monuments meant to celebrate both their new identity and the creation of a German nation-state. As the work of Lutz Tittel has shown, the planning, funding, and eventual form of these national monuments reveal much about the officially sanctioned conceptions of the nation in the second half of the nineteenth century.[3] Thomas Nipperdey has presented a detailed critique and catalogue of the ideological registers to which these structures appealed, including monarchic authority, democratic populism, and a mythic sense of community based on sacrifice, fate, and struggle.[4] George Mosse has investigated the cultural and symbolic use of these monuments in national celebrations, noting that they were centers of national activity as much as static visual embodiments of national identity.[5] This scholarship, along with studies of individual monuments,[6] has contributed to a thorough understanding of monuments as national property.

Although national monuments themselves were meant to give a defining image to the German nation and its new nation-state, only a small percentage of Germans at that time saw them firsthand.[7] If only a tiny fraction of the national population saw these structures, how could they function as symbols of the "nation," as transmitters of the national ideas Nipperdey so clearly explicates? To fill the role of national emblem, they had to be accessible to a much larger population. In other words, these monuments, which were themselves representations of national strength and unity, had to be re-presented for distribution. One means of distributing the monuments was via visual reproductions and replicas, which communicated their stature and "monumentality" secondhand. For millions of nonvisitors, however, contact with these symbols of national greatness was mediated in the popular press. My objective in exploring the circulation of such images in the periodical press is to understand the additional meanings the monuments acquired in the process of their translation from stone and metal into images on paper. As a medium that shaped and disseminated their meanings, the press was central to the monuments' national significance.

Each issue of the *Gartenlaube* contained numerous images depicting such objects as regional German landscapes, foreign peoples in their local costumes, events from military battles, technological innovations, and wildlife. The purpose of these images, alongside the essays and reportage, was to offer the readership a view of otherwise inaccessible sights and events. As we have seen, even the most apparently apolitical of these topics, such as technology and nature, helped define the contours of the German nation. How much more acutely, then, can an investigation of the popular magazines' construction and dissemination of national monuments in pictures and essays reveal the tensions and ambiguities in representing the modern nation? Not only was there a gradual shift in the kind of monuments the *Gartenlaube* celebrated over the years, but the presentation of official monuments that glorified the German nation-state of 1871 stood in contrast to the attention the magazine devoted to geographic regions outside the German Empire (chapter 2).

Some of the first monuments Keil's liberal *Gartenlaube* presented were those dedicated to heroes of liberalism and German culture. In the first decades of its existence, the magazine frequently discussed "monuments of the historical-cultural nation," which depicted representatives of German intellectual tradition such as Hans Sachs, Luther, and Schiller.[8] These were joined by monuments honoring liberals from the Wars of Liberation and the 1848 Revolution such as Ernst Moritz Arndt, Theodor Körner, and Karl Rotteck.[9] With the founding of the new empire in 1871, however, the magazine's liberal repertoire changed. Images of military victories began to outnumber monuments embodying republican ideals.[10] Of course, this shift in the *Gartenlaube*'s presentation corresponded to the change in monument construction after 1871. But the tone of the magazine also indicated a move away from the ideals of the 1848 revolution toward a liberalism that welcomed Bismarck's unification of the nation "from above."[11]

One year after the proclamation of the empire, the *Gartenlaube* presented its readers with a spate of projected monuments honoring the newly unified German nation. Within the first six months of 1872 the magazine described work on the *Siegessäule*, the Victory Column in Berlin; the *Niederwalddenkmal*, the National Monument depicting Germania located in the Niederwald overlooking the Rhine River; and the *Hermannsdenkmal*, the Monument of Hermann (Arminius), the Cheruskan who had led the Germanic defeat of the Roman legions in the Teutoburg Forest in 9 A.D.[12] Celebrating these monuments as "reminders of the glorious deeds of the German people," the *Gartenlaube* participated in the national enthusiasm for monument construction that exceeded that of any other country and seemed to favor the small German solution to the "national question" (1872: 48).[13]

The *Gartenlaube*'s treatment of these monuments was unequivocally affirmative; its objective was apparently to present them to a new mass national audience, not to comment on the appropriateness of their imagery or symbolism. The popular press at large not only introduced these monuments to the public, it kept them alive in the national imagination prior to and long after their completion.[14] The image of Germania on the Niederwald received the most attention from the *Gartenlaube*, a total of eight essays, culminating in three articles in 1883 that reported on its completion and unveiling (see fig. 1). Even before there was a monument to see, the magazine had outlined the significance of its location as a focal point of past national achievements, "from Roman times to the present day" (1872: 314) and characterized its setting as a key to the memory of "Germany's road to greatness."[15] In this regard, the magazine's work anticipated the monumental representation of the nation. It nurtured national collective memory by functioning as a guide for the reader and giving specific suggestions for understanding the monument's explicitly national quality. The *Gartenlaube* insisted on the finished monument's ability to speak unequivocally of the unity of the German people: "When in the future the monument reigns on the mountain's heights, it

Das National-Denkmal auf dem Niederwald.

Zum Andenken an die einmüthige siegreiche Erhebung des deutschen Volkes und die Wiederaufrichtung des deutschen Reiches.

Nach dem Modell des Professor Johannes Schilling in Dresden.

1. The National Monument on the Niederwald (*Gartenlaube* 1874: 534–35)

will require no commentary and no interpreter. It will speak by
itself of how the people rose up as one and regained the long lost
and desired unity" (1874: 536). Despite this assertion of the monument's clear meaning, the magazine provided a model reading of
the monument, acting more as enthusiastic exegete than objective
reporter.

In fact, the *Gartenlaube* frequently offered readers the official view of each monument's design and placement. The Niederwald monument, placed on a bluff overlooking the Rhine River, was a good example. In an introductory essay, one author described not only the proposed dimensions of the structure and its figure of Germania, but also explained its plethora of symbols and the reliefs that would decorate the lower portions (1874: 536). Most essays on the *Niederwalddenkmal* were written by Ferdinand Heyl, an author from the Rhineland who initially proposed the idea of this monument.[16] Heyl's essays, as well as one contribution by the secretary of the local *Niederwalddenkmal* committee, Otto Sartorius, used a wealth of romantic imagery to accentuate the antiquity of the nation symbolized by this structure. References to the surrounding natural countryside reinforced this historical logic; the monument's placement high above the winding river was interpreted as natural and bucolic (1874: 536). In a racial, biological definition of Germanness, the magazine attributed blue eyes to the metal Germania, describing her as the archetypal German heroine with a spiritual connection to the entire German people. The *Gartenlaube* gave the official mythical, romantic view of this monument a national audience—millions of readers throughout Germany and even abroad.

Another monument that attracted inordinate attention from the *Gartenlaube* was in the Teutoburg Forest and represented Hermann (or Arminius), the Cheruskan warrior who gained popularity in the nineteenth century as the first defender of German soil, and thus the first unifier of the German nation. The idea of national origins provided the inspiration for the monument. Through its narration, the *Gartenlaube* brought the story of Hermann's defeat of the Roman legions in 9 A.D. together with that of the monument's designer, Ernst von Bandel, creating parallel histories of national heroism.[17] An 1872 article entitled "Eine schöpferische Ohrfeige" ("A Creative Slap in the Face") traced the inspiration for the Hermann monument back to a boxing of the ears Bandel received as a child from a French occupation soldier in 1806 (1872: 441). Pursuing the image of an enflamed patriotism throughout, the article lent continuity and logic to the vision of this "national hero" who, unable to carry arms, turned his artistic skill into a weapon for the national cause (1872: 444). The *Gartenlaube*'s narration of this story combined the vocabulary of military struggle with that of artistic creation and drew a final parallel between the founding of the empire in 1871 and the construction of this monumental work. These articles combined individual motivation with the story of the nation. They provided the reader with a personal means for understanding each monument as an emblem of national cohesion.

The immediate context of these articles and images varied greatly; part of the *Gartenlaube*'s program of people's education was to expose its broad readership to as much information about contemporary society as possible. This meant that these essays were placed alongside memoirs, historical and biographical essays, or articles on contemporary life, including trends in animal husbandry or changes in school regulations. But the presentation of these impressive monuments added spectacle and grandeur to the issues of the magazine that otherwise dealt with more mundane matters. Discussions and illustrations of the monuments also appeared in the *Gartenlaube* in the context of other definitions and celebrations of the nation, such as reports on national sharpshooting and singing societies, heroic accounts of the war against France, and essays about the specific customs and dress from various German regions. In this context, the monumental public representations of the nation became an integral part of the *Gartenlaube*'s mass mediation of national identity.[18]

Monument as Modern National Commodity

The *Gartenlaube*'s representation of national monuments mentioned above employed established elements of nineteenth-century national discourse. As we have seen in chapter 2, the German press in general borrowed traditional motifs such as national unity and geographical centering that were already prevalent in patriotic songs, paintings, and literature.[19] In addition, however, the *Gartenlaube* took an innovative approach to displaying the nation, focusing on the monuments' and the nation's industrial character. This was remarkable because the segmentation inherent in industrial assembly departed from the notion of the nation as an authentic, organic whole. That is to say, the magazine's depiction of a monument as a constructed, indeed manufactured product of industrial society was at odds with images of the nation as natural and eternal. The *Gartenlaube* thus unwittingly pointed to the ambiguity of the late-nineteenth-century political nation as rooted in the past, yet dependent on modern forms of production and social relations.

This combination of tradition and modernity pervaded the discussion of all monuments. An early example was the *Gartenlaube*'s presentation of the Victory Monument in Berlin as a sign of the capital's and the nation's bright future as much as a symbol of past achievements. Begun in 1865 to commemorate the victory over the Danes in 1864, the *Siegessäule* was not completed until 1873.[20] In 1872, one year before the monument's unveiling, the *Gartenlaube* published an article that placed the structure within the context of Berlin as the new imperial capital. The article began by acknowledging that Berlin, despite its recent growth, still lagged behind other national centers such as London, Paris, and New York. It went on to minimize this lack by emphasizing the future, referring to the monument's usefulness "for generations to come" (1872: 48) and to the beautiful impression it would make upon completion (1872: 50).

This forward-looking presentation of the Victory Column and its surroundings proposed two ideas about the nation. On the one hand, it suggested that the image of the nation, as already conceived in thought, plans, and models, preceded the historical realization of the nation. A future cohesive Germany was only a matter of time, not a problem of compromises and discussions that must be resolved politically. On the other hand, the urban context of the monument integrated military victory into the life of the national community; the park, square, and buildings that would surround the monument were said to reflect the "glory" of a monument whose construction would incorporate the spoils of war, twenty-two captured French cannon barrels. The wealth of the *Siegessäule* (the cannons would be gilded) was associated with the symbolic value of the future palatial buildings that would contain all the luxury and amenities of the modern era. This symbol would enable the capital city to compete in status with the cities mentioned at the outset, and thus, by implication, assert Germany's equal footing with the French, British, and American nations. In the public space of the emerging mass media, the magazine provided the German reader with concrete images of a glorious national future.

The popular press translated the experience of monumentality onto the format of the printed page, allowing readers to confront the immense dimensions of the metal and stone. The visual dissection of the Teutoburg monument in an illustration of its construction presented the magazine reader with details (see fig. 2), in particular of Hermann's head, that would never be visible to hikers standing at the foot of the completed structure. This view in the *Gartenlaube* offered a space for the reader to see the detailed construction of the monument in a manner which then would become part of a common memory. In this image, the placement of Hermann's mammoth head or foot next to Bandel and his workers emphasized the giant proportions of the final product through a human-scale comparison.[21] This picture was also an allegory for the construction of a modern nation that relied on national cooperation.

Just as this visual image depicted the combined efforts of the preindustrial trades of smith and sculptor, the accompanying text affirmed the cooperation of heavy industry in this national project. The article described the various locations where stone for the monument's base was quarried—the Teutoburg Forest, the Murg Valley, Saxony, and the region of the Nahe River—implying that modern transportation was a key to the monument. Ten years later, the *Gartenlaube* reported in detail on the participation of numerous industrial firms (from Frankfurt, Munich, Nuremberg, and Dresden) in the completion of the *Niederwalddenkmal* (1883: 635, 638). In addition, the magazine's extensive discussion of the difficulties and record feats in the transportation by train and the assembly of the massive Germania statue proudly reiterated the absence of accidents and affirmed the centrality of industrial progress to the national effort.[22] This insistence on the immensity of such monuments glorified the potential of industrial technology as well as commercial cooperation.

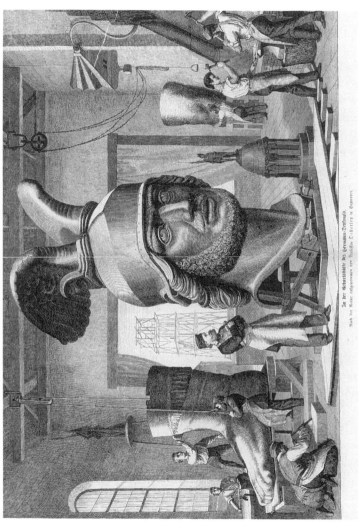

Zu der Geburtsstätte des Hermann-Denkmals.
Nach der Natur aufgenommen von Professor E. Arndt in Hannover.

2. In the birthplace of the Hermann Monument (*Gartenlaube* 1872: 442–43)

The depiction of the industrial processes behind these monuments affirmed Germany's achievement at the end of the nineteenth century and brought together national tradition with modern technological devices, knowledge, and tools. Their presentation in the *Gartenlaube*, however, juxtaposed the magic of German technical and industrial skill that was beginning to put Germany in the forefront of industrial production with distant historic tradition. In the visual rhetoric of these monuments, national icons (Germania and Hermann) were dressed in ancient garb. In the combination of text and illustration, past and present were conjoined in the portrayal of the nation.

Through their circulation in the press these monuments became commercial objects available for consumption. The inclusion of illustrations as spectacles was a frequent part of the magazine's mode of displaying desirable items. The publication of a visual representation allowed each subscriber to own a copy of the artifact. In honor of the Niederwald monument's completion, the *Gartenlaube* published a two-page spread that depicted an elaborately drawn frame encasing a picture of the structure along with seven smaller images of nearby areas along the Rhine River (see fig. 3).[23] This presentation had several implications: visually this image idealized the monument, suggesting the renewal of the nation, rising on the horizon like the sun behind it. Secondly, for the reader of the *Gartenlaube*, this display of both monument and setting might take the place of an actual visit to the site because it showed the monument from a variety of perspectives.

But most significantly, this presentation was framed for posterity. In this form, the national monument became available for consumption and localized representation on living room tables or walls across the nation. The *Gartenlaube*'s own display was complemented by other reproductions of the national monument. Replicas could be acquired at the site or purchased through the popular press. In 1884, the year of the monument's unveiling, the *Deutsche Illustrirte Zeitung* advertised the monument's sale in miniature copies (see fig. 4).[24] This practice made the monument a consumer item just like the digestive tablets, bullets, and sewing machines advertised on the same page. The monument's replication occurred

3. The National Monument on the Niederwald and its environs (*Gartenlaube* 1883: 636–37)

not only in the range of model sizes available, but also in the repeated representation of magazine advertisements.[25] While this commodified reproduction may have destroyed the "aura" of the original, as Walter Benjamin has theorized for later reproduction in photography and film, it nonetheless magnified the original's national impact by making it more widely accessible.[26]

Promoting national tourism was another way in which the *Gartenlaube* participated in the commodification of these monuments. One year after the completion and unveiling of the *Niederwalddenkmal*, the *Gartenlaube* published a one-page article on a special tram that had been constructed to carry visitors up to the monument. This notice included both a laudatory description of the tram's technology and a celebration of the number of tourists it had already shuttled back and forth (1884: 668). The press's focus on reproduction and tourism provided readers with a map to orient their individual trips to the monument, whether these were imaginary or real.

Self-Reflection of the Popular Press

The press's commodification of national monuments pointed to another modern aspect of its construction of the nation: the advertisement of its own contribution to the process. In an announcement from 1875 that accompanied the first picture of the completed Hermann monument, one author claimed that a *Gartenlaube* article from 1860, "Ein vergessenes deutsches Denkmal" ("A Forgotten German Monument"), mourned the apparent loss of interest in the monument while at the same time keeping alive a deeper level of national concern by dint of its coverage (1875: 360). Another article from 1875 explicitly praised the *Gartenlaube* for following the fate of the monument over the previous twenty-two years, beginning with its first essay in 1853 (1875: 555). According to its own logic, the *Gartenlaube* both objectively documented and patriotically inspired national sentiment; it had simultaneously registered a lack of interest on the part of the nation and raised a sense of national consciousness by drawing attention to the abandoned monument.

In carefully representing its own involvement in establishing national unity, the *Gartenlaube* could portray itself as speaking about,

4. Page of advertisements (*Deutsche Illustrirte Zeitung* 1884–85 [vol. I], 488)

for, and to the nation. It succeeded in making its readers both the subjects and objects of its "narration of the nation."[27] Specifically, one eyewitness account made the overt claim to be an important mediator for a large part of the nation that could not be present at a national event. An essay dedicated to the unveiling of the *Hermannsdenkmal* referred to this function of the press: "While the glasses rang here, the news of this glorious celebration was already flying on wings of lightning toward all the winds over land and sea to let all those who celebrate with us take part in this experience with us" (1875: 642). Apparently, the best methods for enabling those others, that is, the *Gartenlaube*'s readers, to take part were a first-person plural narration and a narrative mode similar to the sentimental prose fiction regularly serialized in the magazine. The essay began with this romantic cliché: "A frightening night of storms lay behind us. From midnight to the early morning the bride of winds had raged through the mountain forest and shaken all the oak trees of the Teut mountain in a wild struggle" (1875: 638). This descriptive voice lent a sense of urgency and immediacy to the depiction of monument, setting, and celebration.

The large image accompanying this report offered a comprehensive summary of the national event in one static scene (fig. 5). The viewer of this image was positioned as a member of the crowd, with a perspective at the level of the participants' heads, but at the same time enjoying an unobstructed view of the Kaiser, the designer Bandel, and the monument that would not have been available to many spectators at the actual event. Even the statue of Hermann was depicted in an unrealistic entirety. As part of the larger image, the monument was seen from behind, seeming to lead the masses forward. However, in the form of small models, the statue was simultaneously visible from three other views—right, left, and front.

This image of a faceless mass, positioned between stages, podiums, and banners, raising hats in the air, was itself monumental and anonymous. It nonetheless allowed for immediate identification on the part of the reading viewer through the inclusion of easily recognizable and humorous scenes in the foreground of the picture: a woman selling mugs of beer and a man spraying other spectators while trying to open a bottle. Like the first-person-narrated text, the visual image combined the grand and the individual; it represented the magnitude of the nation at the same time it gave each reader, and thus its audience as a whole, the opportunity to identify simultaneously with the perspective of the narrator and with that of all other readers. In this way, the *Gartenlaube* reader was a privileged viewer of the national event with an almost impossibly

5. Festival scene at the unveiling of the Hermann Monument in the Teutoburg Forest (*Gartenlaube* 1875: 640–41)

clear perspective, while at the same time he or she was just one of many "readers" who depended on the magazine for access to the nation.

The representation of monuments in the mainstream popular press provides one example of how the nation was made accessible to a broad spectrum of the population. The press proposed that the nation was in part based on historical continuity; articles of the 1870s and 1880s portrayed national monuments as integrally tied to the geography and ethnicity of a (supposedly preexisting) national community. At the same time, however, the *Gartenlaube*, itself a product of modern mass production, incorporated new aspects of the nation into its representation. At the end of the nineteenth century, the nation had become a community of consumers, and the *Gartenlaube* acknowledged this fact by foregrounding the technical, commercial, and touristic elements of these national monuments.

Monuments are powerful messengers of collective identity. They embody a variety of political and social ideas depending on the needs of a particular nation at a specific moment in history. Maurice Agulhon has demonstrated how certain elements, such as the inclusion or omission of the Phrygian cap from the French figure of Marianne, can substantially alter the political connotations of the larger image.[28] Other historians have noted that, irrespective of political ideology, monuments commemorating war dead can all be said to share the task of providing communal identity to those who survive.[29] And yet, the ability of monuments to speak to a nation is dependent upon their access to a national audience. The massive monuments of late-nineteenth-century Germany were impressive and effective national spaces, but their impact on the national population was also the product of another public space, the mass media. The *Gartenlaube* characterized these monuments as symbols, formed by national history, but also by industrial production and an economy of consumption. This view paradoxically challenged the idea of the monument as an immovable, eternal emblem of national stability. In its desire to mediate the newest inventions and events, the *Gartenlaube* revealed the constructed, commodified quality of the modern nation.

EXHIBITIONS AND FAIRS: THE NATION FOR SALE

The international trade and industrial fair was a child of the nineteenth century. The movement began in England at midcentury and culminated in the Paris Exposition of 1900. Prince Albert sponsored the first major world exhibition held in London in 1851. "The Great Exhibition of the Works of Industry of All Nations," as it was officially designated, was an overwhelming success, drawing a total crowd of over six million spectators from May to October.[30] The various exhibits themselves covered everything from mined minerals and all sorts of machines to furniture and the fine arts. In addition, the building that housed the entire fair itself provided a major source of attraction. The Crystal Palace, designed by architect Joseph Paxton, was a mammoth yet delicately frail-looking house of glass. Contemporary critics celebrated this structure, as well as the elaborate and multifarious displays it contained, as a modern milestone of industrial design and construction. This exhibition was particularly successful as a tourist site; it enjoyed extensive press coverage in England and abroad. In short, it quickly became an event to be copied.

The London exhibition inspired a flurry of similar fairs over the course of the next fifty years in Europe and the United States. These exhibitions were devoted to displaying the latest developments in fields such as manufacturing, technology, the arts and crafts, and even education.[31] They were international in scope and boasted participants from around the globe. According to some, their purpose was to further international understanding; Prince Albert had argued in 1851 that by revealing the similarity of interests throughout the world, the exhibition would reduce international hostility.[32] However, for the host nation in particular, and for all participating nations as well, each fair was a forum for demonstrating national proficiency, taste, skill, and progress in a variety of competitive fields. The national press coverage that accompanied these exhibitions was an important vehicle for acquiring (or losing) an international reputation.[33]

Significant international prestige could be gained from hosting an immense and well-attended exhibition. The international event that followed the 1851 London Exhibition and aimed to compete with it in scale was the "Exposition universelle" held in Paris in 1855. It was the first held in France, and the French prided themselves on creating an exposition that could outdo the London show. Richard Mandrell notes that both this and a later 1867 Paris exposition were touted as advancing the cause of international idealism, "while narrowly promoting French prestige and material interests" (14). This idea of advancing national interests was not exclusive to the French. For both host and participant nations these international gatherings were tied to the importance of national self-assertion in modern times. For Germany of the 1850s and 1860s, in particular, the lack of a cohesive unified nation-state was seen to be a distinct disadvantage with regard to promoting a strong national identity. In the nineteenth century, Germany did not host one major international exhibition. Thus, perhaps all the more so, participation and success at the international fairs held in other countries were considered important for Germany's self-presentation to a world audience.

The German states were involved in these international exhibitions from the start. Their showing, however, often left much to be desired in the minds of critics from Germany and elsewhere. Reviews of arts and crafts commentators harshly described the German entries as pitiful orphans amidst the luxurious products of France. One German critic of the 1851 fair gave a scathing review of the German exhibits: "One comes into an area where all cows are gray and all flowers black."[34] As late as 1876, German works at the Philadelphia World Exhibition were considered disorganized, of poor quality, and commercially and culturally inferior.[35] Professional critics perceived a weakness and deficiency in German production and skilled craftsmanship that set nations like France and Britain apart from it. Such negative reviews were often accompanied by calls for better education, more rigorous training, and upgraded models for German tradesmen. Beginning in the mid-1860s museums, schools, and associations for the arts and crafts were founded in many major German cities with the goal of improving German skilled labor and craftsmanship.[36] Another response to this perceived deficiency was the organization of a German exhibition in the year 1876 in Munich under the slogan "The Works of Our Fathers." Its goal was to encourage improvement in German production. In order not to expose German products to further comparison, however, this exhibition was limited to German participation. In addition to the Munich fair, a series of regional industrial and arts exhibitions were held in various German lands and these received significant attention in the weekly popular press, including the *Gartenlaube*, whose reviews we will look at below. But, ultimately, proof of Germany's rising image in the international marketplace had to come from its ability to compete with other nations at international expositions.

In addition to serving as a forum in which nations could further their world reputation, international exhibitions had a broader function. They displayed and embodied the achievements of late-nineteenth-century Western civilization; they were showcases for the latest technological and stylistic developments in innumerable areas. As Hermann Glaser has noted, these massive displays popularized a vision of paradise on earth with the greatest accumulation of richness and wealth. They were "complete works of art, that rhapsodically praised consumerism as the true happiness of mankind."[37] Visitors came from far and wide to admire the newest developments in almost every field of manufacturing and the applied arts. The exhibitions drew huge crowds and grew consistently in popularity throughout the century. Attendance at the Paris exhibitions alone rose dramatically over the years, with five million visitors in 1855, eleven million in 1867, sixteen million in 1878, and thirty-two million in 1889.[38] The exhibitions' format and accessibility to large viewing audiences implied that this wealth was now generally available.[39]

The attendance at the international exhibitions by locals as well as numerous foreigners was not surprising. They were impressive events for their day. Part of their draw was not explicitly political in character, but rather a fascination for the newest and the latest, an eagerness on the part of Europeans from many classes to glimpse firsthand the astonishing creations of their modern century. This organized presentation of the latest manufactured goods and craft products seemed to imply that the conveniences of modern life were now available to the masses at large. It marked the beginning of the mass spectacle. Our interest in this spectacle stems from its frequent appropriation for the purpose of celebrating the achievements of individual nations. In the reception and review of these exhibitions in the contemporary press, we can trace the participation of the nation in the modern spectacle of commercial production and consumerism.

The splendor and opulence of these public displays were celebrated by the popular periodicals of the day as the latest in mass entertainment and pleasurable satisfaction. One example of the press's interest was the amount of space the Leipzig *Illustrirte Zeitung* devoted to the Paris Exposition of 1867. In the first seventy pages of the magazine that year there were nine full-page images depicting the grounds and displays, even showing the illustrious and admiring crowds that attended the exhibitions. These images were, of course, also accompanied by weekly reports on various aspects of the exhibition: gala balls for visiting princes, national pavilions of participating countries, and industrial and fine arts exhibitions.[40]

The *Gartenlaube* also focused on these exhibitions throughout the second half of the century. It mentioned the 1851 London world exhibition in its first volume, even though it was not published until two years after the exhibition had taken place. Despite this passage of time, the *Gartenlaube* participated in the excitement of this unprecedented event by commenting in 1853 on the reconstruction of the Crystal Palace (moved from Hyde Park to Sydenham just outside of London). According to this depiction, the palace remained a wondrous display of geological treasures as well as products and manufactured goods from around the globe that should entice and excite the modern individual. At least four articles appeared in 1853 and 1854 devoted to this renewed structure and recounting its immensity in detail. The massive water display was just one element of the building that received the admiring accolades of the *Gartenlaube* (1854: 419–22). One essay compared the new surroundings of the Crystal Palace to the royal gardens and fountains of Versailles and found the newer grounds to be much grander and more majestic (1853: 292–93). This judgment implied that this spectacle meant for the common people (both the visitors and the readers of the popular press) could match and even outdo the royal extravagance of previous centuries. This comparison suggests that the press was replacing the otherwise inaccessible images of aristocratic privilege and exclusivity with a new populist spectacle. The images selected by the *Gartenlaube* described a new luxury supposedly available to the masses.

This spectacle of modern luxury and commercial advancement was enticing for the century's new middle-class readership. Like other new technological inventions and wonders of modern science and industrial production, the international exhibitions as a whole provided a wealth of material for the voyeuristic pleasure of the modern reader. But as the century progressed, the national loyalty of the *Gartenlaube* influenced its discussion of these events. The German lack of "success" at international exhibitions dampened the magazine's enthusiasm for British and French exhibitions. In the late 1860s and 1870s, the magazine favored the German industry and art production presented at the regional German exhibitions. Evidence for this comes from the year 1867, in which Paris held a universal exposition that was twice as large as any previous event.[41] The *Gartenlaube*'s report consisted of four rather cynical "letters" by Michael Klapp that focused on the commercialism of the French exposition. He explicitly accused the French of using their international exhibition to advance their national reputation: "The French have put a whole series of these working machines next to one another and to the delight of the crowds let them all operate at once in a colorful sum *ad majorem nationis gloriam*" (1867: 575). In contrast to this critical and surprisingly meager coverage, in the same year the *Gartenlaube* published three articles on regional German exhibitions that were much smaller. The magazine praised these regional exhibitions as indicators of Germany's strength in manufacture and production.[42]

The occasion of an 1867 exhibition in Chemnitz gave the magazine the opportunity to advertise the diversity of goods produced in German lands and to outline the historical background of German manufacturing. The *Gartenlaube* described in opulent detail the treasures of German production: "An oval mirror with a (porcelain) blossom-garland as a frame! What delicate, lovely forms and what color delight blooms for us here! . . . How unfortunate that the space in the *Gartenlaube* is too limited for us to lead our ladies piece by piece past a rich wreath of images in plaster, marble, serpentine, sandstone, clay" (1867: 541). Such essays emphasized the richness and variety of local German industry and trade (1867: 392–93). From its beginning, the *Gartenlaube* participated in the enthusiastic reception of the idea of displaying wealth and modern production as a sign of Germany's vitality.

The preference for German products is evident in the magazine's contrasting discussion of the machine hall at the Paris exposition and the machine hall in Chemnitz. Michael Klapp presented a highly ambivalent portrait of the machinery, the "industrial words of power" spoken by France and Britain, exhibited in Paris: "All the humming, racing, humming, rattling, stamping, slamming, small and large masters and rulers of modern work, these supplanters of the human hand . . . what a formless screeching of a thousand secret powers that reside in the elements, what a multivocal roar coming from colossuses that can simultaneously be angels and devils, pleasers and destroyers of humans" (1867: 570). The machines of the Chemnitz exhibition described the same year appeared in a drastically different light: "It is high time to turn to the inviting racing and humming of the machine hall: we follow it and stand before the largest room with the grandest contents of the entire industry palace. It is completely true what we very gladly repeat from a reporter: 'The representation of the machine producers is unarguably the greatest and most interesting part of the exhibition, and if one has cause to be proud anywhere, then it is here; nowhere does the rule of human spirit over nature show and prove itself so apparently and concretely as among these wheels, gears, screws, and cranks, which, constantly obeying natural laws, fill a purpose that man has given them'" (1867: 541). In the marked contrast between these two descriptions we can see how the magazine's presentation of technology was more about national allegiance than it was about celebrating the modernization of Western society as a whole.

In addition to the German bias of this reporting, the *Gartenlaube* and other magazines clearly saw their national contribution in serving as a mediator of the latest developments in international technology, manufacturing, and design. Although these articles (as most in the *Gartenlaube*) were meant to inform readers of events that they otherwise might miss, it is worth noting that the magazine presumed some of its readers would visit the sites themselves. To this end, it occasionally printed articles that provided travelers with suggestions about hotel accommodations, food, local transportation to the exposition, and the kind of clothing needed for the visit in the foreign city (1867: 382–83; 1873: 489). By describing the possibility of participating, these essays emphasized the accessibility of such spectacles.

The majority of the periodical press's readers, however, were probably not planning to attend the exhibitions themselves. For these readers, the press provided a summary of the various displays of arts, crafted works, modern luxury items, and products of heavy industry. Such massive spectacles presented a problem for the magazine that favored realistic and detailed depiction. The descriptions simply could not provide a comprehensive account of the variety and diversity of the exhibitions. Indeed, spectacle is by definition so massive and monumental as to defy an all-encompassing summary. Any description of it must thus allude to its diversity while intimating the difficulty of accounting for all aspects of it. Only as something that cannot be completely comprehended does an event or object acquire the awe-inspiring magnitude of a spectacle. The approach that best achieved this in the *Gartenlaube* essays was what I will label the "walk-through" description.

This descriptive approach was systematic; the narrator would begin at one spot in the exhibition and realistically narrate a walking tour of the hall or the grounds, mentioning a selection of what could be seen from vantage points along the route. Even modest exhibitions acquired the grandeur and monumentality of the spectacle with this narrative device. An essay on the Saxon–Thuringian exhibition in Chemnitz employed this strategy, listing wares upon wares and constantly referring to other displays too numerous to describe in detail. This round-trip tour mentioned a multitude of articles within the "view" of the author: statues, ironworks, woven fabrics, musical instruments, furniture, lace, linen goods, porcelain and terra cotta, mining products, alabaster and glass wares, lithography, men's clothing, bookbinding, tobacco and cigarettes, chocolates and candies, beverages, cheeses, ovens and stoves, chemicals, dies, sewing machines, horn items, brushes, brass products, fur and leather, knit products, gloves, rubber items, surgical instruments, watches, umbrellas, women's apparel, ribbons, corsets, oil painting, artificial flowers, carpets and wall-coverings, and so on. This breathless list concluded with the remark: "Our walk is finished, but how many thousand items, that didn't force their way to our eye, have we *not* seen" (1867: 393).

This descriptive device revealed the general layout of an exhibition in a gradual fashion and allowed the narrator to mention different exhibits and list the variety of material products on display. It also, however, enabled the constant and repeated allusion to entire rooms or halls that could not directly be seen from the position of the narrator. This gave the magazine reader the sense of the exhibition's fullness and endlessness. The implication of this technique was that one might eventually pass through the exhibition and find the way out again, but there would always be entire rooms and treasures hidden from view. The exploration of certain spaces implied an inability to see those spaces beyond them, but also the existence of a farther, unseen vastness. Such lists and the stated inability to see everything was meant to give the reader "an approximate image of the richness" of the exhibited products (1867: 393). This narrative of the spectacle in the *Gartenlaube* magnified the wealth of modern production displayed at the exhibitions, especially the regional and national shows in Germany.

The casual stroll through the exhibition also allowed the reader a kind of firsthand experience of the exhibition and thus encouraged reader participation. One essay on the much-later Chicago exhibition (from 1893) summarized the categories of exhibits. At the same time, its author expressed amazement and wonderment at the immensity of the event. He praised the amount of money that had apparently been invested, the size of the buildings and exhibition spaces, and anticipated attendance and income. His language highlighted the new and unprecedented qualities of this space as a modern spectacle: "a wonder," "colossal interior," "immense proportions," "massive portal," "what masses of material did this $1,500,000 building swallow!" (1893: 493). The result was a narrative fascination with the modern scale of grandeur brought together in one place, the kind of awestruck reaction that a first-time viewer would have had. As the "eye" of the reader, the magazine thus played a seminal role in the spectacle of these exhibitions: "I do not want to leave you standing outside in front of the holiest place of world industry" (1867: 509). Once again, it could emphasize its function as mediator between the fascinating yet unseen distant world and the German burgher sitting in his or her living room: "The reader should imagine . . ." (1893: 402).

As we have already indicated, the general interest in the modern commodities at the grand expositions that were presented to a mainstream public was consistently subject to a selective presentation in the *Gartenlaube*. Essays and illustrations gave preferential treatment to the products on display that represented German industrial production and German successes on this international field of competition. Although the international fair had its birthplace in England and encouraged a lively spirit of international cooperation, it also clearly came to be perceived as a forum of national competition. Ever since the London exhibition of 1851, German entries were a regular part of the international exhibitions. The reports in German publications rarely failed to mention the success or relative failure of the German showing at any of these events. Even before 1871 and the political unification of Germany, the press identified the entries in crafts production, machinery, and art from diverse German regions under the common label of the German nation. The exhibitions, although international, thus enabled the popular family magazines to use this spectacle of modern life and production to present a unified, heroic view of the German nation.

Perhaps the clearest example of the *Gartenlaube*'s preoccupation with Germany's performance on this international field was its reporting about two expositions that received repeated attention: the Paris Exposition of 1878 (seven years after the founding of the German Empire) and the 1893 Columbian Exposition held in Chicago. In reporting on these exhibitions, the *Gartenlaube* employed a language of extremes in order to present the German contributions as a significant national event. The most notable aspect of the magazine's essay style was the predominance of military metaphor. In more than one instance, a *Gartenlaube* author portrayed the German participation at an international exposition in terms of military conquest and victory. An extensive article by Fritz Wernick from 1878 summarized the "Teilnahme der deutschen Kunst auf der Pariser Weltausstellung" ("Participation of German Art at the Paris World Exhibition") (1878: 692–99). In praising the unity and coherence of the German hall that exhibited the sculpture, painting, and drawing of numerous artists from many German artistic schools, the author returned repeatedly to the language of battle. The artist Anton von Werner, who was in charge of the selection of German contributions, was described as a second Bismarck, and those who helped him were characterized as his "general staff." This mention of the Prussian German military alluded to the Germany victory over the French in 1870.

The author's conclusion was even more explicit in this regard: "Thus our Germany has won a glorious victory here, too, under different circumstances and on hotly contested ground, yet with the smallest army" (1878: 696). An army of artists thus could defend the nation just like a military army and could win decisive victories for the cause of national unity. This essay even claimed a unity and coherence for the German exhibition that it argued was lacking in the other national halls; the French and Belgians were described as attempting to redecorate their displays in order to compete with the German model, that appeared "in determined, well-planned battle array" (1878: 696). In a follow-up note to this article that appeared one month later, the designer of the German hall, Lorenz Gedon, was also labeled a "general," who patriotically inspired his staff to follow the German victory on the bloody field of battle (another reference to 1870) with victory on the peaceful "field of art" (1878: 768). Again, this commentary ended with the cry, "We have been victorious!" that placed the competition of the international exhibitions beyond the mere success of one commodity over another and attempted to nationalize the content of these competitors.

An article devoted solely to the German house at the 1893 Columbian Exposition in Chicago also praised the Germans for recovering from what had been a "miserable defeat" at the 1876 exhibitions in Philadelphia to "shine here in victory" (1893: 621). This author insisted that "[Germany's] entire exhibition outstrips both in variety and richness and in solidity those of all other peoples" (621). The German building of stone, iron, and wood was acclaimed as capable of lasting centuries, long past those of other nations. The specific exhibits in Chicago that were chosen for detailed attention by the *Gartenlaube* author also encouraged a military interpretation of the nation's competitiveness. One article boasted about Krupp cannons that were on display, listing their individual size, weight, and range. This passage inspired the conclusion: "[T]hus we see Germany represented with dignity and glory at the entire world exposition" (1893: 624). Another German contribution to the Columbian celebration praised in detail two German warships sent to the fleet show at the mouth of the Hudson River in New York. In this article the author sang the praises of one ship's speed, power, and beautiful form (1893: 226, 401). The importance of conveying Germany's national strength to readers back home motivated the selection of these products, since they embodied the power of a united Germany on an international terrain in unambiguous terms. The descriptions of cannons and battleships helped the magazine support its conclusion about the German showing at this exposition, "that the victory of Germany, that is uncontested on all fronts and that was fought on the same ground where we suffered a serious defeat 17 years ago, will have the most blessed results for our art and industry" (1893: 624).

Beyond emphasizing the nation's military power, however, the *Gartenlaube* was concerned with Germany's performance at the Chicago exposition because of its significance for the nation's economic well-being. One essay explicitly described the New World as an important market for European producers, and thus particularly key as a venue for Germans in their competition with French and British products (1893: 624). For each of these exhibitions, the language of conquest was appropriate to the competitive spirit that pervaded the market for new commodities. The items on display in London, Paris, and Chicago were not only competing with each other for awards at the expositions, but also in the marketplace of consumers. Some consumers might first see them in the context of the exhibition halls, others might encounter them in the press, and still others in the gradually expanding phenomenon called the department store. In all cases, the purpose of the commodity display was to announce an item's attractiveness over and against competing commodities. As Guy Debord has so succinctly put it: "Every given commodity fights for itself, cannot acknowledge the others, and attempts to impose itself everywhere as if it were the only one. The spectacle then, is the epic poem of this struggle."[43] In the *Gartenlaube*, this struggle of one commodity over another was additionally given clear national implications and emerged in military garb.

The *Gartenlaube*'s interest in commodity production as a spectacle of the nation at world expositions was paralleled in the press's coverage of industrial and commercial development in Germany more generally. The international context of the fairs in London, Paris, and the United States constituted a framework of fascination for the potentially more mundane discussions of German places of manufacture that were a regular part of the magazine's discussion of modern life. These industrial sites fit well into the spectacular vision already established by the magazine's treatment of the commodity on display. Here, too, certain rhetorical strategies turned the discussion of production and the interest in innovation into a national issue.

Essay series in the *Gartenlaube* on German industry extended over several decades and were repeated according to an established format. This repetition itself suggests that editorial decisions were probably tied to presumed reader interest or the positive response these thematic reports evoked. As in the case of the geographical series that began in the 1850s, the recurring topical focus on "German industrial sites" from the 1860s to the 1890s suggests that the magazine had identified an effective formula for simultaneously promoting its educational agenda and generating reader appeal. This series operated with the same strategies of national integration as essay series devoted to other themes. Defining "Germany's Great Industrial Workshops" both before and after political unification in 1871 under Bismarck, the *Gartenlaube* attempted a textual unification of the nation's political diversity.[44] Articles discussed industrial sites from a wide geographical area: Bochum, Detmold, Hannover, Berlin, Nuremberg, Chemnitz, and Dresden, among others. As in the presentation of a national geography (see chapter 2), here, too, a representative sampling of industrial regions throughout Germany was sought.

Although each essay emphasized the specific achievements or points of interest of the industrial branch under discussion, common strands ran through all the contributions. One similarity was that they highlighted the competitiveness and independence of these German businesses with regard to similar institutions in other countries. One article from 1875 praised the rise of a Bochum steel casting factory. It insisted that the German production of steel had surpassed the English in quality.[45] In 1883 an article featured the entrepreneur Louis Schönherr and his specially designed weaving stool in Chemnitz. The essay praised his factory: "The Schönherr factory is German through and through—no foreign patents, no English masters" (1883: 690). According to the author of this essay, the national character of this factory implied that "the German people owe this man and his factory honor and thanks" (1883: 691). Similar euphoric comments were made about the successes of "the German miner" (1879: 670), and the "significant contribution to the entire fatherland" of a watchmaker from Glashütte (1879: 222). Each branch of German industry was placed in the service of the German nation and acknowledged by the *Gartenlaube* in the name of the entire German *Volk*. This elevation of industry to a national cause consistently reestablished commercial production as an integral part of imagining the nation.

These essays contributed to an integration of the German nation in a second respect. In celebrating national industry, they erased social divisions that might otherwise appear in reports on industrial production. There was, for instance, a noticeable absence of references to workers, other than to list the number of laborers employed in a factory. Most discussions of production processes were objectified, described in the passive voice without mentioning the agency of workers: "Forged iron is by comparison hardly pourable and must be forced into the desired form by hammer and rolling

mill at red heat" (1875: 542). The productivity of machines and auto-
mated power was praised; workers appeared at best in generalized
references. Production was idealized as a positive social situation,
as, for example, in an essay about work in a furniture factory, which
noted that although the company was not yet turning grand profits,
there was "constant work, sufficient wages, and healthy humans"
(1883: 30). Despite the attention paid to Schulze-Delitzsch and his
reformist workers' movement in two articles from 1863 (1863: 504–
6, 516–19), there was little concern in essays on national industry
for the working or living conditions of those whose labor supported industrial production. The *Gartenlaube* was more interested
in depicting German industry as the emblem of the modern, powerful, socially unified nation than it was in presenting intranational
class conflicts. To be sure, the middle-class liberal ideology of the
magazine played a role in this perspective. But it is interesting to
note that whereas the simple shepherd who gave his life for the
nation (see the case of Born in chapter 1), or the lonely work of
an inventor like Wilhelm Bauer (chapter 3) or an artist like Ernst
Bandel, was relevant to the national portrait the *Gartenlaube* was
painting, the spectacularization of national industry left no room
for the industrial worker. The sanitizing of industrial and production processes was an incidental cost of representing the modern
nation as spectacle.

The popular press was not alone in this construction of national
identity. The spectacles it depicted for its readers were in themselves
ostentatious products of a consciously modern nation. The process
of creating national monuments involved physical construction on
an unprecedented scale. It relied on mass support and subscription
efforts to collect sufficient funds. Construction culminated in well-
choreographed celebrations at the unveiling of each structure.[46]
The extensive historical literature on the world expositions of the
nineteenth century attests to their spectacular presentation of the
national idea for many countries, including Germany.[47] Ultimately,
however, the visibility of these activities, despite the tens of thousands who actually visited national monuments or attended the
German exhibitions at international fairs, was a product of their
distribution in the popular press. As a result of the press's reporting,

these emblems of national cohesion and strength were made available to a much larger audience than could otherwise have perceived them. In magazines like the *Gartenlaube*, these monuments and displays were accessible to millions of readers and viewers. Mass spectatorship thus occurred at one remove from the original sites of consumption. In distributing these spectacular images of the nation, the popular press revealed both its strong interest in the modern quality of the nation and its own fundamentally modern character.

If we are to understand the nineteenth century as the beginning of a mass imagining of national identity, it must be through the press as the main channel of disseminating this identity. For a mass appeal, the nation had to be concretized and made tangible in print and small-format images. These reports and images, in turn, had to be "consumable," just as the commodity at international fairs was the object of visual consumption. The mass character of imagining the nation was predicated on the production and distribution of images that could be readily understood. For this reason, it is not surprising that the visual component of the *Gartenlaube* increased over the decades. Whereas in the 1860s and 1870s the number of images in a sixteen- or twenty-page issue averaged between two and three, by the 1890s almost all pages in each issue bore some kind of illustration or decorative image. In chapter 6 we will undertake a closer examination of the illustrations in the *Gartenlaube*, when we discuss the magazine's representation of the nation at the close of the century. This increase in visual material not only facilitated the *Gartenlaube*'s presentation of the nation as spectacle, it also aided the speed and ease with which the magazine could be consumed. Visual absorption increasingly replaced the more methodical involvement of the reader with a written text.[48]

In the process of portraying the nation as spectacle, the popular family magazines themselves became the basis of a spectacularized society. These publications thrived on displaying the wondrous new inventions of their age. At the same time, however, they were themselves a product of technological innovation. Not only in the attendant technologies that supported them, which we outlined in chapter 1, but in their general character as unidirectional communicators to an isolated, individualized, yet mass population, these publications were spectacles.[49] The communicative process of the early mass media in the nineteenth century previewed the operations of the twentieth-century press. In these last two chapters we have seen the *Gartenlaube*'s strategies for appealing to an explicitly modern audience. The presumed uniformity and universality of the magazine's audience was central to the *Gartenlaube*'s presentation of national monuments as well as the technology of war. In the next chapter, by contrast, we will see one example of how the magazine also appealed to particular reading populations. It integrated the gender interests of its women readers into the larger categories that were part of imagining the nation. Even in the process of addressing divergent audience interests, however, the illustrated family magazine maintained a clear and centered definition of the nation as a whole.

5

DOMESTICATING THE NATION

. . . a golden-haired German maiden worked a miracle; and the distracted glances of a wobbly world filled with passionate unrest and bloody conflict were shifted onto the simple and quiet luster of her graceful appearance.–Gartenlaube *1871: 803*

The process of creating a national audience was an intimate part of the attempt in the early mass press to popularize a coherent image of the nation. However, the concept of national identity was neither singular nor simple. As we have seen in the preceding chapters, various political and social considerations were involved in the press's definition of national identity. Regional identities were incorporated relatively easily into the larger category of the nation through the idealization of a national space. Class identities could be smoothed over with discussions of the people's common history or in the obliteration of class conflict in the spectacle of modern industrial production. This chapter focuses on the process of integrating the female gender identity (at the time thought to be beyond the pale of politics) of a large segment of the *Gartenlaube*'s readers into the idea of the nation. In other words, this chapter investigates how gender factored into the problem of nation-building as it occurred in the popular press.

Discussing the processes by which an important subset of the potential national audience was integrated into the national whole means understanding the place of women readers in the popular press of the nineteenth century. The *Gartenlaube* was the most popular periodical publication of its time, but as we have seen in chapter 1 it was also part of a larger trend in the press that explicitly catered to the entire family as its ideal (or targeted) reading audience. We have discussed the apparently cautious and tentative character of Ernst Keil's introduction to his magazine from 1853: "Far from all reasoned politics and all difference of opinion in religious and other matters, we want to introduce you, in truly good stories, to the history of the human heart and the peoples" (1853: 1). This modest, apolitical manifesto could be read as Keil's liberal response to the censorship of the reaction period after the 1848 revolution. In that light, Keil's domestic agenda appears as a preemptive measure against political censorship in a conservative era.

But it was more than that. The ideal reading context proposed by Keil's introduction, "next to the cozy oven" or in a shady bower "when red-and-white blossoms fall from the apple tree" (1853: 1), suggests that the magazine was also explicitly addressing the middle-class family within the privacy of the domestic sphere. The peacefulness of an interior private space and cultivated nature established the prescribed domestic context of the *Gartenlaube* from its beginning. Keil's interest in addressing the middle-class family as a reading audience was part of his ideological project to educate the German people as well as entertain them. But it was also the key to achieving mass circulation, to winning an unprecedented readership. In other words, the magazine's success in defining a national identity and speaking to a national audience in late-nineteenth-century Germany was directly tied to the domestic character of its readership.

Although the *Gartenlaube* described the family as the ideal context for reading, its programmatic statement about what constituted the German reading family was vague. In part, it obviously envisioned the family as a mixed gender group, an audience of both men and women.[1] Its claim to represent the positions of its audience rested upon its ability both to communicate the magazine's interest in the reader and to construct the broadest, most inclusive definition of the reader. The process of appealing to men and women, boys and girls had to take into account the gender characteristics of women and men in nineteenth-century Germany. Historians, such as Karin Hausen, have demonstrated that the social characteristics of women and men in the course of the nineteenth century became ever more clearly differentiated and codified into separate roles and spheres. Women were characterized as passive, emotional, and exclusively qualified for domestic life, while men's active and rational gender characteristics made them ideally suited for the world of work and trade. Hausen argues that these well-articulated gender distinctions acquired the force of a natural law and affected all aspects of family life by the end of the century.[2]

DOMESTICATED READERS

Given this social differentiation, we need to explore the role gender identities may have played in the construction of national identity. If the popular press helped readers envision the nation as a coherent political and social body, we need to ask what social space within such a national "body" it allotted to women. Were feminine characteristics part of the ideal nation posited by the *Gartenlaube*? The women who read such magazines were not citizens in the same regard as men; their legal and political rights were at best limited. Women had fewer rights to hold property, they could not vote, run for political office, and even their right to assemble was highly restricted. This limitation of women's social and political visibility corresponded in the print media to a relative marginalization of women.

And yet, the explicit inclusion of women readers was central to the *Gartenlaube*'s establishment of the middle-class family as the basic building block of German national identity. From the beginning, the editor Keil intended his publication to interest and educate women readers as much as men: the essays about nature should be written, Keil stated programmatically, simply enough for any common craftsman and, especially, for any woman to understand them.[3] As a periodical meant for the whole family, the *Gartenlaube* did not prescriptively identify certain material for female as opposed to male readers. However, given the contemporary notions of appropriate reading material for women and women's reading preferences, the editorial staff most likely had implicit notions concerning the texts that would be read by women, such as popular novels.[4]

In order to identify the place of the woman reader with respect to the *Gartenlaube*, we need to consider the space occupied by women within its texts. The dominant genre in the magazine was the essay. This included biographical sketches and historical exposés. By and large, these focused on prominent men such as military officers, politicians, and poets. In *Gartenlaube* articles devoted to the activities and biographies of important social and historical individuals, women played at best a peripheral role. On average, only one or two in twenty essays dealt with women.[5] In the rare cases when women were the focus of attention, they were usually women of royalty. These essays were not about women per se, but were early examples of the press's voyeuristic gaze into the lives of the rich and famous.

When bourgeois women were featured, it was usually as the wives, sisters, or mothers of notable men. When women became the subject of articles and essays independent of men, it was none-theless most often in the context of their familial and domestic identity.[6] This emphasis on domesticity even found its way into articles on popular science which presented anthropomorphized familial organization and behavior within the animal kingdom. Finally, when women were the explicit addressees of reportage articles, these pertained mostly to feminine, domestic concerns. Even essays that described the women's movement reinscribed these female activists within the context of the family.

Judging the magazine solely in terms of thematic frequency, women seemed to play a marginal role in the composition of the *Gartenlaube*. But other sources indicate that women were central to the success of the magazine on several levels. Whereas men were often the subject of factual, historical reports, women figured prominently in the magazine's fictional contributions, most of which included love stories or domestic scenarios. In one early sample year (1855), for instance, the fictional tales had such titles as "Treue Liebe," "Der gestohlene Brautschatz," "Braut und Gattin," "Eine seltene Frau," "Das spanische Mädchen," "Die Stiefmutter," and "Der Diebstahl aus Liebe" ("True Love," "The Stolen Bridal Treasure," "Bride and Wife," "A Rare Woman," "The Spanish Maiden," "The Stepmother," and "Theft for Love," respectively).[7] Bringing the family together as a reading audience, which the *Gartenlaube* hoped to do, meant appealing to women with topics that addressed them directly.

Some historians of the press have suggested that women's role in the success of the *Gartenlaube* went beyond their readership, that they were mainly responsible for the family's purchase of the magazine.[8] The question that remains unanswered in terms of the magazine's logic is whether Keil's goal to make the *Gartenlaube* accessible to women was intended as a way to sell more issues and create more demand (sensing that women had a voice in domestic purchases), or as a way to reach the entire family for the pedagogical goal of educating a self-assured, enlightened middle class. In either case, the magazine's success was dependent on its ability to acknowledge gender as a part of women's identity and incorporate this identity into a national self.

A summary of the topics concerning women that received repeated treatment in the *Gartenlaube* from the mid-1860s to the 1880s can help us understand both how women readers were seen by the editors and what role they played in the magazine's project as a whole. The repetition of these topics not only indicates their perceived popularity with the readership, it also constitutes a textual space in which the magazine could refer to its own earlier positions, to accentuate its significance both as a mediator of important ideas and as a successful product. Women's topics that the *Gartenlaube* editors considered worth discussing included: physician's suggestions to young women and virgins that were entitled "feminine beauty,"[9] essays on women's fashion,[10] and a topic that incorporated both health and fashion, a discussion of the harmful effects of tight corsets on the liver and other internal organs.[11] A primary concern of the *Gartenlaube*'s presumed female readers was their bodies and appearance.

A second topic that appeared repeatedly was housework and the image of the housewife. Even articles that focused on the characteristics of housewives and women in other nations discussed them in the context of the German housewife. Despite the titles of two

articles from the 1860s, "Die amerikanische Hausfrau" ("The American Housewife") (1866) and "Zur Charakteristik amerikanischer
Frauen" ("On the Characteristics of American Women") (1867),
these essays also assessed the characteristics of German women,
who were addressed in the second person and thus clearly defined
as the audience. This discussion of German issues in the context
of other cultures occurred in *Gartenlaube* essays that referred to
Americans on the frontier or Africans in their villages to make statements about German society. Identity, be it generically German
or specifically feminine German, was often defined by contrast,
through comparison with another model.

Let us turn to essays on American women from 1866 to see not
only what images of women the *Gartenlaube* propagated, but also
how the magazine approached its female readership. They began by
praising the virtues of the American housewife, generalizing that
she is usually attractive, clean, and meticulously concerned about
her dress. The American woman is characterized as a caring, sometimes overly concerned mother, who takes care of the children's
education and is often just as clever and educated as her husband.
As a domestic angel, she makes her home as pleasant and attractive
as possible. But perhaps her most admirable qualities are her ability
to comfort and support her husband in his financial misfortunes
and her marital fidelity in times of forced separation (1866: 120–21).
The first article went on to note that American women who were
not married had pursued a wide range of occupations that could
serve as models for their European counterparts, and that they
seemed close to achieving the right to vote. But these apparently
progressive qualities are qualified at the end of the article, where
the gradual spread of a sensible household economy in America is
credited to the influence of German immigrant women. This move
both privileges proper domesticity and ties it to a national ethnic
identity. Ideal feminine domesticity is a German cultural virtue.

More remarkable than this list of ideal characteristics are the
strategies by which the magazine (1) presumed reader knowledge,
(2) posited the limitations of its female readership, and (3) described women's expectations and desires. The first paragraph of
the 1866 article introduced its subject while suggesting a direct tie

between reader desires and the magazine's willingness to satisfy them: "The female readers of the *Gartenlaube* certainly know something about the fact that the position of the American housewife is not insignificantly different from that of the German and they want to learn more about this" (1866: 120). The very next sentence also addressed female readers directly, but in order to apologize for the length of the article that would require women to read longer than they are accustomed to in one sitting. With this introduction, the *Gartenlaube* revealed two premises. First, it presumed an exclusively female audience for certain articles; this premise was repeated throughout the articles with each successive address to "our German (female) reader" or "our female readers." In the second place, the magazine presumed that women readers had a significantly shorter attention span, a presumption that itself was contested by the fact that women reading the magazine's fictional contributions regularly dealt with much longer passages.

Such interventions posit a unity of female reading identity and judgment. Each of these forms of address suggests reader complicity with the author of the article and with the *Gartenlaube* as a whole. Ultimately, it assumes agreement among readers by implying that the magazine is simply communicating to the woman reader what she already senses as well as what she wants to know. In these articles, the magazine mediates an identity to female readers through the content of a particular passage and through the women's process of reading. Certainly, the similarities and differences between German and American housewives played a role in generating a self-identity in such articles, but the appeal to the identity of the woman as a reader with specific desires and expectations was central to the construction of her identity as a narrative participant. The *Gartenlaube* became not only her access to contrasting images of femininity and Germanness, but also a mirror of her own desires, expectations, and abilities.

Despite a general lack of political and legal rights and activities for women in the nineteenth century, there were nevertheless some women's organizations that offered middle-class women a forum for voicing interests concerning women's education, women's work, and general social equality.[12] The beginnings of this movement coincided with the first three decades of the *Garten-laube*'s publication and were occasionally featured by the magazine. The magazine's reception of this trend was positive. In large part, this support of the "woman's question" was due to the liberal political tendency of the editor, a liberalism that emerged and grew from the demands for middle-class equality and rights in the decade prior to the 1848 revolution. One author of Keil's earlier journals, *Unser Planet*, *Der Wandelstern*, and *Der Leuchtturm*, was Louise Otto, an outspoken advocate of women's emancipation in Germany.[13]

The *Gartenlaube*'s positive coverage of the women's movement praised it above all for its moderation. An early article on the German "*Frauenbewegung*" carefully distinguished it from the older French movement, whose demands it labeled decadent and extremist. The "woman's question" of the post-1848 period in Germany was accepted as legitimate precisely because it could be categorized as "an educational and instructional, an occupational and professional question that emanates from the people" (1871: 818). The author of the essay found the German solution to the woman's question tolerable because the organizers tried to remain free of the "dilettante inclusion" of social politics and personal vanity (1871: 818).[14] Perhaps the most redeeming quality of this activism, in this author's opinion, was the fact that it had not altered the traditional notion of the German family: "the innermost essence of the German home, the German wife, marriage and family remained what it was despite all the changing tendencies of the newer cultural shift" (1871: 817).

While the organized women's movement of the 1860s and beyond was subdued in comparison to demands made in the *Vormärz*,[15] the presentation in this article additionally dampened the political implications of women's activism. The *Gartenlaube*'s intention was not to present a history of this women's organization, a description of its institutions, or the platform of the "Allgemeiner deutscher Frauenverein" ("General German Women's Organization") founded in 1865. Rather, the approach was personal: to affirm for its readers the talent, knowledge, and education of the main female proponents, and especially to show how their "earnestness of heart and character combined with genuine femininity." The author concluded this essay by writing that the *Gartenlaube* believed itself to be serving the interests of its female readers when it presented the portraits of both Auguste Schmidt and Louise Otto-Peters, the two presiding members of the German women's organization (1871: 818). Again, the magazine's strategy with respect to a "woman's topic" was to emphasize femininity and to argue that it was merely satisfying preexisting reader desires.

The women's movement was of interest for the magazine as an intimate story. Women's issues, which could potentially serve to divide the overarching class and national goals of the German middle-class family, were diffused through a process of narrative domestication and personalization in the *Gartenlaube*. An article from 1883 that reported on the thirteenth national convention of the "Allgemeiner deutscher Frauenverein" (1883: 718–22) demonstrates this process. It began as a veritable celebration of the women's organization but then mentioned the fears among German men who posed the question: "What do these strange women want from ours?" The article sought to allay men's anxieties by presenting an objective image of the movement: "Let us take a closer look at these German women . . . let us listen to their speeches for a moment . . . let's step into the meeting hall of the most recent Düsseldorf women's convention!" (1883: 718). What claimed to be an objective overview, however, characterized this political activity as "the morally earnest goals of these female pioneers." In effect, this depiction moderated and contained the changes demanded by the women's movement through two narrative maneuvers.

In the first place, it offered a personal view of these women to make them familiar and thus unthreatening. In this representation, the women became noteworthy for their positive feminine characteristics: they are "angels" for their husbands in time of need, they are unique beauties, delicate and small, selfless in their dedication to others, and, finally, they see their highest happiness in a peaceful, ordered family life and a happy marriage. The novelty of radical demands such as women's right to an education was domesticated. Ultimately, despite the advocacy of women's right and duty to work, the most highly valued job seemed to be that of the German "Hausfrau." Just as a mother lives not for herself but for her family, this article argued that the women's movement does not seek the betterment of women, but rather the improvement of the German people, that is, women's children and husbands. The article closed by suggesting that the radicalism of the French women's movement was not a danger in Germany: "This women's movement, as we have become acquainted with it, can only awaken our sympathies" (1883: 722).

The assertion of domestic familiarity was accentuated by the second narrative strategy in this article, a strategy that was representative of the *Gartenlaube*'s narration in general. As we have already seen in the case of monuments or the inventions of Wilhelm Bauer, the magazine was self-reflexive whenever possible, reminding readers of its previous presentation of new material. An example of this can be found in the repeated announcements to the effect that readers had already encountered these members of the women's movement in the pages of the *Gartenlaube*: "The small woman with the glasses, to whom we now turn, is well-known to our readers. The *Gartenlaube* has recently had the opportunity in the context of the hygiene-exhibition to refer to her achievements" (1883: 720). But the most explicit reference in the article to the work of the magazine itself was the final statement: "And we close with the heartfelt wish that these lines have substantially contributed to distributing and furthering the noble strivings of these German women" (1883: 722). This self-reflexive maneuver is a sign of the magazine's role as a creator and shaper of the German nation, not just a transmitter of others' ideas and values.

In the case of women's issues, the *Gartenlaube* claimed to be the servant and advisor of German women for the betterment of the entire *Volk*. The magazine's notion that its female readers seemed to need more advice in order to properly identify themselves as members of the national community becomes evident in its presentation of fictional texts. As a magazine which began each weekly issue with a serialized novel or novella, the *Gartenlaube* became active in guiding the literary taste and experience of its female readers. One common approach to this education was the publication of letters from literary figures and critics, such as the liberals Karl Gutzkow and Rudolf Gottschall. These letter-essays were conspicuously addressed to an individual woman who had supposedly requested instruction in the state of the literary arts and in judging literature.

In the case of Gutzkow's letters "An eine deutsche Frau in Paris" ("To a German Woman in Paris") about literature, the *Gartenlaube* did not simply document an exchange (be it real or fictional), but rather acknowledged its own role as the sole mediator of this dialogue. Gutzkow began his first letter by mentioning its publication in the magazine: "Not only am I actually writing these letters . . . ; I am circumventing the letter dissemination institutes of the Imperial French General Postmaster . . . and sending you my answers . . . through—the *Gartenlaube*" (1869: 72). This reference alone implies several things. First, it alludes to the magazine's wide distribution, since it presupposes that the German woman subscribes to the *Gartenlaube*, or at least reads it regularly in Paris. In addition, the fact that Gutzkow feels compelled to reconstruct the encounter which led to this literary correspondence reveals that, at least in its present form, this letter is intended not only for this particular woman, but for the entire (female) readership of the *Gartenlaube*. Both of these points, the magazine's distribution and the communication between two Germans about German literature across a national border, suggest that there was also a national function to be discovered in the inclusion of a female reading audience for the *Gartenlaube*. In this instance, the magazine presented a discussion of German literature in the guise of educating a female reader. In fact, it was the German reader who was being educated.

With the pretext of writing to a "lady," both Gutzkow and Gottschall repeatedly referred to certain characteristics of German literature as explicitly national. These letters used many of the techniques that constructed a unified nation found in other texts within the *Gartenlaube*, such as references to typically German landscapes (the sea, oak trees, grapevines, and the Rhine River). In talking about the status and quality of contemporary literature, they also appealed to a common notion of Germanness, such as Gottschall's praise of Auerbach's novel *Country House on the Rhine* as successfully depicting "the mood of nature, the landscape and the life of the people" (1870: 90), while generalizing for his reading audience the romantic associations of the Rhine that he had known as a child: "Thus this fleetingly enjoyed Rhine panorama stands in anyone's recollection, also in yours, Madame!" (1870: 90). Gutzkow sees in his correspondent's renewed encounter with German spirit (which had occurred along this national river) the source for her literary interest: "Yes, you felt the uniqueness of your people, our strength, our tenacious stamina, the iron determination of our will—! You heard the fountains rushing again, from whose depths we fill those cups from which we drink the ecstasy of enthusiasm!" (1869: 73). Using an erotically charged vocabulary, Gutzkow translates the woman's experience into images of a powerful (masculine) nation. In this way, literature and the nation were continually brought together for the reader in the name of enlightening the uninformed female reader.

NARRATIVES OF DESIRE

The purpose of these contributions in the *Gartenlaube* was, as Gottschall himself said of his letters, to give a report now and then on the state of contemporary literature for an interested reader (1869: 745). But a large part of the *Gartenlaube* itself consisted of literature, that is, novellas and novels, serialized for weekly consumption. Indeed, some critics have suggested that the magazine owed a substantial part of its unprecedented success to the popularity of its "star author," the novelist E. Marlitt.[16] The rest of this chapter explores the relationship between two apparently contradictory aspects of Marlitt's extraordinarily popular stories about feminine heroism and fate.

On the one hand, these tales all concluded with an inherently conservative ideology, with the recontainment of female characters within the restricted space of middle-class domesticity. On the other hand, their unprecedented popularity and significance as a regular feature of a popular family magazine meant that they operated according to a dynamic of reader interest or desire. Yet, despite the clearly restrictive implications of these stories for women, their popularity itself was rooted in references to female strength, independence, and even sexual desire. These aspects constituted a direct appeal to a female reader's pleasure. This tension between control and release, between women's domestic and public identities provides the focus for the following discussion of mass fiction as part of the popular construction of a national identity.

E. Marlitt was one of the most popular (that is, best-selling) authors of the last third of the nineteenth century in Germany.[17] With novels such as *Goldelse* (*Golden Else*) (1866), *Das Geheimniß der Alten Mamsell* (*The Secret of the Old Mademoiselle*) (1867), *Reichsgräfin Gisela* (*The Imperial Countess Gisela*) (1869), and *Das Heideprinzeßchen* (*The Moorland Princess*) (1871), she won the hearts of a broad reading audience in the 1860s and '70s. Her stories of female heroines mirrored her own life in important respects, so it is interesting to first look briefly at her biography.[18] Marlitt, whose real name was Eugenie John, was born into a merchant family in Thuringia and grew up as an adventurous and energetic young girl. Her first disappointment in life came when her father was forced to file bankruptcy and her family lost its economic and social status. In the next few years, however, the artistic potential of the young Eugenie John was identified, and she set her dreams on becoming an opera singer, a famous musician who could then support her family and help reestablish its honor. She was taken in by the Princess of Sondershausen, sent to Vienna to study for two years, and was on the verge of launching her singing career when she was cruelly struck by a hearing disorder and forced to give up her dream. This second crisis left her with the compensatory honor of becoming a reader and companion for her sponsor. However, when the Princess had to limit her household expenses, Eugenia returned to her hometown and her father's house.

Marlitt's life and adventures were not over. Her artistic talents moved to the domain of literature, and she began to try her hand at writing stories. She received some encouragement and eventually allowed her brother to submit one of her novellas to the *Gartenlaube*. It was accepted by Keil, who requested more material. Her next work, the novel *Goldelse*, was a tremendous reader success in the magazine. Overnight, E. Marlitt became a national sensation, whose every work was awaited by millions with bated breath.

As the most widely read magazine of its era, the *Gartenlaube* was Marlitt's ticket to success. The serialized publication of her first novel, *Golden Else*, in 1866, not only launched her long-term collaboration with the magazine and its editor Keil, but the novel was credited (as were her later works) with substantially boosting the circulation of this already successful publication. Marlitt quickly became an important selling point for the magazine. The *Gartenlaube* boasted about the popularity of her works in serialized form and as book editions (published by the *Gartenlaube* press), which often had runs in the tens of thousands and were translated into almost all European and some Asian languages.[19] Its advertisements of the new editions of her works often appeared just before Christmas, and the promise that another one of her novels would appear in the magazine in the coming year was frequently used as an enticement for future subscribers.[20]

The commercial interests of the magazine ensured that it included as many of Marlitt's works as she could produce, but the magazine also took care of her financially; she was on an annual salary after the publication of *Golden Else*, and in 1870 Keil built a villa for her. She spent the rest of her life there in seclusion, writing for the *Gartenlaube* until her death in 1887. By the mid-1860s Marlitt had already been struck with rheumatism and arthritis so severe that she was hardly able to walk and was in constant pain. Because of her poor health, the promises of forthcoming novels occasionally went unfulfilled and their publication in the *Gartenlaube* had to be postponed. Marlitt's novels must have been perceived by the magazine's staff as having a positive impact on its audience and potential audience, because Marlitt was by far the most frequently mentioned author in the *Gartenlaube*'s "previews of coming attractions."[21]

But what was so "attractive" about Marlitt's novels? Her stories generally recounted the feminine tale of overcoming adversity, maintaining a virtuous and moral life (much like her own) in the face of a society filled with fraudulence, greed, and sexual lust. Her heroines inevitably break out of their poverty, loneliness, or alienation to win fame, fortune, and, of course, the heart of the hero. Marlitt's works were not only intended for and read by women; readers' letters from men attested to their appreciation of her as well.[22] However, a careful analysis of Marlitt's narrative style demonstrates the manner in which her novels privilege a woman's perspective. Her first novel, which is often characterized as her "best," was *Golden Else* (1866). Because of its popularity, it is both typical of Marlitt's recipe for success and also exemplary as a piece of fiction from the *Gartenlaube*.

Golden Else tells the story of Elisabeth Ferber, whose family has been the victim of bad luck; her father has lost his job and her mother has been meanly denied her inheritance by her aristocratic father for having married into the bourgeoisie. The story begins with Elisabeth working hard to support her parents and younger brother in the face of poverty, thus establishing at the outset both her nurturing, mothering nature and her determination and strength. Most importantly, however, it is her domestic inclination and abilities that set the stage for her later path. When her uncle, forester for a prince, arranges a job for her father, the Ferber family moves from the city to the old ramshackle castle Frau Ferber had reluctantly inherited, where, contrary to their expectations, they soon find comfort and domestic bliss. In this new setting, Elisabeth (also called Golden Else) proves herself to be in every respect the "angel of the house," just as she had been in the city. She is a combination of feminine daintiness (with her elegant, slender white fingers) and domestic energy. Else does household chores with her uncle's housekeeper, fetches her uncle's pipe, and keeps all coffee cups warm and replenished, all the while caring for her younger brother and soon emotionally supporting her new acquaintance, the young invalid aristocrat, Helene von Walde.

From the beginning, then, the novel depicts the middle-class family as a coherent and stable social group able to overcome financial adversity. The daughter is a skilled domestician whose moral training will guarantee the continuance of the family and its values. Tension mounts when a new threat to the security of this middle-class world appears. This threat is sexual desire. The challenge it presents to the coherent family generates the novel's suspense and its presumed appeal to the female reader. The core of the story can best be summarized as follows: at the end of the third sequel, Golden Else surveys the region around her new home through a telescope; with this magnifier of the gaze she spots a man, "young, tall, and slender" (1866: 38) in the company of her future friend, Helene von Walde. This man, Hollfeld, soon becomes attracted to Golden Else and begins pursuing her, at first genteelly and then aggressively, while she, disturbed by his forward behavior, consistently rejects him. Hollfeld's undisguised desire is a threat to Elisabeth's code of modesty, virginity, and domesticity because it expresses itself as uncontrollable lust for the heroine; this is clearly marked as dark, dangerous desire. By contrast, a brighter form of human passion is the heroine's slowly developing attraction to the hero Rudolf von Walde who, despite his aristocratic identity, exhibits bourgeois restraint and respect. The hero desires Elisabeth in return, but, as in most romance novels, both are unaware or are repeatedly made unsure of the other's feelings, so that they run the risk of missing their opportunity to come together.[23]

Both forms of desire increase throughout the novel, but they are constantly paralleled and thus checked by the domestic tendency and activism of the heroine. In one instance, Golden Else's adventurous nature intercedes to disrupt an attempt on Rudolf's life. The tension between good and bad forces peaks when, in the next to last sequel, the mad woman, Bertha, who at one time had been a real victim of Hollfeld's seduction, comes close to killing Elisabeth. Golden Else is rescued from this danger by the man she desires. Thus, at the close of the novel, evil, in the form of uncontrolled sexual appetite, is rejected. The other form of desire (Elisabeth's) is contained as nonsexual and is placed firmly in the service of domestication as the hero and heroine are united, marry, and found a family. All participants in bad forms of desire are banished from the scene or are dead—Hollfeld who is lustful and manipulative and Helene whose love of Hollfeld is blind and whose physical weakness prevents her from fulfilling a domestic role.

In addition, middle-class domestic virtue steps in as a cure for a whole host of moral ills. In the epilogue, the reader learns that the arrogant Baroness Lessen, whose haughtiness and taste for luxury had wreaked havoc in the von Walde home (the Lindhof) before Rudolf's return, is punished by having to lead a modest lifestyle that requires her to do her own domestic chores. Bertha, whose sexual disgrace was paralleled throughout the novel by her failure in domestic activities, is given a second chance to behave domestically and morally as a farmwife in America. What is the moral of this tale? Perhaps that the absence of domestic responsibility in women leads to aristocratic decadence or immorality; perhaps that simple domesticity is victorious on every front as the mark of middle-class superiority. In the logic of the novel, domesticity is a form of self-regulation that is (or becomes) an end in itself.

What is the role of the reader, in particular, the female reading subject, in all of this? Clearly, this story of the victory of upright bourgeois ideals over aristocratic decadence would appeal to a nineteenth-century, middle-class audience in principle. But more specifically, in this novel, as in Marlitt's others, the privileged subjective perspective is feminine in gender. The action in the story consistently follows the path of Elisabeth, presenting the reader throughout with the view of the fictional world that is in her purview at any one time. That is to say, the reader is in the same place as Elisabeth almost all the time; only rarely do we find descriptions that would be beyond her perception. All other characters are introduced through Elisabeth's eyes, and most subjective experiences in the text, such as feeling, recognizing, and seeing, are Elisabeth's. This makes her the dominant source of narrative focalization.[24]

More importantly, however, even the desire that is expressed in the narrative is that of the female gaze. The best example of this is the view the reader gets through the telescope that Elisabeth points at the Lindhof. From the first, this gaze is clearly identified as Elisabeth's: "The massive, serious mountain tops moved closer . . ." (1866: 36). Even the randomness or directness of her gaze is made explicit by the narration: "If until this point Elisabeth had let the telescope wander restlessly from one object to another, she now sought a firm hold and perch for it, because she had seen something which caught her rapt attention" (1866: 37). The next long paragraph gives a detailed description of the garden at Lindhof, then of the young lady (Helene) reclining there until finally Elisabeth's gaze comes to rest on the object of Helene's view, "the face of a man" (1866: 38). This is the culmination of the descriptive passage. Elisabeth's first contact with and searching description of a man begins a series of instances in which women (in the form of Elisabeth or a focalized female narrator) gaze at men, either with desire or fearful of being desired. In either case, however, the view of the woman is prioritized; her desire is narrated.

However, just as female desire is shut down at the end of the novel, so too is the subjective voice of Elisabeth silenced; she gets her man, she "is happy," but she disappears as the agent of the story, as the focalizing subject. Both she and her desire are domesticated. For the female readers of the *Gartenlaube* then, reading could mean pleasure and the space to explore certain positive and negative, threatening and legitimate forms of desire through fictional heroines. In the end, however, it seems that this desire is explored only to be contained by the power of domestic authority. The genius of Marlitt within the context of the popular magazine was her ability to create these desiring women, figures who are both morally strong and the source of focalization, but who eventually (willingly) participate in the domestication of desire.

This is not to say that these narrative economies of desire were unique to the *Gartenlaube* or late-nineteenth-century Germany. Feminist critics like Tania Modleski and Janice Radway have analyzed the ambiguously empowering function of twentieth-century "mass-produced fantasies for women."[25] Likewise, the German novels of Marlitt were not that different from women's literature in other countries at the time. Kathryn Shevelow has argued that early British moral weeklies of the seventeenth and eighteenth centuries marked women's visible entrance into print culture, but also served to idealize women as purely domestic creatures.[26] Nancy Armstrong has convincingly shown the gradual domestication of desire in a wide range of English texts from the eighteenth to nineteenth centuries. Armstrong suggests that the constructed separation of public from private life, which was central to middle-class stability and power, can be traced in the history of domestic fiction.[27] The case of Marlitt is instructive because it highlights the press's role in the ideological separation of men and women into distinct public and private spheres in the nineteenth century. The institution of the mass media had to appeal to the female reader's desire, but also inscribe into it the values of middle-class feminine domesticity.[28]

The larger social context of this domesticity was emphasized by the magazine's interpretation of Marlitt's importance, and that of *Golden Else*, for its readers. Besides the major works of Marlitt that appeared in quick succession, Marlitt herself and her work were repeatedly the subject of articles in the magazine (until 1900). An essay entitled "Bei der Verfasserin der 'Goldelse'" ("With the Author of Golden Else") from 1869 celebrates the simple, withdrawn lifestyle of this modest lady in the personal tone of an intimate visit in her home. Marlitt is depicted as enduring her rheumatism "with a smile of genuine feminine submission and with the peacefulness of a great soul" (1869: 827). The inspiration for her writing is described as a drive to make herself useful to the world as best she can, a motherly attitude of service and sacrifice.

This popularity took on explicitly national overtones in a second article, written after the founding of the empire in 1871. The claims that Armstrong has made for the class-affirming function of such economies of desire can be expanded[29]; the domestication of woman was used to contribute to the solidification of a national identity as well. The character Golden Else was credited with having given innumerable Germans an emotional antidote to the heated conflict of 1866; that was the year *Golden Else* appeared in the *Gartenlaube* and the year of the divisive "Brother War" between Prussia and Austria. According to the *Gartenlaube*, Marlitt's fictional character had a profound effect on its national readers within that historical context: "A golden-haired German maiden worked a miracle; and the distracted glances of a wobbly world filled with passionate unrest and bloody conflict were shifted onto the simple and quiet luster of her graceful appearance" (1871: 803). The magazine attributed to its feminine fiction a role in the process of national unification when it insisted that this virgin's character spoke of the proud "struggle of the century, of the happy consciousness of victory of this national idea." The essay implied that although women are inherently domestic creatures, they also contribute to the national cause by appealing to the healthy instinct of the people, that is, by containing desire while affirming the family and bourgeois values. The *Gartenlaube* had given its readers a domestic ideal that it deemed beneficial to the German nation.

This essay was an advertisement for *Golden Else*. It announced and praised the new illustrated, "exquisite edition" that would appear just in time for Christmas. But it also advertised (after the fact) its own role in introducing the German audience to this novel and, in a broader sense, to Marlitt, its author. The article reminded readers that the "chaste story," which brought a ray of sunlight into hearts and homes of the nation, was first carried through the world "on the shoulders of the *Gartenlaube*" (1871: 804), estimating that one and a half million people read it in the pages of the magazine alone. The subsequent success of the story (which, as a book, had been published in at least six editions by 1871) was proof of the social good sense of the *Gartenlaube* in identifying the taste of its audience, but also in providing its readership with morally uplifting reading material.

The *Gartenlaube* often portrayed the woman reader as the grateful beneficiary of the magazine, who also repaid this debt by giving testimony for the magazine. One example is an essay that appeared in 1875 to commemorate the *Gartenlaube*'s star-author by describing a so-called "Marlitt-page," a reproduction of a large format oil painting that depicted the author surrounded by five of her heroines (1875: 68–70). The article began by praising Marlitt and her model female characters, but then it passed the torch to several Marlitt readers, all women, who gave their "responses" to Marlitt. The reader letters chosen for the article are significant for their appeal to a domestication of reading alongside implicit and explicit responses to the potentially radical demands of the women's movement. One reader was identified simply as a "Swiss girl" who first affirmed her antiaristocratic solidarity with Marlitt's female heroines. She then characterized the enthusiasm of her grandmother and aunts in listening to her read the stories aloud in what was an intimate community of women readers in the idyll of a rural interior setting. This naive testimony was followed by that of an intellectual woman, who was initially skeptical of Marlitt's works because they avoided the "woman's question." But this reader confessed to her eventual conversion; her involvement with these heroines had convinced her that they were the true models for an emancipation of women. They reveal, she claimed, how harmoniously the independence of women can be integrated with "the magic of beautiful femininity" (1875: 70).

Perhaps the most intriguing aspect of this article is again the *Gartenlaube*'s compunction to sell itself. The essay praised the *Gartenlaube* for playing the biggest role in Marlitt's success. The magazine took credit for the readers' access to Marlitt: one German women from Ohio testified, "When the *Gartenlaube* comes, I dash for it and devour the serialized continuations with a ravenous hunger" (1875: 70). At the same time, it pointed to its role of bringing the readers to Marlitt: "Don't we want to let those speak whose letters (from Switzerland and America as well as Germany) have reached Marlitt via the hand of the magazine's editors?" (1875: 68). Marlitt may be the star, but the *Gartenlaube* is the mediator between her and her audience, in both directions. The *Gartenlaube* is thus an early example of a highly self-conscious commodity, a product aware of the need to refer to its own value. It is not surprising that such an article from the mid-1870s coincided with the inclusion, in other weekly magazines, of advertising supplements. The magazine simultaneously viewed itself both as a product that had to appeal to a public and as the creator of that public.

Marlitt, and her heroines, were daring female appropriators of male gender roles, in particular through activism, involvement in public space, and the willingness, even eagerness, to be money earners and not financially dependent. Through the *Gartenlaube*, Marlitt acquired an enthusiastic and unprecedented following in one of the most visible forums of public interaction, the emerging popular press. Despite this explicitly public notoriety, she chose to lead a secluded, almost monastic existence. The magazine safely characterized her literary success and public persona as elements of feminine advice and nurturing.

Marlitt's heroines were also paradoxical figures, at turns strong and withdrawn. They are remarkable for their outspokenness, their willingness to embark on dangerous missions, and their strength and courage in the face of massive opposition. And yet, in the end, each one submits gladly to the male hero, a character of supposedly superior strength and wisdom. As in the case of Golden Else, these female heroines retreat from their adventurous lives, renouncing independence and a public role and apparently finding a new happiness in the domestic role of wife and mother. It is important to note, however, that this later stage of feminine happiness is never described in detail. To be sure, Golden Else exhibits strong "domestic," "feminine" tendencies and skills throughout the book, yet we might pose the question: would her story be worth narrating, would it have the reader appeal if it lacked the tension introduced by female adventure and the "danger" of sexual desire?

Although the narrative domestication of women was not new, the extreme fluctuations of Marlitt's characters were tied to the new medium in which these images were transmitted. In the second half of the nineteenth century, the periodical press became a major force in the creation of popular opinion and the dissemination of new ideas. As an early successful example of the press, the *Gartenlaube* was alert to the need to market its products. Its resulting representations of women were products of the modern commercial exchange, the consumption of images.

In the context of the popular magazine that was interested in the smooth operation of German middle-class society, these tales for and about women had many goals to fulfill, including outlining women's usefulness for the nation. This process of modeling good female citizens meant several things: (1) the confirmation of the family and private sphere as subset of the nation, (2) domestication of energy and intellectual skills, and (3) the containment of sexual desire as the greatest threat to social domestic stability. Yet, the demands of commercial popularity and success (i.e., reader desire) stood in contrast to these ideological principles. As part of a commercial endeavor, these stories had to appeal to the readers' interests and be entertaining. The new medium of popular serialized texts was forced to acknowledge women's desire at the same time it attempted to erase it.

As the main purchasers and consumers of this medium, nineteenth-century women were acquiring a visible public identity within consumer culture. These stories of active and independent women returning to domestic identities were a significant vehicle for selling the magazine; at the same time, the *Gartenlaube* felt compelled to market these stories and Marlitt as valuable merchandise. The result was a repetitive system of production and dissemination that both provided women with a steady flow of predictable fantasy and warned them of the dangers of such fantasy. This new institution of the popular press lay at the beginning of the national mass market, in which women readers and writers for a long time would play a major, if ambiguous, role.

To be sure, the reading desires of men were also seminal to the success and project of the *Gartenlaube*. Yet, women's place in the construction of a national identity was tied to a specific strategy of appeal that could include them in the "domestication" of the nation. The process of domestication that governed women's depiction in essays and historical articles operated in fictional texts as well; in both kinds of texts, this process required first the awakening of reader interest or desire. In essays, this occurred through a direct reference to the female subject's knowledge; in popular fiction (usually serialized), this happened through an appeal to the gaze or narrative perspective of the female reader. In all instances, the appeal of this magazine to women readers acknowledged their desires and interests as a way of subsuming their social identity into that of the (male) nation.

6

COLONIALISM, MYTH, AND NOSTALGIA

I n 1883 *Die Gartenlaube* entered its fourth decade. During the previous thirty years it had experienced steady growth and unprecedented popularity. For the most part, the magazine's presentation of the nation had kept in line with Ernst Keil's political tastes and ideology. Keil, who became more politically moderate in the later years of his publishing success, never completely abandoned his liberal roots. His magazine also adhered to a liberal program, for a while at least, even after his death in 1878.[1] But the recipe of national identity that helped the *Gartenlaube* achieve such remarkable popularity in the 1860s and 1870s encountered a changing political landscape in the German Empire of the 1880s and 1890s.

As new concerns shouldered their way into the political arena and also into the pages of the popular press, the representation of national identity underwent changes as well. As we have already seen, from its first years the *Gartenlaube* characterized the nation in a variety of ways, appealing to the traditional discourse of a constant geography while also emphasizing the nation's industrial potential. In the final decades of the century, it became even more difficult for the magazine to speak unequivocally about the German nation or national identity. From the mid-1880s on, three new topics entered the pages of the magazine: reports on German colonialism, monumental representations of the nation's past, and visual images of an idealized German homeland. The frequency of their appearance suggests their significance for the construction of the German nation, but beyond that they all address, directly or indirectly, the issue of nineteenth-century modernization. This chapter explores the tensions and contradictions in defining the modern nation at the end of the century. Alongside celebrations of national modernization the *Gartenlaube* published surprisingly antimodern idealizations of the traditional, simple life and of a mythic past.

Three pressures generated by modernization might be cited as the context for these images in the magazine. The first was industrial development. In particular, the growth of heavy industries was a central aspect of each European country's economic strength and competitiveness. Although Germany was late to enter the industrial revolution, in the last few decades of the nineteenth century its production of steel, heavy machinery, railways, and armaments had come to equal or surpass that of other Western industrialized countries.[2] Secondly, industrial development was paralleled by a growth in military might. Germany's strength was unchallenged on the European continent after 1871. In the last two decades of the century, it competed for global power and influence. Indeed, the expansion of heavy industry was put to the test for military purposes by the young Kaiser Wilhelm II in the 1890s. The Kaiser, his Admiral Tirpitz, and popularly organized interest groups saw Britain as Germany's main enemy and competitor.[3] For them, the establishment of national strength and authority therefore meant demonstrating German superiority over Britain in terms of military potential. They were devoted to the construction of a German fleet to compete with British sea power.[4]

These two substantial changes in Germany's international stature were taken up by the popular press. As we have seen in chapter 4, Keil's *Gartenlaube* regularly recognized the advances of German industry. The series of essays entitled "Deutschlands Große Industriewerkstätten" ("Germany's Great Industrial Workshops") continued into the 1880s and 1890s, as did the magazine's reports on German industrial fairs.[5] The *Gartenlaube* and other periodical magazines celebrated the newest creations of German shipbuilding, featuring the naval shipyards in Kiel and presenting their readers with detailed illustrations of the latest boats, torpedo devices, and submarines. This final chapter will not discuss this aspect of German modernization in detail (see chapter 4), but will rather turn to the third aspect of modernization that concerned Germany at the close of the nineteenth century: colonialism.

Industrial growth and military power were related to the expansion of German influence outside Europe. The German Empire was involved in the race for global spheres of economic and political hegemony that included such projects as the construction of the Baghdad railway in the Middle East. Most importantly, however, the German Empire became an active and aggressive participant in the European rush for colonial territories throughout the world. In 1884 Bismarck gave his approval for the first colonial protectorates in Africa and the Pacific, areas in which German merchants had been trading for years and campaigning for imperial support against the interests of other European merchants. Within a few years, most of these protectorates acquired official colonial status as part of the German Empire. Like other magazines, the *Gartenlaube* familiarized its readers with the progress of German colonial expansion. From the beginning of official German colonial involvement, the magazine presented essays on each of the territories and acquainted its readership with their climate, topography, inhabitants, crops, and with the general development of German interests abroad.

In addition to presenting colonialism as a key instance of Germany's competitiveness internationally, the *Gartenlaube*'s discussion of the German nation changed in other, perhaps less expected ways. Along with images of industrial development and international influence, the *Gartenlaube* and other mainstream magazines began to print more and more images of the simple life, illustrations that embodied an older, traditional lifestyle. An example from the contemporary monthly periodical *Vom Fels zum Meer* (*From Rock to Sea*) reveals this surprising juxtapositioning of old and new. One issue of this magazine from the year 1886 carried a long exposé on modern sea travel. This article discussed the latest developments of sea travel and depicted numerous German merchant steamers and armored warships, as well as a modern Chinese corvette[6] (fig. 6). Opposite the last of these images, yet still buried in the middle of the article on modern ship construction, was an image of a small rowboat floating calmly near the shore of a lake.

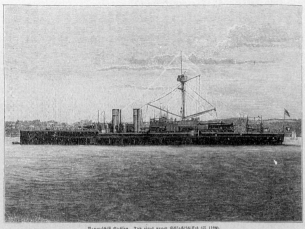

Panzerschiff Sachsen. Typ eines neuen Schlachtschiffes (S. 1128).

breiter werdenden Schichten kenntlich. Der befahrene Matrose wird ein seltener Artikel und Handels- und Kriegsmarine merken bereits allenthalben, daß der Seemann anfängt zu fehlen, und daß ohne Seemann die Seefahrt selbst in den eisernsten Töpfen gefahrvoll ist, und daß Heizer und Handlanger mit ihren tüch-

tigsten Ingenieuren und Führern durchaus nicht allein den Eventualitäten Trotz zu bieten vermögen, die oft genug an sie herantreten, ist viel zu wenig erkannt. Die weiteren Folgerungen sind einfach und logisch. Die Segelschiffahrt ist in den Hintergrund gedrängt worden. An Stelle der Matrosen treten vielfach ge-

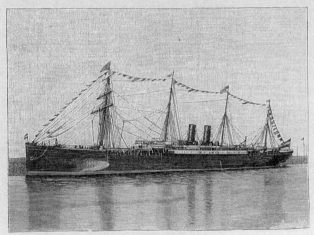

Bremer Dampfer Fulda. Typ eines Schnelldampfers (S. 1128).

6. Armored ship *Saxony*, a type of new battleship (above); Bremen steamer *Fulda*, a type of a rapid steamer (below). (*Vom Fels zum Meer* 1886, col. 1115–1116)

The simplicity of this vessel is heightened by its occupants, a young smiling woman in simple dress and two small children. The boy is holding a string from which a toy sailboat trails among the reeds (fig. 7). While continuing the previous motif of water-going vessels, this illustration presents an idyllic image of the simple life.

The contrast of German steamers and battleships with the row-boat and the child's toy boat is just one example of the intriguing disparity of images of modern German society that pervaded the press in the final decades of the century. It constituted a simultaneous depiction of power and simplicity, modern technology and traditional tranquillity. The contrast of such images might initially strike us as puzzling. Upon further reflection, however, the idealized images of the simple life can be seen as providing a kind of balance or antidote to the destabilizing change of modern industrial activity. These images of traditional existence in Germany affirmed a kind of reassuring national continuity that enabled readers to enjoy the changes of their age, such as rapid industrialization and the expansion of modern military power, without anxiety. The following pages examine the *Gartenlaube*'s presentation of national identity in the last decades of the century as an uneasy and at times contradictory mixture of exoticism, nostalgia, and myth.

GLOBAL NATION: THE COLONIAL ENTERPRISE

The 1880s was not the first time the *Gartenlaube* had devoted attention to German interests abroad. As we have seen in chapter 2, from its first decade the magazine described with interest the great waves of German emigration to distant lands. But despite the magazine's insistence that these Germans were exporting their national identity with them and implicitly expanding the boundaries of the German cultural nation, it was always clear that the emigrants had left Germany to live within the economic and political context of other nations. The impact of emigration on Germany was one of attrition and economic loss. By contrast, the magazine's portrayal of the colonial enterprise (in the 1880s and beyond) stressed the financial benefits and political profitability that colonialism would bring the German nation.

Bei günſtigem Wind. Von Karl Raupp.

7. "With Advantageous Wind" by Karl Raupp (*Vom Fels zum Meer* 1886, supplement opposite col. 1119–1120).

As the century came to a close, this family magazine, like many others, included ever more descriptions of "wild" and "exotic" places in Africa and Asia as part of a growing national interest in gaining German colonies abroad. The perspective on these foreign places was uniformly German, with "other" peoples characterized in the context of German economic and political interests, or serving as a foil to reaffirm German cultural values. This perspective concerning the "colonial world" was, of course, shared by other Europeans in the last decades of the nineteenth century.[7]

For Germany, the idea of foreign colonies was a relatively new concept in the nineteenth century. The pursuit of colonies by the German Empire was delayed in comparison to the acquisitions of France and Britain. This delay was due in part to Germany's limited participation in the era of exploration, its minimal significance as a naval power before the end of the nineteenth century, and the absence of a unified German state prior to 1871. But, additionally, Bismarck's antipathy to the idea of colonial possessions slowed German involvement. Until the early 1880s, the German Chancellor had resolutely rejected the acquisition of colonies. According to Hans-Ulrich Wehler, Bismarck never completely abandoned his early position that colonies would create more problems for the German state than they would bring it in benefits.[8]

Yet, in 1883, the Chancellor apparently had a change of heart about colonial matters. He made it a campaign issue in the 1884 Reichstag elections, and by 1885 Germany had declared protectorates in Togo, Cameroon, Southwest Africa, East Africa, Northwest New Guinea, the Salomon and Marshall Islands, and the Bismarck Archipelago.[9] Bismarck conceived of these protectorates as private syndicates under state protection that would be governed by the companies located there and therefore would not require large investments on the part of the state. However, private individuals interested in colonial enterprise were put off by the costs of governance and soon demanded that the state provide the construction of necessary infrastructure and use its military to put down local revolts.[10] The government acceded and the protectorates became crown colonies by 1889.

There is no consensus among historians about why the German government under Bismarck finally became involved in colonial acquisition in the early 1880s, but one compelling factor was the activism and propaganda of the colonial organizations. In 1884 two colonial organizations existed in Germany. They were the Deutscher Kolonialverein (German Colonial Association, founded in 1882) and the Gesellschaft für deutsche Kolonisation (Society for German Colonization, founded in 1884). There were some differences between these pressure groups, but, in general, both actively pushed for official and military support of German commercial trade that already existed in Africa and the Pacific. The leaders of the German colonial movement, such as Friedrich Fabri and Carl Peters, insisted that colonies would bring the empire enhanced commercial benefit and new investment opportunities. To gain popular support for their cause, they emphasized to the populace at large the usefulness of colonies for German emigration, as new national living space, and for spreading the benefits of German culture.[11] The actual extent of the "popular support" they engendered is, however, rarely documented by scholars.[12] It can probably be said to overlap with the membership and activities of the colonial organizations themselves.[13]

Most historians agree that Germany's colonial involvement was at least to some degree determined by international competition. Early proponents of colonialism such as Friedrich List saw colonies as a way of protecting Germany's foreign interests, including its markets and sources of raw materials.[14] A. J. P. Taylor sees in Germany's move to acquire colonies a strategy of embroiling France and Britain in further competition with each other.[15] For those not necessarily interested in the immediate economic benefits of foreign colonies, German involvement in distant territories in the Pacific or Africa was an ideal means of bringing a shine to Germany's somewhat tarnished international prestige. Contemporary rhetoric considered the creation of a colonial empire to be a way of enhancing Germany's international status and reputation, granting it a place in the sun.

There is little indication that the motive of international prestige itself found any favor with Bismarck. His famous statement from

1888 to an Africa expert suggests that he considered Europe an important and complex enough terrain for international concerns: "Your map of Africa looks nice, but my map of Africa lies in Europe. Here is Russia, and here is France, and we are at the very center; that is my map of Africa."[16] In Hans-Ulrich Wehler's characterization, the colonial project ultimately appealed to Bismarck for two domestic reasons. In the first instance, he saw that successful German trade with distant territories could provide an economic outlet for Germany's repeated recessions by guaranteeing expanded markets for German goods. In the second instance, the growing enthusiasm within Germany for colonial possessions could distract public attention away from the country's internal problems.[17] Recently, Winfried Baumgart has argued persuasively that another element of Bismarck's motivation to found protectorates was to establish a German anti-British policy that could not be revoked by the Anglophile Friedrich III, who was to succeed the aging Kaiser Wilhelm.[18]

Whatever the reasons for Germany's colonial involvement, in retrospect the German colonial empire as a whole has been called "apparently a venture in futility" and "highly unsuccessful."[19] Yet, despite its relatively brief existence (Germany lost all colonies after the First World War) and its lack of economic profit, historians agree its impact was significant and important. To be sure, for the imagination of Germans in the final decades of the nineteenth century, the so-called "colonial question" was powerful food for thought about their nation.

The colonial obsession in the pages of the popular press paralleled official state involvement in the "colonial idea." Before 1884, the issue of colonialism, especially German colonialism, was not discussed much in the mainstream press. This changed dramatically with the newly sanctioned involvement of the German government. In 1884 alone, the *Gartenlaube* published three articles on the progress of German colonization in Southwest Africa (1884: 609–10; 1884: 614–16 [map, 617]; 1884: 665, 667–68); one on Cameroon (1884: 610–13); one on Togo/Little Popo (1884: 349–51); a report by Dr. Robert Flegel on his most recent research trip in Africa (1884: 710–15); and one on events in the Sudan (1884: 181–85). It also published an essay on the international conference on West Africa hosted by Bismarck in Berlin (1884: 805–7). In 1885 articles appeared about African palm oil and ivory (1885: 15–17), and on Zanzibar (1885: 96–102), German East Africa (1885: 210–12), and the Congo (1885: 329–34) in Africa, as well as New Guinea (1885: 48–51) and the Caroline Islands (1885: 642–43) in the Pacific. In 1886 the magazine published brief contributions on German East Africa (1886: 555); Cameroon (1886: 108); the Marshall Islands (1886: 37–38, 572); and three long articles on the "discovery voyages of the German steamer 'Samoa' in New Guinea" (1886: 83–86, 111–12, 192–95). In the last fifteen years of the century, forty-five essays appeared in the *Gartenlaube* on the topic of German colonies.[20] Another six contributions from 1885 through the early 1890s described the productive work of and the risks taken by the German physician Dr. Eduard Schnitzer (alias Emin Pascha) in the Sudan. Several articles focused on the role of other European countries and explorers in Africa.[21]

The fact that the magazine began reporting on German colonialism after it was already a reality stood in stark contrast to its reporting on other national causes. In previous decades it had prided itself on campaigning actively and early for what might seem to be much smaller national concerns, such as Wilhelm Bauer's inventions.[22] This difference raises some interesting issues. The first is that the magazine was apparently not a strong, independent advocate of acquiring a colonial empire.[23] In the second place, it seems that the magazine was not significantly influenced by the active proponents of colonial involvement. The organizations and associations that existed before 1884 do not seem to have caught the ear of the *Gartenlaube* editors. Rather, the magazine was attracted by the reality of colonial protection that Bismarck initiated in 1884. Only after the establishment of protectorates did it begin to publish a significant number of articles on colonialism.

The third point raised by the timing of the *Gartenlaube*'s essays on colonialism is the fact that external forces governed the selection of topics in the popular press. Even if the editors of the *Gartenlaube* did not consider colonial involvement a key national cause, by 1884, with the popular curiosity and euphoria about successful territorial acquisitions, the magazine had to include a discussion of colonialism. It became an issue that editors of the mainstream press could not ignore. Even *Westermanns Monatshefte*, a monthly cultural review that passed over many other potential national causes and rarely included current events, discussed the founding of colonial protectorates after 1884 in substantial detail.[24] This fact suggests a more general conclusion that certain national topics, once they emerge in the public arena, become forces that have to be addressed.

The *Gartenlaube*'s presentation of colonialism was not uniform. As with many topics of national concern, the essays about Germany's colonial involvement were authored by a variety of contributors. They also dealt with the colonial territories that were spread throughout Africa and the Pacific Ocean and thus discussed different issues with regard to each indigenous culture, geography, climate, and the production and transportation of goods. The purpose of the magazine's essays, perhaps even more so than with other, less "foreign" issues, was to introduce its readers to the characteristics of these places, to present an image of the native people and their life, but also to explain the usefulness of this new colonial relationship for Germans themselves. Despite differences among the essays, the *Gartenlaube* unequivocally applauded colonial policy. No essays critiqued the involvement of the German Empire in the race for colonies; none condemned the implications of the activity.[25]

The *Gartenlaube* pursued three objectives in its presentation of the colonial empire to its readers as a positive novelty. In the first instance, it attempted to orient readers geographically and historically about German colonialism and to justify the relevance of colonialism for those readers. Secondly, the *Gartenlaube* and other magazines advertised the colonial project as a national good that would contribute to German national glory and world status. This aspect of the press's coverage conformed most to the interests of the colonial organizations. Finally, the *Gartenlaube* added an oddly antimodern twist to the presentation of German colonies that stood in rather awkward contrast to the processes of modernization upon which colonialism was based and to which it purportedly would contribute. The presentation of colonial (and potential colonial) territory as a re-found paradise was one part of a larger image prevalent in the popular press in the final decades of the century, an image of the nation (as we will see below) as a guarantor of an idealized space in response to the alienation of modern existence.[26]

Popularizing the Colonies

The *Gartenlaube* offered a mainstream alternative to the propaganda about colonialism distributed by the various colonial associations.[27] This is not to say that the perspectives the magazine presented were contrary to the interests of the colonial movement. Indeed, they often overlapped. Yet, the magazine strove to persuade its readers by relying on expert sources who would relay a neutral picture of the colonies and their potential usefulness for the nation. The liberal weekly magazine did not devote articles to the leaders of the colonial movement or any of their organizations. The names of agitators and entrepreneurs like Carl Peters, Adolf Woermann, and Adolf Lüderitz appeared only rarely in the essays, and leaders of the movement were also not contributors to the *Gartenlaube*. The first step in popularizing colonial activity was explaining it to a national audience. The *Gartenlaube* and other mainstream periodicals did this in a variety of ways. They clarified its dimensions, described the location of these foreign places, summarized the impact it might have on German politics and economics, and in general outlined its relevance for the German nation.

The *Gartenlaube* presumed that Germany's colonial territories in Africa and the Pacific were uncharted areas for the magazine's readers. The *Gartenlaube*'s intention was, as traveler and researcher Otto Finsch remarked at the beginning of one essay, to provide objective geographical information: "Our era is especially supportive of the study of geography. Every day names of countries and places surface of which we only heard in passing in school and which we gladly forgot since then along with so much else" (1885: 642). The topics and language of these essays typically provided substantial descriptive information. Apart from justifying German colonial involvement (an aspect we will consider below), the essays were intended to orient the magazine reader with regard to these lands, their climate, and inhabitants. This was done to a certain extent with maps. Half of the essays included maps of colonial territories that helped the reader follow the detailed description in the essays themselves. Another constant companion to the essays were illustrations. These showed a variety of scenes, such as native inhabitants relaxing or working in villages, running from a stampeding rhinoceros, or posing as if in front of a camera. In general, these images were anthropologically sober, presenting realistic portrayals of the people, their art, dress, and surroundings[28] (see fig. 8).

To make the colonies comprehensible, the *Gartenlaube* also turned to contributors who could boast firsthand knowledge of the colonial situation. These "experts" included German explorers such as Otto Finsch or researchers such as Dr. Eduard Schnitzer and Eduard Robert Flegel. Such authors could also best capture the excitement and adventure that would make these places intriguing for German readers.[29] The impression these reports left was, however, sometimes misleading. One example is the series of essays published in 1886 written by Otto Finsch, entitled "Entdeckungsfahrten des deutschen Dampfers 'Samoa'" ("Discovery Journeys of the German Steamer 'Samoa'"). Finsch's three essays offered a kind of firsthand introduction to the land of New Guinea, its people and their customs. They included descriptions of the colors and songs of the local birds, Finsch's initial spotting of local inhabitants, and then details of their basketweaving and construction of buildings (1886: 81–83). Some passages indicate that this was a virgin research trip. Finsch writes, for instance, that after he and his people had finished viewing and studying the village, they went on a walk through the island during which they hunted a few birds. He remarks that these "children of nature" ("*Naturkinder*") who accompanied them were initially frightened by Western guns. This first essay implies both that the village was being studied for the first time and that these villagers had never seen Westerners before (85–86). The series' title also suggests that this was the first excursion of Europeans to the coast of New Guinea. However, as becomes clear in the next essay, the bays and mountains of this area have already been visited and even named by Britons as early as 1700 (Cape King William, Cromwell Mountain) (1886: 111–12). In other words, claims of originality,

Das Iunggesellenhaus auf Bilibili.
Nach einer Skizze von Dr. O. Finsch gezeichnet von A. von Roehler.

8. The bachelor house in Bilibili (*Gartenlaube* 1886: 81)

although not always valid, were a way of heightening the *Garten-laube* reader's sense of participating in the process of exploration through the magazine.

Despite apparent attempts to characterize the native people and their environment objectively, an assumption of German (European) superiority pervaded the description of the natives themselves. This took the form of moral judgments made about the native people and their customs, but also emerged in descriptions of their physical characteristics. It was here that the undercurrent of contemporary racist thought speaks most clearly in the mainstream magazine. This is noticeable in two respects: first, in the racist presuppositions about blacks, in general, and, secondly, in the hierarchical categorization of colonial natives which placed Pacific Islanders above Black Africans.

The condemnation of colonial natives as inferior appears in such offhand comments about African rulers as "[T]he desire to rob and plunder is always present and emerges at any opportunity" (1887: 639). The fact that this terminology of theft and violence was not applied to the contemporary European process of colonization, or even internal European wars that the magazine had regularly followed, reveals a preconception that African disputes were more petty and less legitimate than those in Europe. Another passage exemplifies the disrespectful tone the magazine took concerning Africans. In describing King Bell, perhaps the most powerful man in Cameroon, one contributor wrote: "His form is stately and his face is less Negroid, dignified, serious, and calm, very regularly formed, almost European, but not without striking peculiarity. His demeanor shows self-confidence and a certain refined reserve. Naturally, King Bell also has his defects. In particular, his sense of acquisition is too pronounced for a king and all too frequently in haggling he forgets all other considerations. King Bell is also simply a Negro, but the best of all, relatively loyal and honest, a gentleman so to speak" (1887: 639). The author consistently gives King Bell's finer qualities European names and attributes his uglier characteristics to his Africanness or blackness. He is, in the explicit language of the essay, occasionally good despite being black, in other words an exception to his race.

The magazine's categorization of better and worse followed the racist doctrine of nineteenth-century writers like Gobineau who posited a hierarchy of races and placed the Black race at the bottom and the White (Aryan) race on the top.[30] In contrast to the more condescending tone taken concerning Black Africans, essays like Finsch's on the Pacific Islands often characterized their inhabitants as a cultured people. Finsch praised the Islanders for having "already reached a certain cultural level, that of the Stone Age" (1886: 84). He acclaimed their artifacts as "indeed a true work of art for stone axes and shell tools that honor their creators highly" (1886: 85). Similarly, another essay suggested that South Sea Islanders were receptive to foreign literatures because of their own saga and fairy tale treasures (1885: 85). Furthermore, Finsch wrote of his encounter with the chieftain Goapäna, whose careful inspection of his Western visitor was part of Goapäna's anthropological study.[31] This emphasis on culture and scientific investigation is missing in contributions on Africans.

The essays on the Pacific Islanders and Africans that mentioned physiognomy reveal most clearly a presumption of German readers that black color corresponds to less appealing facial characteristics. In writing about the natives of Zanzibar, one essay announced: "However, the light skin does certainly not always correspond to a more noble facial form" (1885: 96). Another essay also indicated that its readers equated darker skin with less attractive features by talking about New Guineans as "making a Negro-like, but in no way repulsive impression" (1886: 84). The "but" in this description clearly speaks to the expectation of a "Negro-like impression" being repulsive. The implication is that Pacific Islanders rank above Africans because they are, to put it bluntly, "less African." In the context of colonialism, the *Gartenlaube*'s liberal respect for other cultures clashed with a deeply held conviction of German (or white) superiority.

This notion also surfaces in the presumption of European innocence and "native" guilt in colonial problems. One case in point is the magazine's presentation of colonialism in an essay on "Elfenbein und Palmöl" ("Ivory and Palm Oil"). Here, an enlightened author cites ravages to the African elephant population by the "harvesting" of ivory. However, instead of acknowledging the role played by Western demand for ivory in this decimation of a species, he itemizes the "brutal" way in which the natives hunt the animals and he attributes the danger of elephant extinction to that: "The disappearance of the elephant species on our globe is hastened by the wild savageness with which the natives of interior Africa conduct this hunt" (1885: 16). In the name of a concern for nature, the contributor placed the blame for colonial trade not with the European traders or consumers, but with the natives of Africa. All in all, however, these essays about colonial difference express a fascination with the exotic strangeness of these colonial territories. Their possession seems to add an intriguing dimension to the traditional German nation.

The *Gartenlaube* and other magazines employed another means of making colonialism understandable to readers that paralleled the "expert" accounts. They presented the colonial enterprise in historical terms. Within one year of the naming of the first protectorate in 1884, the *Deutsche Illustrirte Zeitung*, the *Gartenlaube*, and *Westermanns Monatshefte* all published extensive articles on the seventeenth-century colonial aspirations of Friedrich Wilhelm I of Brandenburg (the Great Elector). In the *Gartenlaube*, the very first essay on colonialism in West Africa mentioned the two-hundred-year-old fort built by the Great Elector in 1682 (1884: 350). The magazine introduced this historical phenomenon to suggest that Germany had long-standing interests in colonial areas, such as Africa, and to imply that this was also a potential part of the nation.

The essay in the *Gartenlaube* begins with a discussion of ruins in general: "A mysterious power presides over ruins. Centuries are unable to weaken its influence because it is jealously protected by saga and history that know how to rescue the most noble things from debris and dust" (1884: 349).[32] This metaphor was familiar to the magazine's German readers. The image of ruins had played a key role in the German movement for national unification throughout the nineteenth century. In an allusion to such symbols as the legendary "rubble of the Kyffhäuser" mountain, from which Emperor Barbarossa was to emerge to reunite his empire, or the ruins "on the heights of the Wartburg," where thousands demonstrated for national unification and liberal freedoms in the 1830s, this passage suggests that contemporary German colonial interests would draw strength from Germans who had been abroad in previous centuries. The ruins of Groß-Friedrichsburg in West Africa described in this essay helped justify and make plausible a German return to Africa: "Thus, in a decisive moment, the old witnesses of the past reached into the fresh, rich life of the people and pushed the masses onto the road to glory" (349).[33]

The essay proceeds to tell the story of "Germany's oldest colonial aspirations." After the Brandenburg navy proved itself so valiantly in battle from 1676 to 1679, the Great Elector decided to use the navy's power for peaceable means, protecting subjects who negotiated and traded by sea. This included sending a frigate to Guinea in 1681, founding an African trade company in 1682, and constructing a German fortress on the Gold Coast, which was named after the Elector himself, "Great Friedrichsburg." Despite historical military conflicts with a neighboring Dutch company, the essay attributes the decline of this and subsequent nearby enterprises to the eventual lack of interest on the part of the Prussian King Friedrich Wilhelm I, the Great Elector himself. The brave Germans who later made the renewal of colonial interest possible did not belong to the state, but to the German middle class: "The mistakes of statesmen, however, did not discourage German merchants, who initially, without any state support, without any protection, founded trading posts on their own and, following in the steps of tireless German Africa explorers opened the interior of the land to global trade" (350).[34] This description casts the earliest example of German colonial involvement as an important precedent and the beginnings of a grand tradition rather than a historical mistake or anomaly.[35]

The essay also makes an explicit comparison between the seventeenth-century war frigates the "Kurprinz" and the "Moriau" and the contemporary German corvette "Sophie." "Sophie" is characterized as a symbol of the German navy, which, according to the article, was again "strong enough to protect German trade" (350). With the subsequent story of the recent military rescue of German merchants and goods and the capture of an offending African king and his people, the *Gartenlaube* re-created the myth of just colonizers and their strict but fair discipline of unethical and rambunctious natives. Using history, the magazine addressed lingering doubts on the part of its liberal readers in Germany about the expansion of the nation in colonialism, as well as about the uncertain benefits of colonial investment. In other words, the press sought to justify to its readers contemporary colonial practices by positing a continuity with the past.

This same essay concludes by suggesting that the format of the periodical press was particularly conducive to writing in support of the colonial idea. It closes with the comment: "For the German colonial movement, the trip of the war corvette 'Sophie' sketched above must be of great significance. The simple report has a greater effect than one hundred speeches and pamphlets" (1884: 351).[36] Although the *Gartenlaube* was not explicitly writing for the benefit of the German Colonial Association, an association that devoted its energy to lectures and pamphlets in favor of the colonial project, the magazine nonetheless became an ardent supporter of the same cause. In the following months and years, it continued a textual campaign to encourage the establishment of a colonial policy: "A great field of activity is opened here for everyone without consideration of party position, and the lofty goal seems achievable to us without military involvement and the loss of human life. One must not leave those in the lurch who have already begun to trade" (1884: 351).[37] In other words, this historical anecdote suggested that Germany could learn from past mistakes (its inadequate support of the colonial mission) and achieve great success in the present. The modern development of German (and European) society would not seem ominous or unsettling to the magazine's readers if they could make connections to Germany's past. The impact of modernization was softened by a reassuring reference to continuity.

Colonial "Goods"

The second concern of the *Gartenlaube* was to present colonialism to its readers as a national good. The magazine consistently enumerated a host of reasons to support colonial involvement. Despite the absence in the *Gartenlaube* of overt recognition of the various German colonial associations, the magazine presented many of the same arguments for colonialism as these organizations. These arguments justified the magazine's attention to the subject matter and give us insight into its definition of the German nation at the end of the century. In the first instance, the *Gartenlaube* explained the usefulness of colonial territories in terms of the raw materials they would make available to Germans. Despite the magazine's euphoria about colonial goods, its essays were generally clear about the limited imports provided by these territories, usually copra and palm oil. It repeatedly discussed the fact that palm oil and ivory were two key African imports that colonialism yielded. Yet, as a popular magazine, the *Gartenlaube* tried to make clear the relevance of these foreign products to the life of Germans. The same essay that discussed the hunting of elephants did just that for the product palm oil:

> Certainly, the fewest of our readers have thought that their house contained materials of African origin long before the colonial question occupied the minds of Germans, that perhaps in the candles on their night stands there were fat components on the production of which a Cameroon Negro had worked, or that the raw material of the white violet-fragrance soap had once lain on a Woermann [colonial company] barge and made the long trip across the ocean. Who among us, when using the most diverse articles, thinks of the voyages and round-about journeys to which they are subject in the grand machinery of global trade? (1885: 17)

This passage emphasized the importance of colonial products for daily life in Germany, thus making exotic goods such as palm oil more understandable and tangible. Other essays insisted, more predictably, on the general usefulness of these products for German industry and trade.

In addition to the usefulness of colonial products, the magazine praised the profitability of these territories for German business and for German trade, in general. In this context, the hard work of German merchants was characterized as selfless, daring enterprise. It was pointed out that merchants often struggled for years without the support of any German government and had to compete against traders of other nationalities who had substantial official support: "Decades of long work and struggle created them [the German trading posts] without which the newest acquisitions of the Empire would be impossible, useless, and without value" (1884: 610). In welcoming the establishment of German colonies, the magazine called for additional governmental involvement to help these disadvantaged Germans in their international struggle: "The sweat of German researchers, the efforts of German merchants should now bear fruit, and even if we have arrived on the field of colonial achievements late, we have not come so late as to leave empty-handed" (1884: 774). It announced that the German flag flies as a sign of protection for all members of the German nation and proves that "Germany has finally taken the seat it deserves in the council of seafaring peoples" (1884: 774).[38]

The magazine couched the contribution of these merchants in national terms, as work dedicated to improving the overall international standing of the German nation. One article on the Caroline Islands made the argument that the Germans introduced productivity to these islands where the Spanish had long been absent and ineffective: "Trade is, as has already been mentioned, but as needs to be emphasized, almost exclusively and for many years already, in the hands of Germans. Now, however, that the ground has been prepared and with great effort the sown seed is bringing forth its harvest, Spain wants to rake in the fruit of foreign industriousness. We hope that our government succeeds in keeping for Germans what they have acquired!" (1885: 643). In the interest of Germany as a merchant nation, then, the colonies had to be supported. Conversely, according to the logic of the magazine, the lack of military and state support for German enterprises in Africa "was damaging to the development of our trade, . . . was embarrassing for a great people, to whom a large moral share is due for the opening of West Africa" (1884: 609).

These territories were occasionally praised as bearing the additional benefit of their potential as a place for German national expansion. About East Africa one *Gartenlaube* author wrote that there were beautiful, "paradisical landscapes" that seemed made for "European settlement" (1886: 555). At other times, however,

German readers were cautioned against emigrating to inhospitable terrains with unfamiliar climates and threatening diseases. An article from 1884 emphatically advised Germans not to think of moving to the West coast of Africa without "the necessary capital and the necessary experience" (1884: 613). The contemporary journal, *Vom Fels zum Meer*, provided readers with calculations about plantation development. It included four pages of detailed estimates of costs for planting, harvesting, transportation, and sales for the first twenty-five years of a plantation. It even itemized the amount of capital that would be necessary to establish the plantation and offered an estimate of when that initial investment would be returned. The essay concluded, however, that all of this was dependent on a guarantee of security for German colonists and control of the local labor force, two tasks that fell to the German government.

In the presentation of the press, colonialism not only added to the international prestige of the German nation, it also demonstrated the superiority of Germans in world politics. One author, in a *Gartenlaube* article about the European conference on West Africa hosted by Bismarck in 1884, implied that Germans would be more humane than other colonial rulers. Referring to the history of Portuguese and Spanish atrocities in the non-European world, he contended that the new era of colonialism, with German involvement, would be better because "in the place of arbitrariness and force would step order and justice" (1884: 807).[39] The same sentiment, that German colonialism was more enlightened and less brutal than that of other Europeans, pervaded an essay from 1886: "We do not doubt that in this area German culture will with time achieve glowing successes, also in relations with the natives, since our Germanness represents humanity everywhere, while the Englishman pays homage solely to his practical purposes" (1886: 555).

The final justification for German colonialism, then, one related to the notion of German cultural superiority, was that it would improve the lives of the native residents of the colonial territories. In this attempt to legitimize colonial involvement, the liberal tradition of the *Gartenlaube* becomes most apparent. The primary interest of the colonial associations, as well as of merchants and Bismarck's government, was not to improve the lot of the native residents of the colonial territories. Yet, in the pages of the *Gartenlaube* a concern for the welfare of the natives surfaced alongside the interests mentioned above. This apparently selfless concern quickly became an important closing statement to the frequent essays on the colonies. The magazine's second contribution on the colonial enterprise, in 1884, emphasized this altruistic goal: "In addition, it will be one of the most refined tasks of Germany to spread Christianity, German customs, German language, and German influence through missions and teachers among the still uncouth people and thereby to elevate the Negro people physically and morally" (1884: 613). Some articles couched this concern in terms of taking care of the natives, teaching them trades, and "bringing them the blessings of true civilization" (1885: 210, 212). Others suggested that the presence of the German Empire would help rid places like the Marshall Islands of "those shady elements" that contribute to chaos and present the natives with a bad role model (1886: 38). Even a small note on the women of the Marshall Islands closed with this refrain: "Thus a spiritual life will soon develop there that reflects German education in all respects" (1886: 572).

The regularity of such passages, and particularly their placement at the end of many articles, suggests they were meant to allay any misgivings the liberal *Gartenlaube* readers might have concerning colonial involvement. According to the colonial historian Woodruff Smith, serious opposition to colonialism was prevalent among liberals and within the liberal parties in the 1870s and continued into the 1880s.[40] This insistence on the humanizing function of German colonial activity can be read both as an apology and as compensation for the less appealing aspects of the endeavor. The magazine consistently presented German colonial enterprise in a positive and selfless light, as different from other, supposedly more brutal and inhumane examples of colonialism. This assertion of the civilizing purpose of German colonialism also constituted an alternative to a technological, mechanistic, modernized discourse on colonial activity. This alternative appeared in other representations of colonialism in the popular press and is worth considering as a third and final aspect.

Colonies as Refuge from Modernization

In addition to outlining the economic and global political benefits that colonialism would bring to the German nation, the press
characterized these colonial territories as spaces for the nation that
were ideally and innocently premodern. Its essays suggested that
in joining the race for colonies, Germany could not only hope to
acquire a substantial and lucrative economic empire but also a portion of the remaining paradise on earth. Essay after essay referred to
the beautiful wildlife, exotic birds, and marvelous greenery of these
tropical and subtropical areas. As we have already seen, the colonies
were promoted as having the potential for bountiful agricultural
production. Even the images of native fetishes and tools that the
magazine reproduced can be seen as more than a sign of arche-
ological curiosity; they constituted an emblem of the simple and
pure lifestyle of these "nature children." The fact that this splendid
landscape was the potential possession of the German nation meant
it could be displayed as a way of offering German readers an idyllic
refuge from the increasingly complex and potentially alienating
industrialization of the West.

Colonial territories were described as beautiful, peaceful, and
picturesque. To be sure, many articles warned of the dangerous
diseases and inhospitable climates that especially coastal regions
presented to Europeans. But often the essays in various magazines
chose the imagery of a park or natural garden to characterize these
foreign landscapes for the German reader. In the *Deutsche Illustrirte
Zeitung* one author wrote of the African jungle as presenting an
endlessly friendly image, one reminiscent of "a park laid out in the
most grand dimensions" (1884: 502). Another author contributing
to *Westermanns Monatshefte* wrote in glowing terms of the virgin forests and stated that "the whole of inner Africa lies like a
ripe fruit in front of our outstretched hand waiting to be picked"
(1885: 240).

One of the most intriguing of such images is an illustration that
appeared in the *Gartenlaube* in 1884 depicting two German colonial
interests in Africa—Cameroon and Fernando Po (1884: 665). Each
protectorate is shown independently, yet as part of one illustration
(see fig. 9). In the absence of an accompanying essay that might

provide additional information about either territory, this illustration takes on greater importance as an interpreter of colonial space for *Gartenlaube* readers. The economic and civilizing concerns of colonialism are noticeably missing in this visual representation. This view of colonial territories does not advertise the benefits of commerce, the production and trade of valuable colonial products. The only sign of human life is the inclusion of three European ships that rest peacefully on the sea, yet are dwarfed to insignificance by the landscape. Instead, we see colonial space depicted as a tropical paradise, an enchanting wonderland of natural beauty. Mountains, sky, sea, and darker, lush coastal areas and exotic tropical vegetation dominate the illustration. These two sites are presented to the German viewer from a great distance, which does not allow for the representation of local inhabitants or their culture, only the image of massive mountain peaks picturesquely framed by puffy white clouds. These views portray the colonial territory as a wondrous piece of majestic nature, as part of a godly creation, which the name "Götterberg" ("Mountain of the Gods"), the German translation of the native appellation, might suggest.

With its depiction of pristine, unspoiled natural landscapes, this illustration previews the kinds of images distributed on twentieth-century postcards of distant lands. The idealized quality of the presentation is heightened by the fact that the two scenes are presented as paintings, artistic renderings that are mounted and pleasingly displayed for the magazine reader. For a magazine that frequently prided itself for its original illustrations drawn on location, this is a noticeable departure from the norm that perhaps is meant to suggest that these panoramas are almost too beautiful to be real. The paradisical quality of these territories is further accentuated by the flowers, foliage, and fruit that frame them on the page of the magazine. This exotic flora is presented not as threatening or dangerous, but as an enticing, decorative indication of the beauty and fertility of the colonial place. Although one purpose of this illustration was no doubt to introduce German readers to the terrain of these two protectorates, every aspect of this illustration invites them to fantasize about the colonies as undeveloped, and thus unspoiled, paradises.

Küste von Kamerun mit Blick auf den Götterberg.

Kamerun und Fernando Po.

Mangrove- oder Schlammwald.

R. Cronau

Nach Original-Aufnahmen von Dr. Pechuel-Loesche für die „Gartenlaube" auf Holz gezeichnet von R. Cronau.

9. Cameroon and Fernando Po (*Gartenlaube* 1884: 665)

One finds this idealized presentation of the colonial space in the final years of the century, even as other aspects of the German colonial endeavor are becoming more problematic and conflictual. The possibility of violence in Germany's colonies is evident in a note from 1896 in the *Gartenlaube*, which outlines the need for German troops in German Southwest Africa and describes the patriotic contribution of the men who have volunteered to spend several years there as "*Schutztruppen*," or protective troops (1896: 483). The dangerous brutality of the colonial situation was made clear in the German press in general, and in the *Gartenlaube* in particular, by 1900, when the supplements to almost each issue devoted at least one page to the war between the British and the South African Boers. In the same year, however, a longer report on the German colony of Victoria in West Africa included several views of the town and director's house that depicted mostly large, leafy ferns and lush foliage, as if to emphasize the richness of the land (1900: 16–18). The text also continued the use of paradisical imagery, talking of the region as "lovely" and "picturesque" ("*anmutig*" and "*malerisch*") (1900: 16).

In this characterization the colonies become an idyllic terrain that constitutes a rich addition to the German nation. This new, uncharted territory can complement the industrialized or agriculturally domesticated landscapes of Germany proper. In other words, this representation of colonialism appears to erase the components of commercialization and international competitiveness and to offer colonialism instead as a potential space of refuge from the forces of modernization. In contrast to the justifications for colonialism that emphasized the financial profitability of the colonial enterprise for Germany, this idyllic representation seemed to propose just the opposite, that colonial acquisitions can provide modern Germany with a tie to happy, naive places where nature and the simple life flourish.

Most scholars today agree that colonial involvement was always a marginal phenomenon in Germany. Compared to its British and French counterparts, German colonialism was short-lived and had minimal economic significance. Indeed, for all the wealth and military energy invested in the colonial project, few "real" profits emerged from it. It can be argued that Bismarck's deepest reservations were justified and the colonial empire cost the Germans much more economically than it yielded in return.[41] Yet, economic output is not the only or the most significant measure of the colonial project for the historian of nineteenth-century German society. Among the real effects of colonialism in Germany was the emotive and psychological impact of the colonial idea. The importance of colonialism as a celebration of national strength and modernization came through quite clearly in the popular press. Although the *Gartenlaube* had not been an early proponent of colonial involvement, it willingly took up the colonial banner in 1884 and presented it to German readers as a national good. Colonialism served as a convenient means for the magazine to tout Germany and Germanness. But this boastful depiction of national strength and competitiveness was not the only image of colonial involvement that appeared in the pages of the popular press at the end of the century. At times, the colonies themselves functioned as an idyllic sanctuary from the commercial world. This aspect takes on greater significance for the *Gartenlaube*'s construction of the nation when we consider that a variety of other images depicting pastoral, premodern elements of the nation appeared in the magazine at the end of the century. In these images, Germany appeared not as an expanding global power, but as an ancient or rural refuge from the activity of modern trade and international expansion.

VISUAL RESPONSES TO MODERNIZATION

There were changes over the years in the *Gartenlaube*'s depiction of a national geography. Particularly in the last two decades of the century, the presentation of a national ethnicity moved away from the ethnographic survey of folk characteristics that we saw in chapter 2 to a less specific allusion to a common identity. The initial essays (from the 1850s through the 1870s) were a kind of popularized ethnographic study of regional identity. Each followed a general pattern of describing the local customs, costumes, music, and dialect of a German region. These essays introduced clearly identifiable rural areas, such as the Black Forest, Upper Bavaria, Vogtland, and Tyrol.

This traditional view of the nation was contrasted with a modernist version of national cohesion and identity, a definition of the German nation as a product of modernization and as an able competitor with other nations in trade, technology, and industrial production. Despite the magazine's insistence on this modern version of the nation, the traditional view never disappeared. Its articulation in the *Gartenlaube* did, however, undergo an intriguing shift at the end of the century. Parallel to visual depictions of a competitive, modernizing German nation (such as illustrations of German armored battleships) was a whole host of images that showed a more traditional side of contemporary German life and identity.[42]

In the final decades of the century, images in general became ever more important as signs of the national identity the *Gartenlaube* was attempting to mediate to its readers. A noticeable change in the magazine in these years was an increased number of illustrations in each weekly issue. The average number of illustrations in 1855 (the magazine's third year) was 2.2 per issue. In 1875, it was 2.7, although the number of pages in the annual volume had increased, to make the number of illustrations per page about the same. By 1895, however, the number of pages per issue was practically the same as in 1875, but the number of illustrations per week had jumped to 8.3. Essays were now often accompanied by numerous smaller illustrations, but there were also many more large-format illustrations. These generally took up an entire quarto-size page and often covered two facing pages. The increase in large illustrations over the decades was consistent: there was a total of 14 in 1855; 67 in 1875; and 133 in 1895.[43] The increasing ratio of illustrations to text meant that images were a far more significant element of each issue of the magazine at the end of the century than previously. The illustrations that are most revealing about a definition of Germanness and what it meant to be German are those that are neither related to any specific current event nor tied to an essay or story that appears in the same weekly issue. The lack of context for these illustrations suggests that they were meant to stand alone and speak for themselves. The substantial space devoted to pictures suggests that we need to consider seriously the visual representations the magazine generated in order to understand its representation of the nation in the final decades of the century.

Increasingly, the images the magazine gave its readers and viewers projected a nostalgia for an earlier era, a simpler time in which life was not complicated by technological progress, urbanization, and the complex issues of late-nineteenth-century global politics. In other words, these images presented an antidote to the magazine's discussion of industrialization and modernization in Germany, even as they appeared next to them. This is not to suggest that images of premodern identity were meant to overshadow a modern conception of the nation. Rather, their presence could continually reassure the magazine's readers that despite the pace of social change, the nation was a familiar, traditional place. As the older geographical presentation of German regions had presented an outline of the German nation, these later nostalgic images were all about negotiating modern identities and articulating an ambivalence to change.

Mythic Monumentalism

This antimodern posture appeared in two main forms. One kind of illustration portrayed images from a mythical national past. These were generally large-scale illustrations that covered two full 9 × 12–inch pages. This representation of a monumental national past included the large-format reproduction of paintings or drawings depicting heroes of the Germanic era. These included portrayals of legend, as in "Der Streit zwischen Kriemhild und Brunhilde vor dem Münster zu Worms" ("The Argument between Kriemhild and Brunhilde in front of the Cathedral in Worms") or mythic scenes of battles from the period of the great migration of peoples, as in "Thorismund wird nach der Schlacht auf den katalaunischen Feldern von den Westgoten zum König erhoben" or "Die letzten Goten" ("Thorismund Is Elevated to King by the West Goths after the Battle on the Kalaunic Fields" and "The Last Goths"). Other examples included heroes such as the victorious Germanic warriors surrounding their leader Hermann, as in "Heimkehr der Deutschen aus der Schlacht im Teutoburger Wald" ("The Germans

Return Home from the Battle in the Teutoburg Forest"), or Hermann's wife, the heroine Thusnelda, defying her fate at the hands of a Roman legionnaire, as in "Thusneldas Gefangennahme durch Germanicus" ("The Capture of Thusnelda by Germanicus"). These monumental tableaus were not part of essays on the history of the Germanic peoples or the German nation. They were presented as visual images of past national strength and heroism. All the images cited, and more, appeared in the first issue of each new year. Both the prominence of their placement and the short explanatory texts at the end of those issues emphasized the significance of these scenes for the German past.

Generally, these illustrations were reproductions of contemporary paintings done in a monumental, pompous style. The historical figures loomed large in the painting and were often impressively crowded into the visual space of the illustration. This mass of bodies and the pathos and grandiosity of the figures' positions and gestures heightened the significance of the events depicted. Just as important as the composition of these tableaus was the reference to moments from a common national memory. The *Gartenlaube* (as well as the painters from whom it borrowed these images) was by no means the first to promote scenes and events from the Germanic times as the origin of the German nation or the national cause. In chapter 4 we have already described an earlier preoccupation with Hermann, the Cheruskan leader, in the context of constructing a national monument in the first half of the century. But such images of the German past appeared in the popular magazine with greatly increased frequency in the final decades of the century.

Images of great individuals or scenes from the Middle Ages also appeared as tributes to a simpler era in the life of the nation. Thus, we find the romantic image of knights, merchants, and knaves stopping in the midst of a rugged landscape to kneel before a roadside crucifix, "Auf einer alten Handelsstraße in den Alpen" ("On an Old Trade Route in the Alps"), as a decorative element in an issue from 1884 (1884: 77). The relevance of such historical images for the present was made clear by the explanatory text that appeared eleven pages later (1884: 88). This brief passage referred to the manpower and dynamite that made the recent construction of the Gotthard railway possible and suggested that the illustration should remind the magazine's readers of the tribulations of medieval German merchants, who had to travel the old Gotthard road through the Alps to bring their goods to Italy. Two other illustrations depict unspecified events from the Middle Ages such as a medieval domestic chamber in which a minstrel sings for a lady, "Sängers Werbung" ("The Singer's Courting"), or the streets and towers of a medieval city, "Aus einer altdeutschen Stadt" ("From an Old German City"). Their purpose was not to be historically specific, but to provide interesting allusions to an earlier period of German civilization. And "Ankunft der Abtissin Irmingard auf Frauenchiemsee im Jahre 894" ("Arrival of Abbess Irmingard in Frauenchiemsee in the Year 894"), a two-page illustration of a storm-tossed lake with boats carrying Hildegard, the granddaughter of Charlemagne, to her exile, shows that not all of the images depicted peaceable times in the nation's history (1894: 192–93). The inclusion of the year of this dramatic scene (Irmingard's exile was exactly one thousand years before 1894) indicated that the heritage and tradition of the German Empire could be conceived of not only in decades and centuries, but in millennia.[44]

Let us consider one of these images in detail to identify its visual representation of Germanness. "The Capture of Thusnelda by Germanicus" was based on a photograph of a painting by Heinrich König, a Düsseldorf artist (fig. 10). Our discussion of this image must be limited to the illustration as it appeared in the *Gartenlaube*, since this is the view that the magazine's readers would have had. The fact, however, that these larger illustrations were based on paintings that existed in art galleries heightened the significance of these black-and-white etchings. It could well be that these images were not studied consciously by contemporary *Gartenlaube* readers with the attention that we devote to them, but most certainly they had an emotional appeal and, given their consistent appearance in the magazine for at least a decade, they were obviously considered by the editors to make a valuable contribution to the magazine.

At the center of this image are Thusnelda and the Roman warrior Germanicus. The *Gartenlaube* reader who was not already familiar with the story of these two characters could read a summary of their

10. "The Capture of Thusnelda by Germanicus" by Heinrich König (*Gartenlaube* 1889: 4–5)

situation on the last page of the issue. This brief paragraph explains that Thusnelda had been promised as a bride to Germanicus by her father Segest. She, however, loved Hermann the Cheruskan leader and married him. The passage cites a Roman source as saying that Segest later took Thusnelda captive and after being aided militarily by Germanicus, offered his daughter to the Roman. This version is cast in some doubt by the *Gartenlaube* commentator, but supported by the illustration, which shows substantial resistance on the part of Thusnelda's companions to the Romans' arrival and the father-figure gesturing toward Thusnelda, apparently offering her as a present.

The only two figures shown in full length are Germanicus and Thusnelda. Both are depicted as relaxed and in control of their emotions and fate. Thusnelda stands out as the brightest spot in the illustration; this is emphasized by the commentator, who describes her "as beautiful as a goddess and with princely dignity" (1889: 34). Thusnelda's stoical heroism is magnified by the fear, anger, and desperation of her attendants, just as the determination of the Roman leader (who is by contrast to Thusnelda the darkest figure in the image) is accentuated by the curiosity of the troops who stand behind him in disorganized array. These characters, but especially Thusnelda as the Germanic heroine, are idealized, of superhuman beauty, and therefore of tragic significance.

The imposing quality of this event is signified, as it has been argued for the art of the *Gründerzeit* in general, by a monumental presentation of the two figures.[45] Their bodies fill the visual space of the illustration; the Roman guards are even crowded out of the picture to the right.[46] This fullness gives the impression of closeness without requiring the intimacy of a portrait. It highlights the emotional impact of the mythical-historical scene. The viewer's closeness to the scene is also aided by the detail in the illustration, details of bodies, clothing, and armor.[47] The specifics of the illustration further encourage the reader to study the image, because he or she is rewarded by finding previously unnoticed subtleties. In general, however, the posture of the figures, as well as the composition of the illustration as a whole, suggests the powerful heroism that makes this representation of Thusnelda, regardless of its historical accuracy, a useful element of the national story. It indicates an active, defiant, warriorlike spirit that can become part of a myth of national character.

It is also noteworthy that the style of this and similar images departs from the realism of the magazine's earlier illustrations. The impartial presentation of events and characters, as well as the more distant, moderate perspective on human issues that was a sign of a sober realism, gives way here to monumentalism in form and story. The mythical stature of the nation and its past is boldly and directly represented in muscular male bodies and statuesque, robust, proud female figures. In addition, the appearance here of bared female breasts and the leering Roman guards provides a kind of highly charged sensuality to this image of Germanic history. Because of its emphasis on historical roots, this type of image is an example of antimodern nostalgia, but it is also an indication of the contemporary self-assurance, even boastfulness, of the German nation. This change in illustration style suggests that the *Gartenlaube*, when it served as mouthpiece of the aspiring nation (from 1850 to 1870), could only depict the German *Volk* in modest terms, whereas the increasingly dominant, powerful German nation-state of the 1880s and 1890s could strut daringly through the pages of the press.

In an era of great national progress in the arena of international competition, such historical, mythical images constituted a reference to past greatness. The period of Germanic tribes and the notable rulers of the Middle Ages alternated with images of Friedrich the Great and the valiantly portrayed victories of Wilhelm I against the French in 1870. These historical images established a connection between the nation's earlier periods and its present claim to be one of the great powers in the world. This aspect of the popular press in the age of rapid modernization supports the argument of Eric Hobsbawm that a nation's past is so important to its identity and coherence that it must be invented if it cannot be otherwise established.[48]

Rural Nostalgia

Alongside this heroic, monumental view of a national past there appeared a second form of visual nostalgia in the *Gartenlaube*, one that also presented a simpler version of national identity. In contrast to the mythic nation, however, this image was rooted in the present. It was an idealized version of contemporary rural simplicity. This involved the allusion to regional identities and the presumption of an unbroken continuity and tradition in the German countryside (as opposed to the discontinuities of modern urban existence). These images of rural simplicity served as a reassuring alternative to the hustle and activity of modernization.

As we have seen in chapter 2, the ethnic and geographic approach to defining the German nation was prevalent in the *Gartenlaube* from its beginning. This method of describing the nation was in keeping with the work of earlier cultural nationalists who viewed the nation as a constant, stable community, whose contemporary characteristics originated in a distant era. This geographically and ethnically defined concept of the *Volk* that dominated the *Gartenlaube* from the 1850s through the 1870s was rooted in the past. It was part of an understanding of the nation as a lasting community over time. It implied that the health and viability of the nation was dependent on its faithfulness to an original essence. According to this understanding, the political boundaries of the German Empire as a nation-state did not necessarily encompass the true nation for the editors of the *Gartenlaube*.

Cities and industrial production played a major role in defining the modern nation. However, for the traditional conception of the nation defined by its geography, the countryside was central. The conventions and traditions of country life and rural populations were presented as unchanging or constant, and thus they could be used to suggest an eternal quality of the national body. Rural spaces and lifestyles pointed to an enduring history of the nation that compensated the German people for their lack of a coherent and modern political unity.[49]

Up to the 1870s, in the *Gartenlaube*'s geographical essays the life of rural Germans was idealized to a certain extent. The cultural scenes paid attention to such pleasant aspects of village life as holidays, festivals, and celebrations. The illustrations never showed the dismal, dirty, impoverished life of the countryside, but always the cheerful and festive countenance of village existence. If the point of such essays and images was, as we have argued, to educate the national populace in regional differences, they were also meant to make the image of rural life attractive and reassuringly pleasant as well as familiar to all *Gartenlaube* readers.

Beginning in the 1880s, however (notably, after the death of editor Ernst Keil in 1878), this rural or regional representation of the German nation changed. In particular, the visual images that regularly had accompanied the ethnographic essays gradually became more independent of the written text. By the 1880s, such illustrations began to stand alone, often on the first page of a weekly issue. They were frequently no longer an integral part of essays. Sometimes they were accompanied by a notice that appeared at the end of the issue, in the section called "Leaves and Blossoms" that provided some information about the source of the illustration, which was often a painting by a popular artist.[50] By the late 1880s, these images frequently even lacked such brief explanatory notes at the back of the issue.

Many of these images were of simple domestic or rural scenes that suggested a contemporary German innocence, a kind of national character that had been untouched, and thus uncorrupted, by the other modernizing processes that the *Gartenlaube* was so keen to document. In this regard, they are similar to the idyllic peacefulness of some colonial representations, such as the beautiful landscapes apparently untouched by human hands (fig. 9). Because these images from the last decades of the century were often presented without a textual frame, they call for a closer reading. Their symbolism rests in imagery alone.

Let us take the example of the year 1889, the year in which "The Capture of Thusnelda by Germanicus" appeared. This volume was divided into twenty-eight *Halbhefte* (double issues) and thus contained twenty-eight first pages. Sixteen of these twenty-eight first-page illustrations depicted either young maidens or children in peaceful idyllic settings. In the first image, entitled "Es schläft!" ("He Is Sleeping!"), a mother gazes at her sleeping child as she quietly slips away from his bedside. The woman is dressed in simple peasant clothing and the room is sparsely decorated, indicating a modest lifestyle, but the fact that the child slumbers comfortably on a thick pillow and holds a doll indicates physical warmth and an emotionally supportive family existence. Another image shows an elderly botanist in a field inspecting a flower with his magnifying glass, as a young girl tending geese looks on. Many of these images are nature scenes, such as the second mentioned here, or take place within the security of a rural domestic interior. In either case, they are meant to evoke a pleased smile from the viewer, in marked contrast to the illustration of Thusnelda, which calls forth defiant indignation.

An example of the sentimentalized regionalism common in this genre of illustration is the first page of double-issue number 9. The illustration on this title page is called "Die Schwalben sind wieder da!" ("The Swallows Are Here Again!") (fig. 11). Rather than contributing to the characterization of a specific regional culture, as the illustrations in the ethnographic essays of earlier decades did, this scene suggests a generalizable rural event.[51] It depicts an attractive young woman (probably a mother) and two children. The young girl stands in front of her mother with her arms and face turned upward, while the mother and the baby she holds in her arm also look upward. They stand on the porch of a farmhouse and greet swallows that are fluttering around the roofline, probably in the process of building a nest under the broad overhang of the family's house.

The mother and children are surrounded by nature, with blooming plants on the balustrade and woods behind them. Visually, however, they remain within the protective shelter of the house, framed by the balustrade wall and roofline. The family and the birds alike present the viewer with an image of domesticity and rural simplicity, but without any details about what part of Germany this is. In other words, the family represents a generic rural German identity. Without any other context, this smiling mother and her happy children become an image of an unproblematic German existence, a symbol of the contented, healthy nation that is not only untouched by processes of modernization, but is also not visibly desirous of them.

An image entitled "Hopp! Hopp!" ("Hup! Hup!") from the same year is a similarly idealized representation of the German

Halbheft 9.   **Die Gartenlaube.**   1889.

Illuſtrirtes Familienblatt. — Begründet von **Ernſt Keil 1853.**

Jahrgang 1889. Erſcheint in Halbheften à 25 Pf. alle 12—14 Tage, in Heften à 50 Pf. alle 3—4 Wochen vom 1. Januar bis 31. Dezember.

Nicht im Geleiſe.

Roman von Ida Boy-Ed.

(Fortſetzung.)

Alfred las den Brief Joſephes noch einmal.

„Papa, warum lieſt Du immer den ſelben Brief?" fragte der kleine Alexander.

„Weil ſehr viel unangenehme Sachen darin ſtehen," ſagte er.

„Dann wirf ihn doch fort!" Mama ſagte geſtern mittag zu Tantchen: ‚Er iſt ein Menſch, der immer Sonnenſchein haben muß.‘ Damit meinte ſie Dich. Und heute ſcheint die Sonne ſo heiß. Fahre doch nachher mit uns in die Sonne," plauderte das Kind.

Alfred nahm es auf den Schoß.

„Ja, es ſoll immer Sonnenſchein ſein bei uns. Wir beide, Du und ich, wollen Deine Mama ſo lieb haben."

„So lieb," wiederholte der Knabe und drückte feſt, ſeit ſeine Arme um Alfreds Hals, um den Grad der Liebe zu bezeichnen.

„Und den ganzen Tag wollen wir bei ihr ſein, und ſie und ich werden Dich zuſammen alles lehren, was kleine Menſchen lernen müſſen, damit ſie groß und verſtändig werden," fuhr Alfred fort.

„Haſt Du denn dazu immer Zeit?" fragte Sacha und ſah ihn groß an.

„Glücklicherweiſe ja! Aber was nun meinſt Du?" fragte Alfred dagegen und forſchte mit argwöhniſchen Blicken in den offenen Kinderzügen. Sein Herz ſchlug. Jetzt würde von dieſen unſchuldigen Lippen irgend ein bedeutungsvolles Wort kommen, ein Wort, das Gerda vielleicht nicht ohne Abſicht vor den immer wachſam lauſchenden kleinen Ohren geſagt . . .

Aber das Kind ſprach nur nachdenklich: „Ich meine nur ſo. Die Papas von Willy und Wolff und Karl haben immer keine Zeit, mit kleinen Jungen zu ſpielen."

Die Väter ſeiner Spielgenoſſen — Alfred kannte ſie alle wohl, der eine war Bankier, der andere ein hervorragender Parlamentarier, der dritte ein Staatsbeamter.

„Die haben auch alle einen Beruf," erläuterte Alfred.

„Den müſſen alle Männer haben, ſagt Mama," rief das kluge Kind.

Da war es nun doch, das böſe Wort, das Wort, welches gleich auf eine ganze Reihe vergangener und zukünftiger Kämpfe hinwies.

„Wann ſagte Mama das?" rief Alfred heftig.

„Ich weiß nicht mehr. Bitte, mach doch dem Huſaren das Bein gerade," und dabei hielt dem kleine Fauſt einen verbogenen Zinnſoldaten faſt unter Alfreds Naſe.

„War es, als ſie mit Tantchen gerade von mir ſprach?" forſchte Alfred weiter. Aber er bog doch gehorſam das krumme Bein wieder zurück.

Der Knabe war mit ſeinen Gedanken ſchon ganz von dem Geſpräch entfernt. Auch hatte er ſchon jeden Soldaten vom Pferd genommen und wieder draufgeſetzt. Nun mußte etwas anderes kommen.

„Haſt Du ſchwarze Farbe, Papa?"

„Nein! Was ſoll's?"

„Ich wollte aus den Schimmeln Rappen machen."

„Das geht nun nicht."

„Was ſoll ich denn nun anfangen?"

Alfred wußte für das geliebte Kind immer Rath.

„Komm," ſagte er. „Du kannſt zeichnen."

Er ſetzte den Kleinen an den Schreibtiſch, ſtellte einen Karton Briefpapier und einige Bleiſtifte vor ihn hin und bat ihn, ein

Die Schwalben ſind wieder da! Nach einem Gemälde von W. Roegge.
Photographie im Verlage von Franz Hanfſtängl in München.

people (1889: 549). The tile oven, the meerschaum pipe, and the pointed cap of the grandfather, as well as the smiling child he is bouncing on his knees, are all emblems of the simple life and home, which are meant to stand for the German experience and the people's authentic identity. These and many such images recall not only the description of the various regions in Germany, but also the *Gartenlaube*'s explicit characterization of itself (that we saw in chapter 1) as a magazine to be read in the quiet private space of the German family. In these images, the traditional view of Germans as having an old heritage and long-standing geographical stability is tied to a political affirmation of the idealized domestic sphere, the idyllic portrayal of the middle-class family as the source of that cultural stability. It is not surprising that both regional and domestic identity were united in these sentimentalized images.[52]

In this gradual process of sentimentalization through decontextualization, the visual image of the nation became an autonomous, uprooted signifier of national sentiment. It became exchangeable and interchangeable. The past was presented as a romantic image of national strength and character. Regional identity was petrified into a simplistic and idealized picture of authentic Germanness that could constitute a decorative and colorful interlude to the other (modern) presentations of the nation. The nation had been reduced from historical and regional specificity to a stereotype. It had been romanticized and generalized. Again, it is not only the style of individual images, but the prevalence of this type of image in the magazine's weekly issues that suggests a change in the representation of the nation in the *Gartenlaube*. With the constant repetition of such quaint scenarios and settings, each of the presentations came to look the same. The idea of the nation was embodied in a set of predictable scenes, evoking a nostalgic sense of the simple and carefree life. Even the modest means of the simple people depicted here was made picturesque and could be seen as providing an antidote to the contemporary real social misery of hundreds of thousands of Germans. Such images obfuscated problems that existed within the nation, but from its earliest years, the *Gartenlaube* was interested in offering its readers identities and images that united the nation, not those of social conflict. By the 1890s, this interest translated into providing reassuring representations of national continuity and stability. Especially in the face of rapid and alienating modernization at the end of the century, the magazine's sentimental reminder of a present past would have been a great comfort for middle-class German readers.

Epilogue

As the *Gartenlaube* produced more sentimental images of the nation, these images became increasingly independent of written text. The icon of the peasant or mother and child was meant to speak for itself. Domestic and rural aspects of traditional identity that such illustrations conveyed apparently no longer required elaboration or explanation. At the close of the century the *Gartenlaube*'s earlier commitment to informing its readers in detailed essays was gradually giving way to easily consumable illustrations that were meant to encapsulate the essence of a German heritage. Whether such images were accepted by the majority of the magazine's readers as accurate or useful representations of the national self is a question that cannot be answered definitively. It is clear, however, that these decontextualized images constituted a move toward national stereotyping, toward a trivialized version of national identity.

This aspect of the *Gartenlaube* has led some twentieth-century critics to dub the magazine the epitome of kitsch. Hermann Glaser even suggests that the trivialized version of the family and German society in such images from the magazine was the root of a dangerously idealizing mentality. The *Gartenlaube*'s inwardness, he argues, was, as a whole, petit-bourgeois and reactionary; as such it was a precursor to the nationalist and domestic ideology of National Socialism.[1] Glaser's judgment, however, is based upon a limited and selective reading of the magazine. As we have seen in detail, the *Gartenlaube* was just as much a participant in the celebration of nineteenth-century liberalism as it was in this sentimental view of German identity. Its initial purpose was the education of the German reading public to political maturity, and this continued to be one of its major functions at the turn of the century. Idealized portrayals of the *Volk* stood side by side with the magazine's continued interest in such things as battleships, mechanical inventions, and German competitiveness in trade and industrial production.

From the beginning, the *Gartenlaube* had appealed to a broad reading audience. It hoped to attract readers of all ages, of both sexes, of many occupations, and most significantly, from all German regions. It had always used a variety of strategies and themes, such as geography, monument construction, and technological innovation, to define the German nation as the main point of identification for its family readers. In the final years of the century, however, this unifying project became more difficult to sustain. The idea of the German nation became increasingly complex and conflicted. The late 1890s witnessed the rise of extreme nationalist organizations like the Pan-German League and the Navy League as well as the colonial associations. It also brought the development of a large and powerful German working-class party that constituted an important national voice. International conflicts, such as the Boer War and other colonial clashes between European interests, raised further national concerns. In this period of increasing social fragmentation and political tension, the magazine struggled to find a mixture of modern and nostalgic images that could enable its readers to negotiate a modern social identity.

The *Gartenlaube*'s sentimental images of the nation, rather than representing a petit-bourgeois reaction, reveal the complexity of the task of representing the nation. These apparently trivialized views of Germanness at the close of the century must be seen in the context of the magazine's history and the other images it continued to produce. The *Gartenlaube*'s images of an archaic past and of a simple, naive present suggest an intriguing ambivalence with regard to the various aspects of modernization it featured and supported. The inclusion of an increasingly aggressive global national politics as one definition of the nation alongside a reversion to premodern sensibilities reveals the growing impossibility of representing the nation in unequivocal terms by the end of the century. It attests to the multiplicity of topics with which the modern press had to come to terms in order to satisfy a broad, mainstream readership. In the case of the *Gartenlaube*, the goal of maintaining a mainstream audience resulted in the dissemination of increasingly disparate and even contradictory images of the nation.

This phase of the magazine coincided with a gradual but persistent decline in its popularity. The *Gartenlaube* experienced a drop in circulation in the early 1880s, only to gain back some of its readership later in the same decade. After the turn of the century, however, its circulation dropped to around 100,000. Despite mergers with other popular periodicals (with *Vom Fels zum Meer* in 1905 and *Die weite Welt* in 1906),[2] the *Gartenlaube* never again came close to its record popularity of the mid 1870s, when it had reached a circulation of almost 400,000.[3] Could there be a connection between the *Gartenlaube*'s gradual decline in popularity at the end of the century and its representation of the nation and German identity?

We might suggest that the magazine that claimed so boldly to speak for the German nation, to be the most "German" periodical, had lost its ability to represent German identity convincingly when it moved to the stereotypical images of national identity that we saw at the end of chapter 6. Perhaps one could argue that these idealizations of Germans and German scenes were too facile for modern eyes, and that the *Gartenlaube*'s editors had miscalculated the interest of their readers in them. This argument loses plausibility, however, when we consider that this trend toward charming images of the simple folk as a means of representing a national self was not limited to German publications and was in fact beginning to gain in popularity in other countries. One only need reflect on the sentimental and highly popular idealizations of stereotypical American scenes in Norman Rockwell illustrations on title pages of the *Saturday Evening Post* in this century.[4] Given the flexibility and adaptability the *Gartenlaube* had exhibited in its four decades of success, it also seems unlikely that its editors would have intentionally pursued a course that would have cost the magazine readers. Therefore, we need to look to other factors to account for the declining popularity of the *Gartenlaube*.

The most plausible explanation for the decline of the magazine can be found in structural factors. The late nineteenth century brought a changing press landscape. In general, there were three kinds of magazines that experienced substantial growth in the last decades of the century and that stood in competition with the family magazine: a new genre of cultural magazines, women's magazines, and illustrated weeklies. The first competitors to the *Gartenlaube* were magazines that fashioned themselves as trendsetters within the press of cultural ideas, appealing in particular to younger readers. One example was Georg Hirth's magazine *Die Jugend (Youth)*, founded in 1895 in Munich. *Die Jugend* incorporated the decorative arts into its format, even lending its name to the turn-of-the-century art movement called *Jugendstil* in Germany. Its appealing visual design and hopeful affirmative social stance helped it gain a circulation of 74,000 by 1908.[5] An even more successful product of the 1890s, that had a circulation of over 100,000 by 1908, was the liberal organ of political satire, *Simplicissimus*, a younger version of the 1848 *Kladderadatsch*, that appealed to a young readership.[6]

Secondly, the last decade of the century witnessed the rising popularity of magazines directed explicitly at a female audience. These included journals with advice about housekeeping, but fashion magazines were the most popular, with circulations that exceeded 100,000 in 1895.[7] Neither of these periodical genres even tried to appeal to the entire family as their reading audience. And because they targeted a smaller subset of the reading population, they never matched the peak circulation numbers of the *Gartenlaube*. As a modern alternative, however, they challenged the validity and the format of the family magazine genre, and more importantly, they competed directly for readers.

Lastly, perhaps the greatest threat to the existence of the family periodical was the rise of illustrated magazines (such as the *Berliner Illustrierte Zeitung*, founded in 1892) that focused primarily on visual material and were geared toward an urban audience. Such publications had existed before; the *Illustrirte Zeitung* (founded in 1843) had long been a contemporary of the *Gartenlaube*. But at the end of the century many of the financial and technical difficulties associated with reproducing images had been overcome, and the *Berliner Illustrierte Zeitung* took advantage of this, basing its astonishing popularity on reader interest in illustrations that could be affordably published. It had a circulation of 100,000 by the turn of the century, 800,000 by 1906, and 1,000,000 by 1914.[8] As we have seen, the *Gartenlaube* reflected this growing general interest in illustrations, as it included an ever greater number of illustrations in each decade of its existence. But in its traditional format it was no match for the genre of magazine that from the start privileged image over text.

The construction of a unified, homogeneous nation is, of course, always a fiction. But it was a fiction upon which the *Gartenlaube* had managed to base decades of popularity and influence. The final years of the nineteenth century brought changing interests and interest groups to the fore in Germany. The family gradually faded as an attractive reading market for the popular press. With it disappeared the *Gartenlaube*'s ideal of unifying a nation of readers with a single periodical. The magazine continued to publish its version of German identity, but the foundational story of the nation it had helped fashion and disseminate for so many decades lost its appeal. At the close of the century, the representational challenges of national identity translated into the end of an era for the *Gartenlaube*.

Despite the *Gartenlaube*'s decline around 1900, its first four decades of publication established it as a remarkable success story and as the first example of the mass periodical press in Germany. Its enormous popularity in the years leading up to and following the political unification of Germany in 1871 make it a rich source for historical investigation of national identity. In particular, it allows us to consider three interrelated issues in the creation and dissemination of national consciousness at the beginning of the modern era.

In the first instance, the example of the *Gartenlaube* reveals how the early mass press could combine reportage, narrative, and visual image to give expression to a cohesive idea of the nation. Because it was relatively autonomous of formal institutions of state power, this medium had the flexibility to address various aspects of national identity. That flexibility, or adaptability, enabled it to reach a broad cross section of the national population with its vision. Secondly, the variety of national themes that emerged in this one periodical over the years allows us to see the importance of other social identities as the context for discussions of national identity.

This nineteenth-century case of the popular press points to the ways in which class, gender, and regional identity, among others, must be included in a successful, marketable image of the nation.

Finally, the case of this nineteenth-century mainstream magazine points to the fact that the construction of a national identity in the modern era must involve both traditional and innovative representations. The *Gartenlaube* relied heavily on historical sources and material for its construction of a German identity. But as a magazine that hoped to attract and maintain a broad, mainstream audience, it also had to adapt its presentation to include current issues, such as the processes of modernization. Although much has changed in the media in the last hundred years, these principles that we identify in the popular press of the nineteenth century can help us understand the forces at work constructing images of national identity in our own time.

Notes

1. "Wer kennt unsere 'Gartenlaube' nicht?" (*Gartenlaube* 1895: 548). For the sake of historical clarity all references to the *Gartenlaube* will be cited according to the year of publication (rather than volume number) and page number. All translations from the *Gartenlaube* and other nineteenth-century periodicals are my own.

2. See the editor's introduction for readers on the first page of the first issue: "Grüß Euch Gott, lieben Leute im deutschen Lande!" (*Gartenlaube* 1853: 1). For a discussion of this program see chapter 1.

3. Joachim Kirchner suggests the numerous "family magazines" founded in the second half of the nineteenth century were inspired by the success of *Die Gartenlaube* and imitated its format. There are at least two publications that even borrowed the name of this model magazine, *Amerikanische Gartenlaube* (founded 1864) and *Österreichische Gartenlaube* (founded 1866). Joachim Kirchner, *Das deutsche Zeitschriftenwesen: Seine Geschichte und seine Probleme*, part 2, *Vom Wiener Kongress bis zum Ausgange des 19. Jahrhunderts* (Wiesbaden: Otto Harrassowitz, 1962), 227.

4. For a detailed overview of the liberal political tradition in nineteenth-century Germany see Dieter Langewiesche, *Liberalismus in Deutschland* (Frankfurt: Suhrkamp, 1988).

5. Jürgen Habermas's *Strukturwandel der Öffentlichkeit: Untersuchungen zu einer Kategorie der bürgerlichen Gesellschaft* (Darmstadt: Luchterhand, 1962), written over thirty years ago, is still the best introduction to the Enlightenment ideal of an open, bourgeois public sphere. It has been translated into English as Jürgen Habermas, *The Structural Transformation of the Public Sphere: An Inquiry into a Category of Bourgeois Society*, trans. Thomas Burger (Cambridge: MIT Press, 1989).

6. In this regard I agree with James Sheehan that in dealing with German history one must not be constrained by the political limits of the "small-German" nation-state. See James J. Sheehan, "What Is German History? Reflections on the Role of the Nation in German History and Historiography," *Journal of Modern History* 53 (1981): 1–23. I disagree with Jürgen Kocka, who suggests that it is impracticable and unrealistic to consider the notion of a German "Kulturnation" beyond the limits of the German

nation-state after 1871. See Jürgen Kocka, "Probleme der politischen Integration der Deutschen 1867 bis 1945," in James J. Sheehan and Otto Büsch (eds.), *Die Rolle der Nation in der deutschen Geschichte und Gegenwart* (Berlin: Colloquium, 1985), 118–20. The present book is intended as an argument in favor of at times defining national identity outside the limitations of political state formation.

7. George Mosse's 1975 book still provides an excellent introduction to the variety of populist national movements and organizations in nineteenth-century Germany: George L. Mosse, *Nationalization of the Masses: Political Symbolism and Mass Movements in Germany from the Napoleonic Wars through the Third Reich* (reprint, Ithaca: Cornell UP, 1991). For a detailed discussion of the gymnastics and choral societies in the first half of the century see also Dieter Düding, *Organisierter gesellschaftlicher Nationalismus in Deutschland (1808–1847). Bedeutung und Funktion der Turner- und Sängervereine für die deutsche Nationalbewegung* (Munich: Oldenbourg, 1984).

8. Benedict Anderson, *Imagined Communities: Reflections on the Origin and Spread of Nationalism* (London: Verso, 1983).

9. This process was aided by three other factors: the changing social status of Latin, the Reformation, and the use of vernacular languages by growing state administrations (Anderson, *Imagined Communities*, 42–44).

10. Ernest Gellner, *Nations and Nationalism* (Ithaca: Cornell UP, 1983), 19–38. These notions also play a major role in Eric Hobsbawm, "Introduction: Inventing Traditions," in Eric Hobsbawm and Terence Ranger (eds.), *The Invention of Tradition* (Cambridge: Cambridge UP, 1983), 1–14. See also Eric Hobsbawm, *Nations and Nationalism since 1780: Programme, Myth, Reality* (Cambridge: Cambridge UP, 1990).

11. Gellner concludes: "A modern society is, in this respect, like a modern army, only more so. It provides a very prolonged and fairly thorough training for all its recruits, insisting on certain shared qualifications: literacy, numeracy, basic work habits and social skills, familiarity with basic technical and social skills" (Gellner, *Nations and Nationalism*, 27–28).

12. In response to the notion (of Elie Kedourie) that nationalism itself engenders or encourages homogeneity, Gellner insists: "It is not the case that nationalism imposes homogeneity out of a wilful cultural *Machtbedürfniss*; it is the objective need for homogeneity which is reflected in nationalism" (Gellner, *Nations and Nationalism*, 46).

13. Anderson notes that this conception of simultaneity has "been a long time in the making." Yet, the influence of print-capitalism as a modern institution furthered this modern sense of time like no other single factor (Anderson, *Imagined Communities*, 24).

14. Richard Terdiman, *Discourse/Counter-Discourse: The Theory and Practice of Symbolic Resistance in Nineteenth-Century France* (Ithaca: Cornell UP, 1985), 123. Terdiman points out that this condition of complete salability was nonetheless at odds with the ideological foundations of the press, the intended appearance of the daily paper as partially for sale and partially unpurchasable.

15. Hobsbawm, "Introduction: Inventing Traditions," 4.

16. For an introduction to reader-based approaches to literary texts see Jane Tompkins (ed.), *Reader-Response Criticism: From Formalism to Post-Structuralism* (Baltimore: Johns Hopkins UP, 1980), and Robert Holub, *Reception Theory: A Critical Introduction* (New York: Routledge, 1984).

17. In Anderson's book, the concept of the reading subject inspired a new definition of the social community as an imagined phenomenon. Anderson's example is the American reader: "An American will never meet, or even know the names of more than a handful of his 240,000,000-odd fellow-Americans. He has no idea of what they are up to at any one time. But he has complete confidence in their steady, anonymous, simultaneous activity" (Anderson, *Imagined Communities*, 26).

18. The popular press has been used by other scholars as a key to a society's or nation's sense of self. Some examples from the case of the United States include Jan Cohn, *Creating America: George Horace Lorimer and the Saturday Evening Post* (Pittsburgh: U of Pittsburgh P, 1989), and Loudon Wainwright, *The Great American Magazine: An Inside History of Life* (New York: Alfred A. Knopf, 1986). These two works are predominantly preoccupied with the history of the magazines and their editors, yet both acknowledge the national significance of such popular publications in presenting images of the nation to a broad readership. Brent O. Peterson has contributed to the understanding of immigrant identity in the United States with his work on a popular German-language magazine from the late nineteenth and early twentieth centuries: Brent O. Peterson, *Popular Narratives and Ethnic Identity: Literature and Community in the Abendschule* (Ithaca: Cornell UP, 1991). Another recent work that focuses on the importance of *National Geographic*, the third most popular magazine in the United States, in the creation of national signification is Catherine A. Lutz and Jane L. Collins, *Reading National Geographic* (Chicago: U of Chicago P, 1993).

19. Anne Norton, *Reflections on Political Identity* (Baltimore: Johns Hopkins UP, 1988), 47.

20. Homi K. Bhabha, "DissemiNation: Time, Narrative, and the Margins of the Modern Nation," in Homi K. Bhabha (ed.), *Nation and Narration* (London: Routledge, 1990), 291–322.

21. These theories of the subject as an active, self-imagining agent have come predominantly from the recent British scholarship on nationalism and national identity. Fewer theoretical categories have emerged from recent German work. German studies of nationalism have come in large part from historians who are pursuing first and foremost the question of historical continuity and tradition. In fact, a school of young historians in the 1960s made its mark by proposing the thesis that Germany followed a particular path (*Sonderweg*) in the nineteenth and twentieth centuries, different from the western European models of England and France. This thesis had major ramifications for the way these historians viewed German nationalism in the twentieth century. Germany was explained as an aberration of sorts, as a deviation from the norm. A younger generation of (British) historians challenged this reading of the German past. David Blackbourn and Geoff Eley, in particular, have argued against a particularist approach to Germany's history. See David Blackbourn and Geoff Eley, *The Peculiarities of German History: Bourgeois Society and Politics in Nineteenth-Century Germany* (New York: Oxford UP, 1984).

22. For a lucid explanation of some of the basic concepts of narrative see Schlomith Rimmon-Kenan, *Narrative Fiction: Contemporary Poetics* (New York: Routledge, 1989). A seminal source for explanations of narrative terminology is Gérard Genette, *Narrative Discourse: An Essay in Method*, trans. Jane E. Lewin (Ithaca: Cornell UP, 1980).

23. Important work in the area of popular literature within the field of literary studies alone has been appearing for at least two decades. See the first German publication of Peter Uwe Hohendahl's important work on the place of popular literature in the creation of a national literary canon in the nineteenth century: Peter Uwe Hohendahl, *Literarische Kultur im Zeitalter des Liberalismus, 1830–1870* (Munich: Beck, 1985), translated by Renate Baron Franciscono under the title *Building a National Literature: The Case of Germany, 1830–1870* (Ithaca: Cornell UP, 1989). Other work on the notion of "Trivialliteratur" can be traced back to the late 1950s and early 1960s.

24. The most important work in the area of literacy, reading habits of the lower classes, and the periodical press has been done by Rudolf Schenda, *Volk ohne Buch: Studien zur Sozialgeschichte der populären Lesestoffe, 1770–1910* (Frankfurt: Vittorio Klostermann, 1970); Dieter Barth, *Zeitschrift für Alle: Blätter fürs Volk: Das Familienblatt im 19. Jahrhundert: Ein sozialhistorischer Beitrag zur Massenpresse in Deutschland* (Münster: Institut für Publizistik, 1974); and Rolf Engelsing, *Analphabetentum und Lektüre: Zur Sozialgeschichte des Lesens in Deutschland zwischen feudaler und industrieller Gesellschaft* (Stuttgart: Metzler, 1973).

25. Simon During is one case in point. For During the contemporary nature of the field's object of study is, it seems, one of the few issues that need not be discussed in defining the field. "Cultural studies is, of course, the study of culture, or more particularly, the study of *contemporary* culture." See Simon During, introduction to *Cultural Studies Reader*, ed. Simon During (New York: Routledge, 1993), 1.

26. Louis Snyder quotes Arnold Toynbee as stating that the nation is surrounded by a thick, almost impenetrable intellectual smog, suffused by paradox, contradiction, and inconsistency: Louis L. Snyder, *The Meaning of Nationalism* (New Brunswick NJ: Rutgers UP, 1954). With regard to the multiple manifestations of nationalism Boyd C. Shafer notes: "Just as the realities of nationalism have reflected human experience, so have the definitions. It is simply not true that when one has studied the nationalism of one time and place one has studied the nationalisms of all times and places" (Boyd C. Shafer, *Faces of Nationalism* [New York: Harcourt Brace Jovanovich, 1972], 3). Anthony D. Smith writes: "At best the idea of the nation has appeared sketchy and elusive, at worst absurd and contradictory" (Anthony D. Smith, *National Identity* [Reno: U of Nevada P, 1991], 17).

27. This work, by the so-called American father of the study of nationalism, Carleton Hayes, was also comparative. See Carleton Hayes, *The Historical Evolution of Modern Nationalism* (New York: Richard Smith, 1931).

28. Hans Kohn's own experience as a refugee from Nazi Germany fueled his interest in the "problem" of nationalism. See Hans Kohn, *The Idea of Nationalism: A Study of Its Origins and Background* (New York: Macmillan, 1946).

29. Louis L. Snyder's work in the 1950s is key here; see Snyder, *The Meaning of Nationalism*. The category of communication first appeared in this context in the work of Karl Deutsch, *Nationalism and Social Communication: An Inquiry into the Foundations of Nationality* (Cambridge: Technology Press, 1953).

30. In addition to the works already cited by Anderson, Gellner, Hobsbawm, and Anthony Smith, of central importance are Hugh Seton-Watson, *Nations and States: An Enquiry into the Origins of Nations and the Politics of Nationalism* (Boulder: Westview, 1977); John Breuilly, *Nationalism and the State* (Chicago: U of Chicago P, 1985); and Anthony D. Smith, *The Ethnic Origins of Nations* (Oxford: Blackwell, 1986). A traditional *Geistesgeschichte* approach that consults intellectual history in order to identify the roots and path of nationalism can be found in Liah Greenfeld, *Nationalism: Five Roads to Modernity* (Cambridge: Harvard UP, 1992).

31. George L. Mosse, *The Crisis of German Ideology: Intellectual Origins of the Third Reich* (1964; reprint, New York: Schocken, 1981). Fritz Stern, *The Politics of Cultural Despair* (Berkeley: U of California P, 1961).

32. See Geoff Eley on the German Navy League and Roger Chickering on the Pan-German League: Geoff Eley, *Reshaping the German Right: Radical Nationalism and Political Change after Bismarck* (New Haven: Yale UP, 1980); Roger Chickering, *We Men Who Feel Most German: A Cultural Study of the Pan-German League 1886–1914* (Boston: Allen and Unwin, 1984).

1. UNIFYING A NATION OF READERS

1. Eva-Annemarie Kirschstein offers the most complete data on the *Gartenlaube*'s circulation history. Kirschstein, *Die Familienzeitschrift: Ihre Entwicklung und Bedeutung für die deutsche Presse* (Berlin: Liebheit und Thiesen), 87–90.

2. The *Gartenlaube* grew consistently and rapidly through the 1870s. Its circulation then tapered off a bit in the 1880s. A summary of the *Gartenlaube*'s circulation statistics is included below in this chapter in the discussion of the magazine's beginnings and development.

3. The family magazine was also a leader in terms of circulation and market success in most other Western countries. For the case of American magazines of this period see Frank Luther Mott, *A History of American Magazines, 1850–1865* (Cambridge: Harvard UP, 1938).

4. See Jürgen Habermas's discussion of a middle-class "publicity," or the "public sphere" (which he translates into German as "Öffentlichkeit"). Habermas, *Strukturwandel*, 13–41.

5. Habermas cites the coffeehouse and the salon as English and French spaces in which this public sphere operated; in Germany it was the scholarly "*Tischgesellschaften.*" Habermas, *Strukturwandel*, 46–52.

6. "Bald wird die Zeitschrift, zuerst die handgeschriebene Korrespondenz, dann die gedruckte Monats- oder Wochenschrift zum publizistischen Instrument dieser Kritik." Habermas, *Strukturwandel*, 58–60. Periodical production was initially a part of scholarly life that only gradually entered the sphere of the middle classes in the eighteenth century. See Margot Lindemann, *Die deutsche Presse bis 1815: Geschichte der deutschen Presse*, part 1 (Berlin: Colloquium, 1969), 277.

7. Eva-Annemarie Kirschstein offers a concise history and overview of the *Moralische Wochenschriften* for the history of the German press and the family magazine in particular. Kirschstein, *Die Familienzeitschrift*, 9–25.

8. For the German situation there has been some difference of opinion as to whether the moral weekly magazines of the early eighteenth century can be considered indigenously German or imports from the more established middle-class culture in England. "Immerhin ist die Theorie, daß England das Herkunftsland der Moralischen Wochenschriften sei, durch die Entdeckung der bereits erwähnten *Erbaulichen Ruh-Stunden* von 1676 zumindest stark erschüttert, wenn nicht widerlegt worden." Lindemann, *Die deutsche Presse*, 1:236.

9. See Lindemann, *Die deutsche Presse*, 1:232–34. See also Kirschstein, *Die Familienzeitschrift*, 9–25.

10. See Lindemann, *Die deutsche Presse*, 1:278.

11. Joachim Kirchner calls the rise of the periodical press in general at the end of the seventeenth century a momentously new event. Joachim Kirchner, *Das deutsche Zeitschriftenwesen: Seine Geschichte und seine Probleme*, part 1, *Von den Anfängen bis zum Zeitalter der Romantik*, 2d ed. (Wiesbaden: Otto Harrassowitz, 1958), 1.

12. See the first issue of Gottsched's *Der Biedermann* from 1727—"Dem löblichen Frauenzimmer zu gefallen soll auch öffters was mit einfließen."

13. The moral weeklies are considered the formal precursors of the nineteenth-century family magazine. Although, as Gerhard Menz points out, the terms "Familienblatt" or "Familien-Zeitung" appeared in serial titles only in the nineteenth century, Dieter Barth comments that some publications of the eighteenth century already identified the family as their targeted readership. Gerhard Menz, "Familienzeitschriften," in Walther Heide (ed.), *Handbuch der Zeitungswissenschaft* (Leipzig: Hiersemann, 1940), 1:263–64. Barth, *Zeitschrift für Alle*, 9.

14. Some scholars have estimated a significant popularity and distribution. Lindemann, for instance, has suggested (presenting findings basing on Joachim Kirchner) that the *Patriot* (from Hamburg) may have had an occasional circulation of 6,000. Lindemann, *Die deutsche Presse*, 1:237. She neglects to mention, however, that the large majority of weeklies probably never exceeded a circulation of 400 and that their longevity seldom exceeded two years. Barth insists that one cannot speak of these magazines as "broadly popular" given such generally small publication numbers. Barth also points out that the levels of literacy and leisure in the early and mid–eighteenth century were too low to let the audiences of the moral weeklies account for more than a fraction of 1 percent of the population. Barth, *Zeitschrift für Alle*, 35.

15. Moral weeklies often included mottoes from great texts in French or Latin that indicated an elevated level of educational background among

their readers. An exception to this was the third issue of Gottsched's *Der Biedermann*. This issue was directed at women readers and consequently had a German rather than Latin motto.

16. Rolf Engelsing, *Massenpublikum und Journalistentum im 19. Jahrhundert in Nordwestdeutschland* (Berlin: Duncker and Humblot, 1966), 37.

17. Historians must rely on regional data and deduce national trends from such information as the number of individuals who can sign their marriage license or the number of military recruits who are able to read and write. See Engelsing, *Analphabetentum*, 96–100. For a summary of the role of education and literacy in the development of a readership see Hohendahl, *Literarische Kultur*, especially chapter 9, "Das literarische Publikum," 303–39. See also Lutz Winckler, *Autor—Markt—Publikum: Zur Geschichte der Literaturproduktion in Deutschland* (Berlin: Argument, 1986), 34–54.

18. Schenda, *Volk ohne Buch*, 444–45.

19. Hans-Martin Kirchner, "Wirtschaftliche Grundlagen des Zeitschriftenverlages im 19. Jahrhundert," in Joachim Kirchner, *Das deutsche Zeitschriftenwesen*, 2:380.

20. The population in Germany between 1816 and 1871 (not including the new territory of Alsace-Lothringen) increased from 23.6 million to 39.5 million. It increased to 63 million by 1910. Wolfgang Köllmann, *Bevölkerung in der industriellen Revolution: Studien zur Bevölkerungsgeschichte Deutschlands* (Göttingen: Vandenhoeck and Ruprecht, 1974), 40.

21. Schenda, who is quite reserved in his literacy estimates, provides substantial evidence to suggest that peasants and workers, in particular, rarely read books. Schenda, *Volk ohne Buch*, 445–51. "Der enorme Zuwachs von potentiellen Lesern . . . rekrutiert sich aus den finanziell leistungsschwächsten Schichten der nationalen Bevölkerungen. Diese können ihre mühsam erworbenen ABC-Kenntnisse nur anwenden, wenn ihnen der Lektüre-Markt billigste Ware liefert. Die Drucker und Verleger haben diese Exigenz durchaus erkannt und Einblattdrucke, Heftchen-Serien und Periodika zu niedrigsten Preisen hergestellt." Schenda, *Volk ohne Buch*, 473.

22. Hans-Martin Kirchner, "Wirtschaftliche," 382.

23. In Prussia alone the amount of hard-surface road increased from 75 km in 1800, to 3,250 in 1816, to 15,680 in 1852, and to 53,700 in 1871. The expansion of a rail network was even more dramatic: in all German states combined there were 6,044 km of railroad in 1850, 11,660 in 1860, 19,694 in 1870, and 33,707 in 1880. Hans-Martin Kirchner, "Wirtschaftliche," 382.

24. See the substantial detailed information in Hans-Martin Kirchner, "Wirtschaftliche," 388–409.

25. Schenda, *Volk ohne Buch*, 107.

26. Schenda, *Volk ohne Buch*, 135.

27. Joachim Kirchner, *Das deutsche Zeitschriftenwesen*, vol. 2.

28. Joachim Kirchner, *Das deutsche Zeitschriftenwesen*, 2:4–64. Most of these magazines did not survive past 1830.

29. Hans-Martin Kirchner, "Wirtschaftliche," 443–45. See also James Moran, *Printing Presses: History and Development from the Fifteenth Century to Modern Times* (Berkeley: U of California P, 1973), 105–11.

30. See Hans-Martin Kirchner for a detailed discussion of paper production and prices in the nineteenth century. Hans-Martin Kirchner, "Wirtschaftliche," 431–41.

31. "Die zuerst in England, dann in Frankreich und in Deutschland verwirklichte Verlagsidee ließ lach Eröffnung des 'Pfennig-Magazins' im Jahre 1833 die Gemüter nicht mehr zur Ruhe kommen. Sie wurde die Grundlage für die Schaffung der modernen Massenpresse" (Joachim Kirchner, *Das deutsche Zeitschriftenwesen*, 2:69). This magazine began publication one year after its English model: "Penny Magazine of the Society for the Diffusion of Useful Knowledge."

32. Joachim Kirchner, "Redaktion und Publikum," *Publizistik* 5:6 (1960): 465; Barth, *Zeitschrift für Alle*, 42–44; Kirchstein, *Die Familienzeitschrift*, 61–64. The circulation of 100,000 reached by the *Pfennig-Magazin* certainly earns it the appellation of a mass periodical, yet it was, as Dieter Barth has argued, an anomaly, not representative of a trend, as the success of the *Gartenlaube* was in the 1850s through 1870s. Barth, *Zeitschrift für Alle*, 52.

33. Joachim Kirchner, *Das deutsche Zeitschriftenwesen*, 2:141; Barth, *Zeitschrift für Alle*, 45–47; Kirchstein, *Die Familienzeitschrift*, 64–65.

34. Dieter Barth, "Das Familienblatt: Ein Phänomen der Unterhaltungspresse des 19. Jahrhunderts, Beispiele zur Gründungs- und Verlagsgeschichte," *Archiv für Geschichte des Buchwesens* 15 (1975), column 124.

35. Kirchstein, *Die Familienzeitschrift*, 62.

36. This list includes a few German-language magazines published in other countries, such as the United States and Switzerland (Kirchstein, *Die Familienzeitschrift*, 153–63). In Germany alone the documented number of magazines of any type rose from 371 in 1826, to 845 in 1858, to 1,961 in 1875, only to reach over 5,000 by the turn of the century. Statistics by Erich Lorenz, cited in Heinz-Dietrich Fischer, "Die Zeitschrift im Kommunikationssystem," in Fischer (ed.), *Deutsche Zeitschriften des 17. bis 20. Jahrhunderts* (Pullach: Verlag Dokumentation, 1973), 20.

37. Dieter Barth, "Zeitschriften, Buchmarkt und Verlagswesen," in Horst

Albert Glaser (ed.), *Deutsche Literatur: Eine Sozialgeschichte* (Reinbek: Ro-wohlt, 1982), 71.

38. Barth, *Zeitschrift für Alle*, 206.
39. Quoted in Barth, *Zeitschrift für Alle*, 206.
40. Anderson, *Imagined Communities*, 26–36.
41. The *Gartenlaube*'s circulation was just as large as those of comparable magazines in the United States. Of the illustrated weeklies cited by Frank L. Mott, *Harper's Weekly* had a circulation of 120,000 at the end of 1861, *Franks Leslies' Illustrated*, 164,000 in 1860. As in Germany, average circulations were much lower, 3,370 for quarterlies, 12,000 for monthlies, and 2,400 for weeklies. Mott, *History of American Magazines*, 2:10. The circulations of popular illustrated magazines exceeded circulations of other periodical publications of the 1860s in France as well. These figures were in general also more modest (20,000–50,000), although two periodicals topped the 100,000 mark: *Le Petit Journal* and *Le Journal illustré*. *Histoire Générale de la Presse Française, de 1815 à 1871* (Paris: Presses Universitaires de France, 1969), 2:311.
42. Langewiesche, *Liberalismus*, 35–37.
43. The history of Keil's journalistic activity is best summed up in Karl Feißkohl, *Ernst Keils publizistische Wirksamkeit und Bedeutung* (Stuttgart: Union Deutsche Verlagsgesellschaft, 1914). An even more enthusiastic version of Keil's life was published in the *Gartenlaube* in 1878 in honor of his death. Albert Fränkel, "Ernst Keil: Ein Lebens- und Charakterbild" (1878: 569–81).
44. Feißkohl, *Ernst Keil*, 20.
45. Feißkohl, *Ernst Keil*, 24.
46. Keil first founded a publishing house in 1845 with a "volksthümlich-praktische und dazu freisinnig-humane Richtung." Within two years all of his publications were banned. Keil's original plan was to publish *Der Leuchtturm* in Leipzig, but officials prohibited this, so he moved it to Zeitz (Feißkohl, *Ernst Keil*, 30). This magazine also endured persecution, moving to three different provincial cities, then to Magdeburg, Bremen, and finally Braunschweig. With the beginning of the 1848 revolution and the temporarily increased freedom of the press, *Der Leuchtturm* returned to Leipzig (Feißkohl, *Ernst Keil*, 39–40).
47. Feißkohl, *Ernst Keil*, 41–52.
48. Feißkohl, *Ernst Keil*, 59–63.
49. The *Gartenlaube* itself summed up Keil's contribution after his death in 1878 in a eulogy written by Albert Fränkel. "[D]ie Erhebung des Keil'-schen Unternehmens zu einer literarischen Weltmacht [war] ein deutliches

Beispiel und imposantes Zeugniß . . . von der volksthümlichen Macht der demokratischen Strömung und des national Einheits- und Freiheitsgedanken" (1878: 571).

50. Not only was Ernst Keil a dedicated publisher in the spirit of democratic liberalism, but numerous editors of the magazine were also members of the liberal-democratic Nationalverein. See Heidemarie Gruppe, *"Volk" zwischen Politik und Idylle in der "Gartenlaube" 1853–1914* (Frankfurt: Herbert Lang, 1976), 27–33.

51. "[I]n einer ziemlich gleichmäßig gebildeten, gleichmäßig tugendhaften Gesellschaft mit gleichen Interessen."

52. After 1849 state control of the press was more difficult because there was no longer precensorship of materials. Censorship also varied in strictness from one German state to another. However, the continued perception of the press as a dangerous vehicle is clear in texts such as the Prussian Press Law of May 12, 1851. According to this law, editors had to receive administrative permission to publish and make deposits up to a few thousand Thaler to guarantee payment of potential fines. For the periodical press, confiscation could cause delays that made a publication less valuable and reduced its subscription appeal. See Eberhard Naujoks, "Von der Reaktionszeit bis zum Reichspressegesetz (1849–1874)," in Heinz-Dietrich Fischer (ed.), *Deutsche Kommunikationskontrolle des 15. bis 20. Jahrhunderts* (Munich: Saur, 1982), 114–30.

53. The historian Thomas Nipperdey uses this term to describe nineteenth-century associations, but his characterization of these organizations as a space for public discussion of morals and principles distinct from political state institutions also applies to a publication like the *Gartenlaube*. See Thomas Nipperdey, *Deutsche Geschichte, 1800–1866* (Munich: Beck, 1983), 195. This notion is related to what Jürgen Habermas identifies as the literary public sphere in his *Strukturwandel* (44). Habermas even makes passing reference to *Die Gartenlaube* (196).

54. "Es gibt Zeiten, wo sich jede Überzeugung in die Familie flüchtet. . . . Der häusliche Herd ist uns keine gedankenlose Plauderstube . . . er ist und wird uns bleiben das sichere Asyl ernster Lebensauffassung . . . eine allgemeine Vereinigung der Menschen als Menschen, wenn auch Parteiung sie zerrisse." Quoted in Eva Zahn, "Die Geschichte der *Gartenlaube*," in Heinz Klüter (ed.), *Facsimile Querschnitt durch die Gartenlaube* (Stuttgart: Scherz, 1963), n.p.

55. See Brent Peterson's discussion of various family magazine mastheads in the context of discussing a German-American nineteenth-century family

magazine, *Die Abendschule*: Peterson, *Popular Narratives and Ethnic Identity*, 10–37.

56. Although other family magazines could not boast this success, several of them (including *Illustrirte Welt*, *Über Land und Meer*, *Illustrirte Chronik der Zeit*, and *Das Buch für Alle*) did reach printings of over 100,000 in the nineteenth century, something that very few newspapers managed to do (Barth, *Zeitschrift für Alle*, 437). *Daheim*, the closest imitator of the *Gartenlaube*, but as a conservative alternative, only reached a circulation of 60,000 in the 1880s (Hans-Martin Kirchner, "Wirtschaftliche," 228). By way of contrast, literary journals of the same period rarely had circulations above 6,000–8,000 (Hans-Martin Kirchner, "Wirtschaftliche," 220–24). Barth cites circulations of *Westermanns' Monatshefte* at 7,000–8,000 copies in the 1860s, and of *Deutsches Museum* at only 600 in 1856 (Barth, *Zeitschrift für Alle*, 56–58).

57. Kirschstein, relying on the numbers printed in the *Gartenlaube* itself, registers circulations slightly different from Dieter Barth, who also referred to the records of the *German Magazine Catalog* (*Deutscher Zeitschriften-Katalog*) since 1850. Kirschstein, *Die Familienzeitschrift*, 88; Barth, *Zeitschrift für Alle*, 473.

Year	Kirschstein	Barth
1853	5,000–6,000	
1854	5,000	
1856	42,000	
1857	60,000	
1858	70,000	
1860	100,000	86,000
1861	100,000–105,000	105,000
1862	120,000–137,000	138,000
1863	155,000–160,000	157,000
1864	180,000 (after No. 27, fewer)	125,000 (180,000 projected)
1865	150,000	
1866	142,000	
1867	210,000–230,000	210,000–230,000
1869	270,000	
1871	310,000	
1875	382,000	382,000
1883	224,000	284,000
1884	250,000–260,000	
1885	270,000	270,000
1895	275,000	
1905	100,000	

58. Barth, *Zeitschrift für Alle*, 437.

59. Because the sources for circulation statistics were generally the magazines themselves, these numbers cannot be considered fully reliable (Barth, *Zeitschrift für Alle*, 54–55). The same thing is true for the publication figures available for American periodicals (Mott, *History of American Magazines*, 9–10). Statistics were also not provided consistently; there are years for which the *Gartenlaube*'s circulation is not available.

60. For a discussion of Marlitt's work and reputation in the *Gartenlaube*, see chapter 5.

61. Despite some disparity between numbers cited, all historians agree that Keil's magazine peaked in the mid-1870s. The greatest overestimation of the *Gartenlaube*'s circulation came from a contemporary. Heinrich Wuttke cited the number 460,000 in his book, *Die deutschen Zeitschriften*, an inflated circulation that even the magazine felt compelled to correct (*Gartenlaube* 1875: 276). See also Kirschstein, *Die Familienzeitschrift*, 89.

62. Rolf Engelsing, "Die Zeitschrift in Nordwestdeutschland, 1850–1914," *Archiv für Geschichte des Buchwesens* 6 (1965): 1005.

63. Rosenstrauch estimates a readership of five million by 1876, which would be approximately 12 percent of the population. Hazel E. Rosenstrauch, "Zum Beispiel *Die Gartenlaube*," in Anamarie Rucktäschl and Hans Dieter Zimmermann (eds.), *Trivialliteratur* (Munich: Fink, 1976), 169–89. Rolf Engelsing is a bit more conservative, suggesting the magazine reached at least two million readers, or about 5 percent of the German population over a period of ten years. See Engelsing, *Analphabetentum*, 119.

64. *Time* publishers published a study conducted for *Life* magazine in 1950, apparently to convince potential advertisers that the scope of *Life*'s contact to American readers was larger than reflected by the circulation of any given issue. See *A Study of the Accumulative Audience of Life* (New York: Time, 1950). The demographic agency of Alfred Politz Research, Inc., argued that even if only 20.3 percent of their sample (and the national population) read one issue of *Life*, 53.1 percent read any one of thirteen issues (*Study*, 20). This kind of presumed increase, calculated as it was for the magazine itself, should be viewed with some skepticism. Yet, it does make an important point that different issues of a periodical might be read by different individuals.

65. Joachim Kirchner, *Das deutsche Zeitschriftenwesen*, 2:228. *Daheim*'s publisher, August Klasing, saw his magazine as a "Christian *Gartenlaube*" (Barth, *Zeitschrift für Alle*, 345).

66. The *Österreichische Gartenlaube: Organ für Familie und Volk, Freiheit und Fortschritt* was published in Graz. Its inability to copy the original's

success is evident from the fact it only existed from 1866 to 1869. An *Amerikanische Gartenlaube* was also founded in New York in 1864. See Joachim Kirchner, *Das deutsche Zeitschriftenwesen*, 2:227.

67. Rolf Engelsing cites the overwhelming and consistent popularity of the *Gartenlaube* as far away as Bremen. See Engelsing, "Zeitschrift in Nordwestdeutschland," 937–1036. Engelsing contends that regional and local entertainment magazines could not compete with national publications like the *Gartenlaube*. Engelsing, "Zeitschrift in Nordwestdeutschland," 992.

68. "Die *Gartenlaube* wird in allen Winkeln der entdeckten Erde, in Amerika, Afrika, Australien, selbst im inneren Asien und in Nordsibirien gelesen, soweit eben auch dort die deutsche Zunge klingt" (*Gartenlaube* 1866: 90). See also Ulla Wischermann, *Frauenfrage und Presse: Frauenarbeit und Frauenbewegung in der illustrierten Presse des 19. Jahrhunderts* (Munich: Saur, 1983), 183. The issue of a geographical nation that includes Germans throughout the world is the focus of chapter 2.

69. Its standard fare included writing of general interest: serialized fiction, poetry, biographical sketches of cultural and political figures, and essays that popularized scientific knowledge and technological innovations. It featured essays on animal life, geography, and the cultures of various peoples.

70. Kirchstein, *Die Familienzeitschrift*, 74.

71. Kirchstein, *Die Familienzeitschrift*, 77–78.

72. Examples of specialized journals come from a diversity of fields, such as legal scholarship, pedagogy, theology, medicine, technology, political and economic associations, military concerns, philosophy, philology, historiography, music and the arts, and publishing, among others. For a detailed summary of such *Fachzeitschriften* in Germany in the nineteenth century see Joachim Kirchner, *Das deutsche Zeitschriftenwesen*, vol. 2. Kirchner's study is broken down by historical period according to key political dates. It covers the years 1816–30, 1831–50, 1851–70, and 1871–1900.

73. See Kirchstein, *Die Familienzeitschrift*, 82.

74. Part 4 of Keil's outline for the magazine revealed his concern to achieve simplicity yet avoid a condescending tone: "Diese belehrenden Briefe dürfen indes durchaus keinen schulmeisterlichen Anstrich haben, sondern müssen durchweg leicht verständlich, elegant, womöglich in novellister [!] Form geschrieben werden, so daß sie die gewöhnlichsten Handwerker, besonders aber die Frauen verstehen können." Quoted in Kirchstein, *Die Familienzeitschrift*, 82–83.

75. Kirchstein, *Die Familienzeitschrift*, 97.

76. Numerous reports on Schulze-Delitzsch appeared in the 1860s and

'70s. An early one from 1863 introduced him as "Ein Freund der deutschen Arbeiter" (*Gartenlaube* 1863: 517). Other essays appeared in *Gartenlaube* 1856: 295; 1859: 580, 719; 1860: 366; 1861: 752; 1862: 206; 1863: 704, 735; 1864: 104; 1866: 240; 1867: 254; 1868: 766; 1869: 103; 1874: 292, 586; 1879: 808.

77. Barth reports an average yearly subscription cost of 6 Marks for family magazines from 1850 to 1870. This was the annual subscription rate for the *Gartenlaube* in 1860. Additional fees were charged for postal delivery. Barth, *Zeitschrift für Alle*, 100–101.

78. In Oldenburg, in 1859, of 1,013 apolitical magazines, individual copies of the *Gartenlaube* were the most numerous. Engelsing, "Zeitschrift in Nordwestdeutschland," 1009.

79. Engelsing, "Zeitschrift in Nordwestdeutschland," 1023–24.

80. One passage Wischermann cites is from M. Wegrainer, *Der Lebensroman einer Arbeiterfrau von ihr selbst geschrieben*, published in Frankfurt in 1979, on page 26: "Die Mutter war vierundsechzig Jahre alt. Sie hatte nie ein lesenswertes Buch gelesen, nur hin und wieder eine Romanfortsetzung in 'Fels zum Meer' oder der 'Gartenlaube,' wenn zufällig eine alte Nummer in die Wohnung geraten oder eine Seite vom Metzger als Einwickelpapier benutzt worden war." See Wischermann, *Frauenfrage und Presse*, 27.

81. This was the beginning of what researchers since have called the high point ("Blütezeit") of the magazine, 1860–75. Kirschstein, *Die Familienzeitschrift*, 94.

82. The year 1861 is a good sample year to consider the *Gartenlaube*'s presentation of German material about German life for its readers. In this year there were no national wars or major crises that skewed the representational percentages of topics.

83. The average length of a weekly issue in this year (as for most issues throughout the 1860s) was 16 pages. The total page count for the year 1861 was 832.

84. The second article of the year 1861 was a commemoration of the German popular struggle in the Wars of Liberation against Napoleon. Pages four through eight tell the story of "Eleven Blood Witnesses of German Freedom," members of the patriotic Schill Freecorps who were executed outside of Wesel in 1809, and they include a heroic image of a brave youth defiantly standing up in a hail of French bullets (*Gartenlaube* 1861: 4–8).

85. "Aus den Zeiten der schweren Noth."

86. The *Gartenlaube* published eleven different contributions about

Germany's defeat by Napoleon and on the Wars of Liberation in 1861. Two of these were split into two articles, meaning that there was an average of one article on this topic alone every four weeks.

87. "Born schwieg. In ihm stürmte und wogte es. Er dürfte nicht zum Verräther werden! . . . Mit gefesselten Händen wurde er an den Abhang der Anhöhe geführt. Vor seinen Augen luden drei Soldaten ihre Gewehre, er wandte sich ab. Eine halbe Stunde Zeit war ihm noch vergönnt, sich zu besinnen. Schweigend setzte er sich nieder und richtete den Blick starr in das Thal und auf die fernen Berghöhen. Seine Wangen waren bleich. Welche Gefühle mußten in ihm vorgehen!—eine Thräne trat in sein Auge—er drängte sie zurück."

88. In a vein similar to the tone of the essays in the years 1806–13, the magazine published four extensive articles about the German national struggle against Denmark for Schleswig (*Gartenlaube* 1861: 137, 568, 664, 712).

89. The fact that serialized fiction might have appealed more to women readers and illustrations to younger members of the family will be discussed in more detail in chapter 5. Indeed, the interest of younger readers in the illustrations might be supported by the fact that in one copy of the *Gartenlaube* from 1861 that I viewed, several illustrations, including mastheads, had been used as a coloring book (of course, it is impossible to know when this coloring took place).

90. "Aus dem Jammer und der Schande der bonapartischen Herrschaft erwuchs dem jungen Manne die fromme, treue Liebe zum Vaterlande."

91. The contextual importance of these essays is strong. In the next issue, the *Gartenlaube* ran an ad for the *Deutsche Turn-Zeitung*, proclaiming that it was not a party paper, but rather a "Sprechsaal" for all who were interested in gymnastics (1861: 560).

92. See 1862, "Das erste deutsche Bundesschießen in Frankfurt a. M.," 441, 477, 492, 521, 542; "Die deutsche Turnmacht," 781; "Bauern-Sänger-fest," 644. For 1863, "Turnfest in Leipzig," 348, 476, 588, 603; "Der deutsche Schützenzug nach La Chaux de Fonds," 509, 519.

93. "[F]ür die Prosperität eines Familienblattes [war] eine der Redaktion obliegende Wendigkeit, sich den Bedürfnissen der Leserschaft anzupassen, d. h. für einen ihr zusagenden Lesestoff Sorge zu tragen" (Joachim Kirchner, "Redaktion und Publikum," 467). "Von allen deutschen Journalisten ist Keil derjenige, der sich auf den 'Kundendiest' an Käufer und Abonnent glänzend wie keiner zuvor verstand" (Wilmont Haacke, *Feuilletonkunde* [Leipzig: Hiersemann, 1943], 1:129). Hans-Martin Kirchner contends that scholars are in the dark with respect to the popularity of the *Gartenlaube*

over a similar magazine like its mother paper, *Der illustrirte Dorfbarbier*: "Wir tappen in der Finsternis, wenn wir erfahren wollen, warum dieselbe Redaktion und derselbe Verleger mit einer Zeitschrift, die Gartenlaube hieß, einen Massenerfolg erzielte, während er mit dem Illustrirten Dorfbarbier über Achtungserfolge nicht hinauskam." See Hans-Martin Kirchner, "Wirtschaftliche," 465.

94. "Stärker als die meisten anderen Medien der Kommunikation hat die Zeitschrift das Recht, ihren Leser in jeder Ausgabe wie einen guten Bekannten zu begrüßen. Wie spricht die ideale Zeitschrift den Menschen an? Ohne aufdringlich zu wirken, duzt sie ihn." Wilmont Haacke, *Die Zeitschrift—Schrift der Zeit* (Essen: Stamm-Verlag, 1961), 14.

95. Haacke, *Zeitschrift*, 32.

96. This interest in the nation did not exclude criticisms of current practices. The national gambling craze was one phenomenon that attracted the close scrutiny of the *Gartenlaube*. See, especially, the years 1861 and 1862.

97. Engelsing, *Massenpublikum*, 27–29.

2. PLOTTING A NATIONAL GEOGRAPHY

1. According to the first biographer of Ernst Keil and reviewer of Keil's career in publishing, this "letter from an emigrant" was written by Keil himself (Feißkohl, *Ernst Keil*, 71). If Feißkohl's surmise about Keil's authorship is correct, this practice was not without precedent. It was a common convention for the eighteenth-century moral weeklies to be composed entirely by one author. See Lindemann, *Die deutsche Presse*, 1:236.

2. For interesting discussions of the term "Heimat" see Celia Applegate, *A Nation of Provincials: The German Idea of Heimat* (Berkeley: U of California P, 1990), and Alon Confino, "The Nation as a Local Metaphor: Heimat, National Memory and the German Empire, 1871–1918," *History and Memory* 5 (spring/summer 1993): 42–86.

3. For discussions of the Holy Roman Empire of the German Nation in the context of the history of German national identity see Otto Dann, *Nation und Nationalismus in Deutschland, 1770–1990* (Munich: Beck, 1993), 28–36, and Michael Hughes, "Fiat Justitia, Pereat Germania? The Imperial Supreme Jurisdiction and Imperial Reform in the Later Holy Roman Empire," in John Breuilly (ed.), *The State of Germany: The National Idea in the Making, Unmaking, and Remaking of a Modern Nation-State* (New York: Longman, 1992), 29–46.

4. Harold James, *A German Identity, 1770–1990* (London: Weidenfeld and Nicolson, 1989), 10–11. James proposes that economics was at the root of

the development of "a German identity" over the course of the last two centuries. His conclusion, based on this thesis, is "that we should put our faith in something other than economics or economic success" (4).

5. Wolfgang Hartwig provides a detailed list of the cultural organizations and groups that were strong proponents of upholding and maintaining a German cultural heritage. These included the language societies (*Sprachgesellschaften*) founded in the seventeenth century as well as academic circles of the eighteenth century. Wolfgang Hartwig, "Vom Elitebewußtsein zur Massenbewegung: Frühformen des Nationalismus in Deutschland, 1500–1840," in Hartwig, *Nationalismus und Bürgerkultur in Deutschland, 1500–1914* (Göttingen: Vandenhoeck and Ruprecht, 1994), 34–54.

6. Moser published an anonymous pamphlet entitled "Von dem deutschen Nationalgeist" ("On the German National Spirit") in 1765. Lessing was concerned with the generation of a national German theater.

7. It is worth noting that Herder and many subsequent national thinkers used the German terms "people" ("*Volk*") and "nation" ("*Nation*") interchangeably.

8. Although he adamantly rejected the notion of various human races, characterizing all of humankind as biologically one, Herder did seek to explain the differences among peoples.

9. Johann Gottfried Herder, book 7, xiii, 258–65. In *Johann Gottfried Herder on Social and Political Culture*, trans. and ed. F. M. Barnard (Cambridge: Cambridge UP, 1969), 285.

10. Johann Gottfried Herder, *Sämtliche Werke* 13:37–38; cf. 14:92–93. See also Carleton Hayes, "Herder and the Doctrine of Nationalism," *American Historical Review* 32 (July 1927): 723.

11. See Hayes, "Herder," 724.

12. Hayes, "Herder," 726.

13. Johann Gottlieb Fichte, *Addresses to the German Nation* (New York: Harper and Row, 968), 129.

14. See Dann, *Nation and Nationalismus*, 51–72. This familiar argument is summarized in Greenfeld, *Nationalism*, 360–71.

15. A synopsis of Jahn's text in English can be found in Louis L. Snyder (ed.), *Documents of German History* (New Brunswick: Rutgers UP, 1958), 137–43.

16. A complete English translation of Arndt's poem can be found in Snyder, *Documents*, 144–46.

17. This characterization clearly included German Austrians in the idea of the German nation. See Peter Alter, *Nationalismus* (Frankfurt: Suhrkamp, 1985), 107. Alter points out that this conception of a Greater Germany

(*Großdeutschland*) was still prevalent among the large majority of German nationalists in the 1830s and 1840s. Other authors of the 1840s, such as Max Schneckenberger and Nikolaus Becker, wrote in more explicitly chauvinistic tones about a geographical centering of Germany. Their impassioned lyrics about defending the Rhine River as German made no attempt to hide an anti-French aspect of defining the nation. In the context of their time, however, these songs were all tied to the predominantly liberal goal of establishing a unified German nation-state based on liberal principles and often with little concern for the authority of existing German kingdoms and principalities.

18. The phrase "aus dem engeren Vaterland" appeared repeatedly in the magazine and designated one of the German lands, that is, Bavaria or Saxony. By using this term, the magazine could incorporate regional patriotism into the love of the larger "fatherland." Such instances of using regional *Heimat* identification to forge a national consciousness substantially predate the material cited by Confino (Confino, "Nation").

19. An essay entitled "Ein thüringisches Volksfest" was not accompanied by a picture (*Gartenlaube* 1855: 54–55).

20. As we will see in other contexts, this practice of writing in the first-person plural was common in *Gartenlaube* essays. By indicating its national component here, I do not mean to suggest that it was always intended to include all Germans. However, its very function was always to include the reading subject in the activities or attitudes of the narrating subject, be it taking in a vista: "Blicken wir wieder einmal um uns, wie wir dem Ende des Bollwerks schon nahe gelangen, so gewähren uns beide Ufer des stattlichen Stromes, . . . einen höchst mannigfaltigen Anblick" (1855: 574), or implying common cultural mores such as the one above concerning belching in public. The likelihood that there was a clear class-identification at work in such cultural generalizations (whether or not they were accurate) cannot be overlooked. Prohibitions against belching might easily have been limited to an urban German middle- and upper-middle-class sensibility.

21. Frederick Jackson Turner, "The Significance of the Frontier in American History," in Turner, *The Frontier in American History* (1920; reprint, New York: Henry Holt, 1945), 3.

22. Cultural geography, as a subdiscipline, has become more concerned with the symbolic qualities of landscapes and the social and political meanings they acquire rather than descriptive morphologies. Dennis Rumley and Julian V. Mingh, "Introduction," in Rumley and Mingh (eds.), *The Geography of Border Landscapes* (London: Routledge, 1991), 4.

23. Alter, *Nationalismus*, 107–12.

24. See Thomas Nipperdey, *Deutsche Geschichte, 1800–1866* (Munich: Beck, 1983), 770–76, and Wolfgang J. Mommsen, *Das Ringen um den Nationalstaat: Die Gründung und der innere Ausbau des Deutschen Reiches unter Otto von Bismarck 1850 bis 1890* (Berlin: Propyläen, 1993), 154–63.

25. "Ein Besuch in Rendsburg" (*Gartenlaube* 1864: 75–78); "Von Rendsburg nach Schleswig" (*Gartenlaube* 1864: 142–43); "Von Schleswig nach Rendsburg und meine Gefangennahme bei den Preußen" (*Gartenlaube* 1864: 157–59); "Von Schleswig nach Missunde" (*Gartenlaube* 1864: 187–90); "Schloß Gottorp" (*Gartenlaube* 1864: 204–6); and "Ein Brief unseres Specialartisten" (*Gartenlaube* 1864: 220–22). The essay that immediately preceded "Schloß Gottorp" reveals how this anti-Danish sentiment spilled over into other articles; this one (*Gartenlaube* 1864: 201–3) was entitled "Eine Erinnerung an die Deutsche Flotte" and closed with the exclamations "Pereant die Dänen!" and "Hoch Deutschland zur See!"

26. "Der neue Herzog von Schleswig-Holstein" (*Gartenlaube* 1863: 793–95); "Schleswigscher Bauer" (*Gartenlaube* 1863: 809–13); "Schleswig-Holsteinsche Gräber" (*Gartenlaube* 1863: 813); "Die Schlacht bei Idstedt" (*Gartenlaube* 1860: 616); and "Die Frau Kriegsministerin—Eine Butterpatrouille" (*Gartenlaube* 1863: 62–64). Memories from previous battles in 1850 include "Ein Soldaten-Diner" (*Gartenlaube* 1861: 137); "Der Lurbaß" (*Gartenlaube* 1861: 568); "Der alte Torfbauer" (*Gartenlaube* 1862: 53); and "Tann'sche Freischaaren in dem Gefechte bei Hoptrup" (*Gartenlaube* 1862: 181).

27. "Die Bauern in Angeln" (*Gartenlaube* 1861: 664–66); "Ein deutscher Märtyrer in Schleswig" (*Gartenlaube* 1861: 712); "Das danisirte Irrenhaus" (*Gartenlaube* 1862: 24); "Der Märtyrer von Oland" (*Gartenlaube* 1862: 149); "Die danisirte Domschule" (*Gartenlaube* 1862: 393); "Ein schleswig'scher Edelmann" (*Gartenlaube* 1862: 825–28).

28. "In einer lothring'scher Weinschenke" (*Gartenlaube* 1872: 173); "Auf dem Ottilienberg" (*Gartenlaube* 1872: 322).

29. "Das Elsaß, seine Spiele und Tänze" (*Gartenlaube* 1874: 373–76); "Pancratius Sanitabringius im Elsaß" (*Gartenlaube* 1874: 574–78); "Familienfeste im Elsaß" (*Gartenlaube* 1874: 658–62); "Sankt Petrus in Elsaß-Lothringen" (*Gartenlaube* 1875: 423); and "Die Seebacher Bauer im Elsaß" (*Gartenlaube* 1876: 704).

30. Between 1870 and early 1872 the *Gartenlaube* published 142 illustrations of the war alone. The pages of text outnumbered this significantly.

31. At the end of the series, the author emphasizes the usefulness of illustrations to explain regional culture: "Wenn obige Bilder, die mein Freund Pixis durch die drei hier veröffentlichten prächtigen, wahrheitsgetreuen

Zeichnungen illustrirt hat, Anklang gefunden haben sollte, überlasse ich die Schilderung des Meßti oder der Kirchweih, der Majstuben und anderer originellen Gebräuche im lieben Elsaß einer späteren Mußezeit und scheide mit freundlichen Grüßen aus dem schönen Elsaß von dem freundlichen Leser. August Jäger" (*Gartenlaube* 1872: 662).

32. For a succinct discussion of the various positions around 1848 see Dieter Langewiesche, "Germany and the National Question in 1848," in Breuilly, *The State of Germany*, esp. 73–77.

33. Langewiesche, "Germany and the National Question," 75.

34. For a discussion of the numerous political, social, and economic factors in favor of the smaller German solution see William Carr, "The Unification of Germany," in Breuilly, *The State of Germany*, 80–102.

35. Four articles were published, one each in 1881, 1882, 1883, and 1884.

36. This prevalence lends strong support to Anthony Smith's work on ethnic identity as the foundation for a national identity. See Anthony D. Smith, *National Identity*, and Anthony D. Smith, *The Ethnic Origins of Nations*.

37. *Gartenlaube* 1866: 90. See also Wischermann, *Frauenfrage und Presse*, 183.

38. Historians of other cultures have insisted on alternative definitions of the nation (other than that of space). The history of the Jewish people or the centuries of African enslavement and displacement have required scholars of those groups to consider the notion of a people in diaspora. One result has been the creative notion of a temporal rather than a spacial nation, the discussion of communities in time rather than space. Although the "nation in time" is more applicable to the diasporas of Jewish and African peoples, it might also be useful for a discussion of what national identity meant to Europeans who left their homelands (voluntarily or due to financial pressure or incentives) to begin new lives on distant continents.

39. For a discussion of nineteenth-century emigration in the context of Germany's population as a whole see Peter Marschalck, *Bevölkerungsgeschichte Deutschlands im 19. und 20. Jahrhundert* (Frankfurt: Suhrkamp, 1984), 45–48.

40. For a history of German emigration see Klaus J. Bade, "Die deutsche überseeische Massenauswanderung im 19. und 20. Jahrhundert: Bestimmungsfaktoren und Entwicklungbedingungen," in Klaus J. Bade (ed.), *Auswanderer—Wanderarbeiter—Gastarbeiter: Bevölkerung, Arbeitsmarkt und Wanderung in Deutschland seit der Mitte des 19. Jahrhunderts* (Ostfildern: Scripta Mercaturae, 1984), 1:259–99.

41. Many of the notices about conditions for German emigrants in spe-

cific countries ended with an appeal to other publications, such as daily papers, to print the same information and thus disseminate it as far as possible. An extensive essay by Friedrich Gerstäcker gave the unusual permission for reproduction, something that was often explicitly proscribed by the magazine.

42. The ships that drop them off "würden nichts weiter thun, als ein dem Mutterlande verlorenes Element an jenen Südgestaden absetzen, damit es sich brasilianisire, d. h. als Dünger für eine Mischlingsrace diene, der es versagt ist, jemals eine erhebliche Rolle in dem großen Völkerdrama zu übernehmen."

43. *Gartenlaube* 1863: 361–64. "Die brasilianische Regierung begünstigt deutsche Einwanderung" (1862: 456).

44. In places where Germans had settled, the most pressing concern of the media was generally how the Germans had fared. Thus, we find an essay devoted to the Native American attack on the city of New Ulm, Minnesota, because it was a predominantly German settlement. The "sad news" offers the *Gartenlaube* the opportunity to devote a long essay of four pages (an eyewitness account) to a detailed description of the German settlement's defense and ultimate loss of their town (1863: 743–47). The enlightened interest in the other residents of that area took a distant backseat to this national concern.

45. According to Klaus J. Bade, 89 percent of German emigration between 1847 and 1914 was to the United States and only 2 percent was to Brazil (Bade, "Massenauswanderung," 270).

46. This essay, published at the end of the year 1879, just in time for Christmas, couched the description of his time in Brazil as a series of Christmas vignettes (*Gartenlaube* 1879: 848–52).

47. "Drüben im Lande der Palmen feiert man auch Weihnachten, aber das ist nur ein schwacher Abglanz der Weihnachtslust, welche hier von Jung und Alt empfunden wird" (*Gartenlaube* 1879: 848).

48. "Ich sitt so verlatten, so trurig, allen / Wo de Palmenbom ragt in dat Land" (*Gartenlaube* 1879: 851–52).

49. "Die Schätze, welche die unermeßlichen Wälder an den Ufern jener Riesenströme des Amazonas, Orinoco und Parana heute noch bergen, und wodurch unserer Industrie ganz neue Materialien an prächtigen Hölzern, textilen Fasern, Farbstoffen, Harzen, Oelen, unserer Heilkunde neue Arzneimittel an die Hand gegeben werden könnten, die Aufschlüsse, welche den Naturwissenschaften aus einem eingehenderen Studium wenig bekannter Thierformen erwachsen würden" (*Gartenlaube* 1875: 478).

50. Mary Louise Pratt, *Imperial Eyes: Travel Writing and Transculturation* (London: Routledge, 1992).

51. Pratt, *Imperial Eyes*, 15–37.

52. Indeed, the author even exhorts his audience to visit this wonderful, exotic, "uncharted" Brazil, that is, this terrain even becomes the ideal space (material) for tourism (*Gartenlaube* 1875: 479).

53. "Ein Straßenbau und die Anlage einer deutschen Colonie in Brasilien. II" by F. Keller-Leuzinger (*Gartenlaube* 1884: 299–301).

54. Keller-Leuzinger proclaims that German engineers, "welche die große Arbeit im Laufe von sieben Jahren glücklich zu Ende führten," had been called in to construct the road after the French had proved incapable at the task (*Gartenlaube* 1884: 299).

55. A similar argument has been made about the place and operation of the magazine *National Geographic* for the construction of national identity in the United States. See Lutz and Collins, *Reading National Geographic*.

3. IN DEFENSE OF THE NATION

1. See Hobsbawm, "Introduction: Inventing Traditions," 1–14.

2. "Wer mit Aufmerksamkeit dem in neuerer Zeit so rege gewordenen Streben nach Verbesserung in der Landwirthschaft gefolgt ist, wird erfahren haben, wie sehr vor nicht zu langer Zeit unsere deutschen Feldbauer, an dem Althergebrachten hängend, noch zurück waren gegen die anderer Länder" (*Gartenlaube* 1853: 94). The fact that this article on the "Dampf-Grabe-Maschine" was one of the *Gartenlaube*'s very first contributions shows how technology from the start was a defining factor for the nation.

3. The temporal delay came from the fact that the production of an issue of the magazine like the *Gartenlaube* took approximately three weeks.

4. The use of technology to establish identity was not uncommon in the nineteenth century. Michael Adas cites a wealth of information that reveals the European attitude of superiority over and against other non-Western, non-European peoples in the age of industrialization. This sense of superiority was affirmed for those contemporaries by the technological advances that they claimed had their source in Europe (Michael Adas, *Machines as the Measure of Men: Science, Technology, and Ideologies of Western Dominance* [Ithaca: Cornell UP, 1989]). We will turn to the issue of European assessment of the colonial world when we talk about the 1890s in the *Gartenlaube*. For the moment let us take note of the fact that technological innovation was also used by nineteenth-century writers to assert the superiority of a

particular European nation over all others. For an instance of this see A. H. Keane, *The World's Peoples*, published in 1908 and cited in Adas, *Machines as the Measure of Men*, 150.

5. For a brief history of the German movement to secure the coasts with boats and rocket-launched lines see the essay by Christian Ostersehlte, "Die 'Deutsche Gesellschaft zur Rettung Schiffbrüchiger,'" in Volker Plagemann (ed.), *Übersee: Seefahrt und Seemacht im Deutschen Kaiserreich* (Munich: Beck, 1988), 96–98.

6. This was the description of the historical situation in the *Gartenlaube* (1866: 313).

7. For instance, in the year 1865 there was a total of ten articles in the *Gartenlaube* on the sea, innovations for use at sea, and storms at sea. It is interesting to note that in its desire to present this issue, the *Gartenlaube* even repeated the use of an image: in 1865 on page 357 the same picture appeared as in the first article (1861: 812). See also the section on Wilhelm Bauer below.

8. The number of articles in the *Gartenlaube* would support the same conclusions.

9. Many of these articles gained the tone of authority since they were written by a ship captain named Werner. His first essay was about the new "rescue boat" (*Gartenlaube* 1864: 252–55). This was followed up in the next week by "more about the rescue boat" and the promise to inform the reading audience about the history of the rescue organization (*Gartenlaube* 1864: 287–88).

10. Two direct appeals to the readership to support the rescue organization were made in issues 22 and 24. These appeals were kept in front of the reader in the next half year by the frequent listing of contributions. Four other articles by the same ship captain Werner about the life and dangers on a seagoing vessel appeared throughout the year.

11. It has been pointed out that *Daheim* began as a conservative and religious competitor to the *Gartenlaube*. See Barth, "Das Daheim und sein Verleger August Klasing," *Jahresbericht des Historischen Vereins für die Grafschaft Ravensburg* 66 (1968/69): 47. Yet, the fact that *Daheim* clearly modeled itself after the most successful illustrated magazine of the time suggests that it hoped to emulate the *Gartenlaube*'s success, which was already substantial by the early 1860s. In the eyes of the public this popularity was clear; readers wrote to the *Gartenlaube* in the 1860s with requests to find individuals (such as a wounded soldier of the 1866 war, or an heir of a German-Australian who had died, leaving behind a small fortune) because, as one

wrote, it was "the most widely distributed German magazine anywhere" (*Gartenlaube* 1867: 288).

12. *Daheim* 1864: 40.

13. *Daheim* 1864: 56.

14. *Daheim* 1864: 255.

15. *Daheim* 1864: 288.

16. *Daheim* 1864: 305.

17. One example of how the magazine casually kept the issue in front of its readers was the inclusion of a map published in 1865 that identified all the ship strandings on the Prussian Baltic coast in the previous eight years (from 1857 to 1864). This was meant to outline the magnitude of the national problem for the readers (*Daheim* 1865: 517).

18. *Daheim* 1865: 429–30.

19. "In dieser Beziehung hat die Technik in der Neuzeit die wichtigsten Verbesserungen geschaffen und um glückliche Erfolge zu erzielen, müssen deshalb neue Boote beschafft werden" (*Daheim* 1865: 429).

20. *Daheim* 1865: 430.

21. *Daheim* 1865: 430.

22. "Das Boot 'Daheim' ist das erste Francisboot, auf das jenes Princip angewandt wurde und obwohl der Versuch zuerst viele Gegner fand, so haben die angestellten Proben sein vollständiges Gelingen dargelegt und höchstwahrscheinlich werden fortan alle Rettungsboote an unserer Küste in dieser Weise gebaut" (*Daheim* 1865: 760).

23. *Gartenlaube* 1868: 501–2; and *Illustrirte Zeitung* 1866: 214.

24. See *Daheim* 1865: 620–22, 651; and *Gartenlaube* 1861: 654, 696; 1864: 334; 1871: 874.

25. *Daheim* 1878, no. 46; 1882, no. 28; and *Gartenlaube* 1872: 259; 1879: 559; 1880: 60.

26. See *Daheim* 1871, no. 31; 1875, no. 40; 1881, nos. 11, 45; 1887, no. 51; 1888, no. 18; 1889, no. 49; and *Gartenlaube* articles on the "Flotte": 1861: 654, 696; 1864: 334; 1877: 626; 1881: 751; 1884: 518; 1890: 692; 1893: 240; 1897: 213; 1900: 412.

27. Anne Norton argues that the liminal role of such figures as the Arab Bedouin and the American cowboy makes them useful as representatives of the larger culture (Norton, *Reflections on Political Identity*, 57–62). Another general source for nationwide concern with the coast would have been the wave of emigration from Germany overseas mentioned in chapter 2. However, most of the incidents reported in these essays discussing rescue devices involved ships attempting to land in Germany and not those departing.

28. The centerpiece of all of these programmatic articles on Bauer was statistics, just as had been the case with the devices of warfare and strategies for defending the public's safety. Numbers identified the value of material lost in shipwrecks, the amount of equipment needed to lift a sunken vessel, the square pounds of pressure required to fill the balloons ("underwater camels") used in Bauer's process, the amount of money that these innovations (which only seem to be expensive) would save a government, and so on. "Wer die Summen beachtet, . . . der wird einer 'Neuerung' nicht abhold sein, die auch in diesem Punkte eine bedeutende Ersparniß oder wenigstens eine zweckmäßigere Verwendung der Staatsgelder möglich macht" (*Gartenlaube* 1862: 567). Each page was loaded with such statistics again emphasizing and celebrating the magnitude of the project to be accomplished and thus defining it as a national agenda. "Daß es sich der Mühe lohnt, diesen Zweig der Industrie einer möglichsten Ausbildung zuzuführen, darüber belehren uns die jährlichen Berichte über die Hunderte von Schiffbrüchen, die Tausende von verlorenen Menschenleben und die Millionen von Werthverlusten" (*Gartenlaube* 1862: 58).

29. The magazine's plea to its readers (the German *Volk*) for more involvement was in keeping with this advocacy in the place of the state. See *Gartenlaube* 1862: 463.

30. Adas, *Machines as the Measure of Men*, 365–80.

31. In the year 1866, issue numbers 29 and 30 of the *Gartenlaube* each devoted 9 of 15 pages to the war between Prussia and Austria. Over the course of eight weeks, beginning with the second week of July, the magazine covered the war and related issues in 57 of its 135 pages. *Daheim* spent a longer period on the war, from the second week of July through September 1866 it devoted 74 of a total of 156 pages to the conflict.

32. This article explained that the apparatus used to load the horses was called the "Hessian ram" because it was first used by the Prussians in 1862 to move horses into Hessia (*Gartenlaube* 1866: 428).

33. *Illustrirte Zeitung* 1866: 428.

34. An article in *Daheim* in 1866 warns its readers at the outset of the "horror" that will follow in the war reportage: "Und nun, Leser, bereite dich vor, ich will dir ein Schauspiel zeigen, das du nie zu träumen gewagt. . . . Schauer und Nacht werden deine Seele mit Grausen und Jammer erfüllen!" (*Daheim* 1866: 648). This report then tells the story of a Bavarian soldier who had been shot through both eyes (*Daheim* 1866: 648–51). Likewise, the *Gartenlaube* published gruesome summaries of soldiers' conditions in the field hospitals. One report described how doctors worked "von Abend die Nacht hindurch die schwersten Verwundungen in

Masse zu untersuchen und zu verbinden, fortwährend Amputationen an Armen und Beinen vorzunehmen, Sterbende und Todte von Lebenden zu scheiden, im Blute förmlich zu waten und zu baden" (*Gartenlaube* 1866: 445).

35. *Daheim*'s front page proclaiming "Peace!" (in September 1866) summarized the damage to "almost every family in the German fatherland" with the assertion: "es gilt vor allem die Versöhnung der entzweiten Stämme" (*Daheim* 1866: 761).

36. In the twentieth century as well, technological progress and individual inventions have frequently been identified with the strength of the nation and national enthusiasm. Peter Fritzsche's book, *A Nation of Fliers*, explores both the German fascination with developing flight technology and in particular the popular national fervor that developments in the field of aviation encouraged (Peter Fritzsche, *A Nation of Fliers: German Aviation and the Popular Imagination* [Cambridge: Harvard UP, 1992]). Fritzsche's book begins with Graf Zeppelin's experiments around 1900 and thus deals exclusively with the twentieth century. Fritzsche contends that the activities that surrounded aviation in the twentieth century helped establish a national sense of self by erasing class boundaries and emphasizing the communal and cooperative.

37. "Was inzwischen aus der Krupp'schen Werkstatt und aus dem immer noch erfinderischen Kopfe des Zündnadelgewehr-Helden in Sömmerda hervorgehen wird, das kann man freilich nicht wissen. Jedenfalls dürfte England noch lange Zeit brauchen, ehe es den Einen und den Andern erreicht" (*Gartenlaube* 1866: 821).

38. The historian Eugen Weber has discussed convincingly how innovation and technology contributed to the French national sense of self in the late nineteenth century. In his discussion of the impact of roads, the railway, and industry on the development of the nation, Weber concluded, "There could be no national unity before there was national circulation. . . . So roads, of stone or steel, welded the several parts into one." Eugen Weber, *Peasants into Frenchmen: The Modernization of Rural France, 1870–1914* (Stanford: Stanford UP, 1976), 218.

4. SPECTACLE FOR THE MASSES

1. Guy Debord, *Society of the Spectacle* (Detroit: Black and Red, 1983), paragraph 24.

2. Debord, *Spectacle*, paragraph 173.

3. See, for example, his discussion of the participation of local and

national organizations in the construction of the Niederwald monument. Lutz Tittel, *Das Niederwalddenkmal: 1871–1883* (Hildesheim: Gerstenberg, 1979).

4. Thomas Nipperdey, "Nationalidee und Nationaldenkmal in Deutschland im 19. Jahrhundert," *Historische Zeitschrift* 206 (1968): 529–85. Although he advises against drawing parallels between styles in the monuments and specific political significance, Nipperdey outlines a series of typological attributions that are based on a combination of thematic and formal aspects of the monuments. Yet, in presenting a typology of national structures from the nineteenth century, Nipperdey allows for what he calls an unevenness or irregularity of artistic development.

5. Mosse, *Nationalization of the Masses*. Mosse's attention to the use of these structures has inspired similar investigations of folk culture in the national context. See Peter Sprengel, "Die inszenierte Nation: Festspiele der Kaiserzeit," *Germanisch-Romanische Monatsschrift* 40 (1990): 257–78.

6. See Tittel, *Das Niederwalddenkmal*; Georg Nockemann, *Hermannsdenkmal* (Lemgo: Wagener, 1975); Hans Schmidt, *Das Hermannsdenkmal im Spiegel der Welt* (Detmold: Hermann Bösmann, n.d.).

7. Using local documents from the city of Detmold, Hans Schmidt estimates that the annual number of visitors to the *Hermannsdenkmal* averaged between 1,500 and 1,800 from 1875 to 1880, and about 2,000 for 1890. After Detmold acquired a train station the number skyrocketed to 20,500 in 1895, and 41,000 by 1909 (Schmidt, *Das Hermannsdenkmal*, 42–43). According to these statistics, very few Germans were able to visit the monument in the first two decades of its existence.

8. The term is Nipperdey's, from his "Nationalidee," 551–59. The *Gartenlaube* discussed monuments in honor of Goethe and Schiller (1857), Kant (1858), Luther (1861, 1867, 1868), Carl Maria von Weber (1862), Schiller alone (1863), Gellert (1865), and Hans Sachs (1868).

9. In the *Gartenlaube*, in 1861, 1863, and 1868, respectively.

10. The magazine pursued some continuity in celebrating older liberal heroes by promoting the statues for Jahn (1872) and Waldeck (1876).

11. Gruppe provides a convincing chronology of the magazine's political tendencies (Gruppe, *"Volk"*, 24). This chronological approach governs her entire investigation of politics in the *Gartenlaube* in the nineteenth century. She distinguishes between the traditional liberalism of the period 1853–70, the national-liberalism of the period 1871–78, and the general conservative position after Keil's death in 1878 and continuing until 1900.

12. These monuments were discussed and depicted on pages 48–50, 311–16, and 441–45, respectively. The *Hermannsdenkmal* in the Teutoburg

Forest was planned as early as the 1830s, begun in the 1840s, and even discussed in the pages of the *Gartenlaube* in the 1850s and 1860s, but only in the context of the new *Kaiserreich* did it receive frequent and extensive attention and become part of the magazine's own construction of the nation.

13. See Tittel, *Das Niederwalddenkmal*, 1.

14. The weeklies *Daheim* and *Illustrirte Zeitung* also commented on the monuments. Monthly magazines, however, such as *Westermanns Monatshefte*, devoted little space to the construction and unveiling of monuments, probably due to their inattention to current events in general.

15. "In the future a wanderer will stroll through these vineyard hills from the south and the north of our great and beautiful empire with a joyful heart, and when his gaze sweeps out from the foot of our national monument into the majestic lands, he will think about the grand struggle, about the victory attained with many and unfortunately heavy sacrifices" (*Gartenlaube* 1872: 316). Not surprisingly, this is the same language the author Ferdinand Heyl used in his essay in the April 13, 1871, *Rheinischer Kurier* to plead for the construction of such a monument.

16. Heyl's earlier essay in the *Rheinischer Kurier* (April 13, 1871) inspired local and national officials to form committees for the construction of a national monument. See Tittel, *Das Niederwalddenkmal*, 4–8.

17. This conjoining of two other national "stories" complements the generation of national myths and a common past that Eric Hobsbawm has called the "invention of tradition." Hobsbawm, "Introduction: Inventing Traditions," 1–14.

18. The magazine's presentation of monuments was thorough. In the last decade of the century, the *Gartenlaube* discussed Bismarck monuments in nine articles. It devoted three to the Kyffhäuser monument and several to other monuments honoring Kaiser Wilhelm I.

19. Tittel has pointed out that the popularity of "Die Wacht am Rhein" in and after the 1870 war (including its recommendation as a national hymn) was indicative of the central role the Rhine River began to play in a national German consciousness. See Tittel, *Das Niederwalddenkmal*, 4.

20. Besides the Berlin *Siegessäule*, the *Gartenlaube* presented its readers with depictions of the *Siegessäule* and *Friedenssäule* on the Augustusplatz in Leipzig (1876: 635–37, 642) and the *Siegesmonument* in Freiburg (1877: 713, 716).

21. The same strategy appeared in the Leipzig *Illustrirte Zeitung*, a weekly smaller in size but with more current events and a greater percentage of illustrations than the *Gartenlaube*. The cover picture of the August 7, 1875, issue depicted the immense head of the statue resting on the ground. It

dwarfs Bandel, who stands with hammer in hand next to it and beside an even smaller model of the entire piece (see *Illustrirte Zeitung* 1875: 97). In the case of the Germania statue in the Niederwald, this comparison was achieved in verbal rather than visual terms: "Her small finger can just be grasped by two adult hands, her thumbnail is nine centimeters wide and eleven centimeters long . . . and ten couples can dance in the interior of her torso" (*Gartenlaube* 1883: 553).

22. "But the trip is supposed to be complicated by numerous difficulties; never before have so many immense and weighty pieces been transported by German trains" (*Gartenlaube* 1883: 552).

23. A similar, but much more explicitly jingoistic centerfold poster of the *Hermannsdenkmal* appeared in the *Illustrirte Zeitung* in 1875. Using emblems to encircle the image of the monument, it equated the Rome vanquished by Hermann with the Paris defeated by contemporary Germany. Supplement to issue from August 7, 1875, of the *Illustrirte Zeitung*.

24. *Deutsche Illustrirte Zeitung* 1885: 488.

25. In the first volume of the *Deutsche Illustrirte Zeitung* (one-half year), this ad appeared five times.

26. Walter Benjamin, "The Work of Art in the Age of Mechanical Reproduction," in Benjamin, *Illuminations* (New York: Schocken, 1969), 217–51.

27. Homi K. Bhabha describes the narration of the nation more explicitly as "complex strategies of cultural identification and discursive address that function in the name of 'the people' or 'the nation' and make them the immanent subjects and objects of a range of social and literary narratives." See Bhabha, "DissemiNation," in Bhabha, *Nation and Narration*, 292.

28. Maurice Agulhon, *Marianne into Battle: Republican Imagery and Symbolism in France 1789–1880* (Cambridge: Cambridge UP, 1981).

29. Reinhart Koselleck explores the historically constant function of war memorials in his essay "Kriegerdenkmale als Identitätsstiftungen der Überlebenden," in Odo Marquard and Karlheinz Stierle (eds.), *Identität* (Munich: Wilhelm Fink, 1979), 255–75. Using quite a different set of materials, Thomas Lacquer has suggested that through the naming that occurs in the production of a monument to the fallen hero, "a space is created in which those left behind remake their lives and culture by infusing meaning into the inert, meaningless, interchangeable remains of the dead" (from a paper presented at the "Pomp and Circumstance Conference," MIT, May 1–2, 1992). See also the published version: Thomas W. Lacqueur, "Memory and Naming in the Great War," in John R. Gillis (ed.), *Commemorations: The Politics of National Identity* (Princeton: Princteon UP, 1994), 150–67.

30. See Brigitte Schroeder-Gudehus and Anne Rasmussen, *Les Fastes du*

Progrès: Le guide des Expositions universelles 1851–1992 (Paris: Flammarion, 1992).

31. Richard D. Mandrell, *Paris 1900: The Great World's Fair* (Toronto: U of Toronto P, 1967), 9–10. Mandrell mentions several smaller affairs organized in New York and Dublin in 1853 and Germany in 1854.

32. Mandrell, *Paris 1900*, 8.

33. The idea that a nation's status might be embodied by and heightened by an international fair carried well into the twentieth century. See Lisa Rubens, "Re-presenting the Nation: The Golden Gate International Exhibition," in Robert W. Rydell and Nancy E. Gwinn (eds.), *Fair Representations: World's Fairs and the Modern World* (Amsterdam: VU UP, 1994), 121–39. For a discussion of the role smaller museum exhibitions have played in constructing national identity see Bruce Wallis, "Selling Nations: International Exhibitions and Cultural Diplomacy," in Daniel J. Sherman and Iris Rogoff (eds.), *Museum Culture: Histories, Discourses, Spectacles* (Minneapolis: U of Minnesota P, 1994), 265–81.

34. Written in 1851 by L. Bucher. Quoted in "Kunsthistorische Skizzen aus der Industrieausstellung aller Völker," in *Packeis und Pressglas. Von der Kunstgewerbebewegung zum deutschen Werkbund* (Giessen: Anabas, 1987), 66–67.

35. See John Heskett, *German Design, 1870–1918* (New York: Taplinger Publishing, 1986), 18.

36. Heskett, *German Design*, 19–23.

37. Hermann Glaser, *Die Kultur der Wilhelminischen Zeit: Topographie einer Epoche* (Frankfurt: Fischer, 1984), 103.

38. Schroeder-Gudehus and Rasmussen, *Les Fastes du Progrès*, 64, 76, 96, 112, respectively.

39. Glaser, *Die Kultur*, 104.

40. *Illustrirte Zeitung* 1867 (vol. 48): 14, 15, 19, 24, 48, 49, 52, 68, 69. The presentation of the exposition easily overshadowed images and reports of the coronation ceremonies of Kaiser Franz Joseph as King of Hungary.

41. The 1867 exposition in Paris doubled the square area for exhibits, the number of visitors, and the profits of previous exhibitions in London (1851 and 1862) and Paris (1865). See Schroeder-Gudehus and Rasmussen, *Les Fastes du Progrès*, 58, 64, 71, 76.

42. *Gartenlaube* 1867: 300–302, 391–93, 538–41.

43. Debord, *Spectacle*, paragraph 66.

44. Between 1865 and 1893 the *Gartenlaube* published twenty articles in the series "Germany's Great Industrial Workshops." Although they did not appear as frequently as those on regional identities, the fact that they were

numbered as essays in an ongoing series alerted readers to a continuity of interest. Numerous other essays on inventions, industrialists, and manufacturing appeared outside this series as well.

45. The article concludes with the following assertion: "in bezug auf Qualität und Arbeit steht das deutsche Eisenfabrikat höher. Wenn England in den wichtigsten Branchen der Stahlfabrikation die erste Stelle an Deutschland längst hat abtreten müssen, so knüpft sich die Ehre dieses Erfolges deutschen Fleißes an die Firmen Friedrich Krupp in Essen und 'Verein für Bergbau und Gußstahlfabrikation in Bochum'" (*Gartenlaube* 1875: 546).

46. See Tittel, *Das Niederwalddenkmal*, and Mosse, *Nationalization of the Masses*.

47. See Robert W. Rydell, *All the World's a Fair: Visions of Empire at American International Expositions, 1876–1916* (Chicago: U of Chicago P, 1984).

48. Advertising was an important part of the commodity spectacle. In the *Gartenlaube* these did not appear in great numbers until the end of the century. The collection in the Berlin Staatsbibliothek, for instance, has advertising sections beginning in the late 1890s. However, other competing publications, like *Daheim* and the Leipzig *Illustrirte Zeitung*, had them already in the 1870s.

49. Debord's thesis about the urban isolation that was part of twentieth-century spectacular society applied to the functioning of the *Gartenlaube*: "The widespread use of receivers of the spectacular message enables the individual to fill his isolation with the dominant images—images which derive their power precisely from this isolation." Debord, *Spectacle*, paragraph 173.

5. DOMESTICATING THE NATION

1. Ulla Wischermann relies in part on the magazine's long-standing masthead to identify the intended address of the *Gartenlaube*. The masthead depicted an extended family sitting together in the shade of their leafy garden arbor ("*Gartenlaube*"). In this idealized image, the magazine is read aloud for the family by the grandfather (Wischermann, *Frauenfrage und Presse*, 26).

2. Karin Hausen, "Die Polarisierung der 'Geschlechtscharaktere'—Eine Spiegelung der Dissoziation von Erwerbs- und Familienleben," in Werner Conze (ed.), *Sozialgeschichte der Familie in der Neuzeit Europas* (Stuttgart: Klett, 1976), 369.

3. Kirschstein, *Die Familienzeitschrift*, 82–83, and Barth, *Zeitschrift für Alle*, 177.

4. See Schenda's citation of Wilhelm Hauff who studied the behavior of readers in a lending library with 4,000–5,000 volumes. Schenda, *Volk ohne Buch*, 205.

5. The year 1875 had an unusually high percentage of biographical essays on women, four of twenty.

6. There were a very few interesting exceptions to this general rule, such as two essays about women travelers, but these rare essays had a more exotic rather than serious tone to them.

7. These seven stories comprised about half the fictional contributions in 1855 and were generally serialized in serveral issues. They covered eighteen issues and a total of seventy-one pages.

8. Engelsing suggests that the taste of the housewife was the decisive factor in families' subscriptions (Engelsing, "Zeitschrift in Nordwestdeutschland," 1009). His sources for this contention are, however, quite thin, primarily a quote from Peter Hilles's novel *Die Sozialisten*. This is the kind of primary information that is difficult, if not impossible, to locate or verify. It is not necessarily refuted by the constant, ideal image (self-representation) of the magazine, depicted on its mastheads from the beginning, of a grandfather figure reading aloud to a family around the table. Even in this image, women (of all ages) are present and well represented as auditors.

9. *Gartenlaube* 1866: 214, 265, 358.

10. *Gartenlaube* 1864: 65, 159, 176; 1867: 653; 1880: 803, 804, 805, 820, 821.

11. *Gartenlaube* 1853: 277; 1863: 216; 1872: 773.

12. See Richard J. Evans, *The Feminist Movement in Germany, 1894–1933* (London: Sage Publications, 1976).

13. Like many women of this era, Otto published her political ideas under a pseudonym; hers was Otto Stern. For a discussion of Otto's life and writings see Ruth-Ellen Boetcher Joeres (ed.), *Die Anfänge der deutschen Frauenbewegung: Louise Otto-Peters* (Frankfurt: Fischer, 1983), 52–138.

14. It is not clear from the magazine if this author is a man or woman. The name is signed with initials only, F. v. D. In her book, Wischermann also offers no insights about the gender of the author. Wischermann, *Frauenfrage und Presse*, 43.

15. Evans, *Feminist Movement in Germany*, 24–30.

16. Kirschstein, *Die Familienzeitschrift*, 92–93. "Der ungeheure Erfolg der Marlittromane und die Riesenauflage der 'Gartenlaube' griffen hier in-

einander. So kam es, daß die beiden Namen 'Marlitt' und 'Gartenlaube' zu einem einheitlichen, volksthümlichen Begriff wurden." See also Hermann Zang, "Die 'Gartenlaube' als politisches Organ, Bellestristik, Bilderwerk und literarische Kritik im Dienste der liberalen Politik 1860–1880" (Ph.D. dissertation, U of Würzburg, 1935), 108.

17. Bertha Potthast, "Eugenie Marlitt: Ein Beitrag zur Geschichte des deutschen Frauenromans" (Ph.D. dissertation, U of Cologne, 1926), 130–31.

18. Summaries of Marlitt's life were published in the *Gartenlaube*. In 1887, as a tribute to its star author after her death, the magazine published a commemorative essay entitled "E. Marlitt" (1887: 460–63). Again, in 1899, it published a series of four articles that once again recounted the path of her life and career (1899: 136–40, 156–59, 170–72, 197–99). Bertha Potthast begins her dissertation on Marlitt's novels with a sentimental characterization of the author's life. See Potthast, "Eugenie Marlitt," 3–22.

19. According to Potthast, *Golden Else* ran to eight book editions by 1871, each with a press run of from two thousand to three thousand. Likewise, *The Secret of the Old Mademoiselle* had six editions in the five years after its initial publication in the *Gartenlaube* (Potthast, "Eugenie Marlitt," 130–31). The *Gartenlaube* itself eagerly announced each new translation of Marlitt's novels. Within two years of its first serialized publication, *Golden Else* had been translated into English, Russian (1868: 272), Dutch, and French (1868: 736).

20. At the end of 1871, the year her new novel *The Moorland Princess* appeared in the magazine, three other Marlitt novels in book editions were "recommended as a Christmas present!" (1871: 808). See also the last issues for the years 1868, 1869, 1870. The last issue of 1868 promised *Gartenlaube* readers the appearance of "*Imperial Countess Gisela* by E. Marlitt" in the coming year.

21. In 1878, because the *Gartenlaube* had received so many requests from readers for information about Marlitt's next novel, the magazine even published an excerpt from a letter by Marlitt for her readers. In the letter, she apologized for not having completed her novel and included as one of the reasons her deep sorrow at the death of friend and publisher, Ernst Keil. She assured her readers that she would try "doubly hard" to keep her promise to him (1878: 616).

22. See examples cited by Kirschstein, *Die Familienzeitschrift*, 101–2.

23. In her work on popular romances, Tania Modleski has characterized this plot development as common for the male hero. Modleski points out that although the hero is initially contemptuous of or indifferent to the

heroine, the reader is familiar with the formula and therefore "always able to interpret the hero's actions as the result of his increasingly intense love for the heroine." Tania Modleski, *Loving with a Vengeance: Mass-Produced Fantasies for Women* (New York: Routledge, 1982), 40.

24. Gérard Genette defines the focal character as the one "who sees" rather than the one who narrates. Gérard Genette, *Narrative Discourse: An Essay in Method* (Ithaca: Cornell UP, 1980), 185–98. For another concise definition of focalization see Shlomith Rimmon-Kenan, *Narrative Fiction: Contemporary Poetics* (New York: Routledge, 1983), 71–85.

25. As part of her goal of deciphering the narrative pleasure women might get from Gothic novels, Harlequin romances, and soap operas, Modleski insists that "the price women pay for their popular entertainment is high, but they may still be getting more than anyone bargained for" (Modleski, *Loving with a Vengeance*, 34). Radway rejects the traditional consumption analogy for interaction with popular literature. By asserting that comprehension while reading is an act of making meaning, she insists that women readers of romance novels are empowered as active reading subjects, even if they also recirculate many notions common to patriarchal society. She suggests that "escape" both refers to conditions left behind and invokes utopian possibility. See Janice A. Radway, *Reading the Romance: Women, Patriarchy, and Popular Literature* (Chapel Hill: U of North Carolina P, 1991), 12.

26. Kathryn Shevelow, *Women and Print Culture: The Construction of Femininity in the Early Period* (New York: Routledge, 1989).

27. Nancy Armstrong, *Desire and Domestic Fiction: A Political History of the Novel* (New York: Oxford UP, 1987).

28. Just as domesticity is a kind of self-regulation, so, too, the process of reading constitutes a manner of discipline. In a discussion of the English case, Louis James has suggested that, especially for the female servant, reading can be seen as a "disciplined activity." Louis James, "The Trouble with Betsy: Periodicals and the Common Reader in Mid-Nineteenth-Century England," in Joanne Shattock and Michael Wolff (eds.), *The Victorian Periodical Press: Samplings and Soundings* (Toronto: U of Toronto P, 1982), 353.

29. Armstrong, *Desire and Domestic Fiction*, 66.

6. COLONIALISM, MYTH, AND NOSTALGIA

1. This was most evident in a eulogy about Keil written by his longtime contributor Albert Fränkel and published that year in the *Gartenlaube*. It is also apparent in essays (published well into the 1890s) praising the liberal

traditions of the Wars of Liberation, the liberals of the 1848 revolution, and the Frankfurt Parliament. See, for instance, the essay on Keil's long-time contributor Friedrich Hofmann (1886: 497–99) or on the history of the *Burschenschaft* (student fraternity) movement (1882: 411, 464, 472; 1890: 528, 592).

2. Within two decades (from 1870 to 1890) industrial production in the German Empire rose from fourteen billion to forty-five billion marks (Hans-Ulrich Wehler, *Das Deutsche Kaiserreich, 1871–1918*, 3d ed. [Göttingen: Vandenhoeck and Ruprecht, 1977], 48). In the same time span, German production of bituminous coal, iron, and steel increased 300 percent (Holger H. Herwig, *Hammer or Anvil, Modern Germany 1648–Present* [Lexington MA: Heath, 1994], 159). Herwig cites the relative industrial potential of Britain compared to Germany in 1880 as 3:1 and in 1900 as 4:3 (Herwig, *Hammer or Anvil*, 161). See also Friedrich-Wilhelm Henning, *Die Industrialisierung in Deutschland, 1800 bis 1914* (Paderborn: Schöningh, 1973).

3. See Robert K. Massie, *Dreadnought: Britain, Germany, and the Coming of the Great War* (New York: Random House, 1991), 160–85.

4. See Eley, *Reshaping the German Right*.

5. *Gartenlaube* articles on German industries appeared in 1882: 143, 931; 1883: 28, 687; 1885: 425; 1892: 648; 1893: 330. Industrial fairs held in Germany alone were described in 1894: 456, 516; and 1897: 312.

6. The article, which was approximately eleven pages long, was accompanied by seven illustrations in columns 1111–12, 1113–14, 1115–16, 1117–18, and 1119–20 of *Vom Fels zum Meer*, vol. 2 (April–September 1886).

7. The significance of images of the non-Western world for Europe's view of itself has been analyzed in Edward W. Said, *Orientalism* (New York: Random House, 1978). For a recent discussion of the British case of African colonialism, see the study of popular and material culture in Annie E. Coombes, *Reinventing Africa: Museums, Material Culture, and Popular Imagination in Late Victorian and Edwardian England* (New Haven: Yale UP, 1994).

8. Bismarck wrote in a letter to Roon in 1868, "die Kosten, welche die Gründung, Unterstützung und namentlich die Behauptung der Kolonien veranlaßt, übersteigen, wie die Erfahrungen der Kolonialpolitik Englands und Frankreichs beweisen, sehr oft den Nutzen, den das Mutterland daraus zieht, ganz abgesehen davon, daß es schwer zu rechtfertigen ist, die ganze Nation zum Vorteil einzelner Handels- und Gewerbezweige zu erheblichen Steuerlasten heranzuziehen." Quoted in Hans-Ulrich Wehler, *Bismarck und der Imperialismus*, 3d ed. (Cologne: Kiepenheuer and Witsch, 1973), 191.

9. For a history of Germany's colonial involvement see Woodruff D. Smith, *The German Colonial Empire* (Chapel Hill: U of North Carolina P, 1978).

10. Wehler, *Das deutsche Kaiserreich*, 175.

11. Woodruff D. Smith, *The German Colonial Empire*, 22–27. Smith bases much of his analysis of German colonialism on the contention that the "emigrationist" version of colonialism won over middle-class support for colonial involvement.

12. Despite the campaigning done by colonial lobbies, the "colonial idea" never had much impact on the working class. See Helmuth Stoecker and Peter Sebald, "Enemies of the Colonial Idea," in Arthur J. Knoll and Lewis H. Gann (eds.), *Germans in the Tropics: Essays in German Colonial History* (New York: Greenwood, 1987), 66.

13. For a discussion of the organizations from the early 1880s that merged into the Deutsche Kolonialgesellschaft (German Colonial Society) in 1887, see Richard V. Pierard, "The German Colonial Society," in Knoll and Gann, *Germans in the Tropics*, 19–37.

14. Woodruff D. Smith, *The German Colonial Empire*, 13.

15. A. J. P. Taylor, *Germany's First Bid for Colonies, 1884–1885* (London: Macmillan, 1938), 6.

16. Cited in Winfried Baumgart, "German Imperialism in Historical Perspective," in Knoll and Gann, *Germans in the Tropics*, 151.

17. Wehler concludes "häufig wirkte der 'Kolonialrausch' sozialpsychologisch als eine Form des Eskapismus vor den sozialökonomischen Problemen der Depressionszeit und der einschneidenden Transformation zur Industriegesellschaft" (Wehler, *Bismarck*, 470). Wehler's thesis about Bismarck's "social imperialism" has perhaps gone the furthest to link the phenomenon of colonization to other national concerns. It also presumes that the colonial movement's argument for colonial space for the German people was largely an unrealized dream.

18. Baumgart, "German Imperialism," 156–57. Baumgart presents convincing evidence to support this theory, which suggests that Bismarck feared a "Gladstone cabinet" after Wilhelm's death before it was known that the heir to the German throne was himself deathly ill.

19. See "Introduction," Knoll and Gann, *Germans in the Tropics*, xiii, as well as Woodruff D. Smith, *The German Colonial Empire*, ix.

20. At least three of these were not listed in the magazine's general index. *Vollständiges Generalregister der Gartenlaube vom 1. bis 50. Jahrgang (1853–1902)*, collated by F. Hofmann and J. Schmidt (Leipzig: Ernst Keil, 1882 and 1903; reprint, Hildesheim: Gerstenberg, 1978).

21. The popular press was interested in the colonial world in general, as the repeated discussions of Stanley's travels to Africa and his discoveries demonstrate. See *Gartenlaube* 1878: 113; 1882: 782; 1883: 794; 1885: 329 (open letters on 714, 726, 748); 1887: 576; 1890: 16, 130, 140, 428. However, the greatest interest was devoted to the progress of Germany's colonial mission.

22. See chapter 4.

23. This would bear out the argument put forward by Woodruff Smith that colonialism was not a favored objective of German liberal politics in the nineteenth century. Smith suggests that one of the reasons Bismarck warmed to the idea of colonial involvement when he did was that it was a way of attracting a middle class (which had been hard hit by the depression) away from their traditional adherence to liberal economic thinking that included aversion to the protectionism inherent in colonial relations. Woodruff D. Smith, *The German Colonial Empire*, 17–18.

24. In one six-month period *Westermanns Monatshefte* published "Deutschlands Interessen im Niger- und Kongogebiet" (1885: 239–59, 325–44); "Erinnerung an Gustav Nachtigal" (1885: 742–55); "Die brandenburgischen Kolonien in Westafrika" (1885: 828–37); and book reviews of *Um Afrika* by Wilhelm Jost and *Deutsch-Afrika* by Richard Oberländer (1885: 840).

25. The sharpest criticism within Germany of German colonial involvement and colonial policy came from the Social Democratic Party and its leaders, Bebel, Wilhelm Liebknecht, and Kautsky. See Stoecker and Sebald, "Enemies of the Colonial Idea," 59–72.

26. Because the present discussion of the German nation is limited to the nineteenth century, it will not touch on the more conflicted years of Germany's colonial period, such as the brutal wars against the Herero people of German Southwest Africa from 1904 to 1907.

27. Richard V. Pierard discusses some of the publicizing strategies of the German Colonial Society, such as speeches and pamphlets, after its founding in 1887. Pierard, "German Colonial Society," 28–33.

28. The illustrations for these essays were either based on photographs or drawn by those who traveled to these places. A few were drawings based on the ethnographic collections of the Godeffroy Museum in Hamburg.

29. Some of these expert travelers were indeed invested in the colonial idea, such as the explorer Otto Finsch, who in 1885 was acting as an agent for the government in the exploration of the Pacific. See *Gartenlaube* 1885: 48.

30. See Léon Poliakov, *The Aryan Myth: A History of Racist and Nationalist Ideas in Europe* (New York: Basic Books, 1974), 215–54.

31. "Auch für europäische Ethnographie interessirte sich Goapäna" (*Gartenlaube* 1885: 50).

32. "Eine geheimnißvolle Macht waltet über Ruinen. Jahrhunderte vermögen nicht ihren Einfluß zu schwächen, denn eifersüchtig wird sie von der Sage und der Geschichte beschützt, die aus Schutt und Staub das Edelste zu retten wissen."

33. "So griffen oft in entscheidendem Augenblick die alten Zeugen der Vergangenheit in's volle frische Völkerleben und drängten die Massen auf die Bahn des Ruhmes."

34. "Die Fehler der Staatsmänner entmuthigten jedoch keineswegs die deutschen Kaufleute, die anfangs ohne jede staatliche Unterstützung, ohne jeden Schutz hier auf eigene Faust Factoreien gründeten und, dem unermüdlichen deutschen Afrikaforscher auf der Spur folgend, das Innere des Landes dem Welthandel erschlossen."

35. It is interesting to note that other periodical magazines also recurred to this historical precedent to help support a contemporary colonial initiative. See *Westermanns Monatshefte*, "Die brandenburgischen Kolonien in Westafrika" (1885: 828–37).

36. "Für die deutsche Colonialbewegung dürfte die oben skizzirte Reise der Kriegscorvette 'Sophie' von großer Bedeutung sein. Der schlichte Bericht wirkt mehr als hundert Reden und Flugschriften."

37. "Hier öffnet sich ein großes Wirkungsfeld für Alle ohne Rücksicht auf Parteistellung, und das hohe Ziel dünkt uns erreichbar ohne kriegerische Verwickelungen und Opfer an Menschenleben. Man darf nur diejenigen nicht im Stich lassen, die bereits zu handeln begonnen haben." Another precedent that suggested the appropriateness of German colonialism was the story of the great German cosmograph, Martin Behaim. The *Gartenlaube* published an essay on this German also early in 1884. It described how this "child of Nuremberg" was asked by the Portuguese government to accompany the expedition that in 1484 discovered the Kingdom of the Congo (1884: 176–79).

38. Similiarly, the *German Illustrated Newspaper* argued that Germany was justified in establishing political rule in the South Sea (Samoa) because all trade relationships of significance there were already in German hands (*Deutsche Illustrirte Zeitung* 1884: 23).

39. In this same essay, the author boasted that the "fame of English discoverers and researchers does not glow more brightly than that of German and French travelers to Africa" (*Gartenlaube* 1884: 807).

40. Woodruff D. Smith, *The German Colonial Empire*, 10–19.

41. See Lewis H. Gann, "Marginal Colonialism: The German Case," in Knoll and Gann, *Germans in the Tropics*, 1–17.

42. "Das neue deutsche Panzerschiff 'Brandenburg'" (*Gartenlaube* 1894: 133).

43. These numbers are based on a tabulation of illustrations appearing in the *Gartenlaube* in the three years 1855, 1875, and 1895. The table below lists (in order) the number of pages in the annual volume, the total number of illustrations, how many of these occupied a full page, and how many a double-page spread.

Year	Pages	Illustrations	Full Page	Double Page
1855	700	115	10	4
1875	860	142	57	10
1895	894	432	107	26

44. This illustration is followed by a brief text on the last page of the issue that explains who this notable woman was (*Gartenlaube* 1894: 196).

45. See the characterization of *Gründerzeit* artistic style in Richard Hamann and Jost Hermand, *Gründerzeit* (Berlin: Akademie Verlag, 1965), 91.

46. Jost Hermand has suggested that "eine den Raum sprengende Versammlung weniger Personen" was typical of late-nineteenth-century artists and that it increased the intensity and drama of the scenes depicted. Hermand uses this description for the works of Wilhelm Leibl, but it is equally true of the monumental illustrations in the *Gartenlaube*. Hamann and Hermand, *Gründerzeit*, 79.

47. This is another argument made by Hermand concerning the art of the period. Hamann and Hermand, *Gründerzeit*, 84.

48. Hobsbawm, "Introduction: Inventing Traditions," 1–14.

49. The "Land und Leute" series was apparently considered quite successful in the *Gartenlaube*'s repertoire. As we have mentioned, it ran for approximately three decades. This kind of series was also copied by the magazine's competitors; *Daheim* in its very first year included similar essays, and the *Illustrirte Zeitung* included many such contributions as well. Even monthly magazines like *Westermanns Monathefte* made use of these ethnographic, geographical short essays.

50. Such notes were printed in a section entitled "Blätter und Blüthen."

51. Most, but not all, of these title images depicted rural scenes. A few presented city scenes, but these were then idealized and exclusively positive presentations of city life, such as streets covered with snow or images of parks.

52. These title images frequently represented mother and child. This was a visual presentation of the national self that even suited the depiction of the Empress and her five young Princes quite well (*Gartenlaube* 1889: 165).

EPILOGUE

1. "Die Konzeption der Zeitschrift, jedoch, die—sicher unbewußt—eine entleerte und damit verkehrte Innerlichkeit als Kulturfassade verwendete, war dem Wesen nach kleinbürgerlich reaktionär. So war es nur eine Frage der Zeit, bis auch der nationalistisch-chauvinistische Inhalt dazukam." Hermann Glaser, *Spießer-Ideologie: Von der Zerstörung des deutschen Geistes im 19. und 20. Jahrhundert und dem Aufstieg des Nationalsozialismus*, 2d ed. (Frankfurt: Fischer, 1985), 64.

2. Barth, *Zeitschrift für Alle*, 337.

3. Joachim Wachtel cites the magazine's circulation in 1906 as 100,000. Joachim Wachtel, *Heißgeliebte Gartenlaube: Herzerfrischende Wanderungen durch ein deutsches Familienblatt* (Feldafing: Buchheim, 1963), 15.

4. For a survey of popular Rockwell illustrations from the magazine, see *The Saturday Evening Post Norman Rockwell Book* (Indianapolis: Curtis, 1977).

5. Joachim Kirchner, *Das deutsche Zeitschriftenwesen*, 2:353.

6. Joachim Kirchner, *Das deutsche Zeitschriftenwesen*, 2:354. Ann Taylor Allen notes that whereas the editor-in-chief of *Kladderadatsch* in 1900 was 63 and the average age of five key staff members was 48, the comparable ages for members of the *Simplicissimus* staff were 30 and 28. Ann Taylor Allen, *Satire and Society in Wilhelmine Germany: Kladderadatsch and Simplicissimus, 1890–1914* (Lexington: U of Kentucky P, 1984), 13.

7. Joachim Kirchner lists three successful titles and their circulations in 1895: *Mode und Haus*, 155,000; *Deutsche Mode-Zeitschrift*, 60,000; and *Große Modewelt*, 105,000. Joachim Kirchner, *Das deutsche Zeitschriftenwesen*, 2:361–62.

8. Joachim Kirchner, *Das deutsche Zeitschriftenwesen*, 2:357.

Index